About the author

Dr. David Lewis is an acknowledged world leader in the application of neuroscience to the buying brain.

Dubbed the "father of neuromarketing," David started his pioneering work back in the late 1980s at the University of Sussex, attaching electrodes to the scalps of plucky volunteers in order to track the electrical responses of their brains to various television commercials.

Since these pioneering days, David—with his colleagues at cutting-edge research consultancy Mindlab International—has used increasingly sensitive and sophisticated technologies to reveal how the human body and mind react when we shop. He has also witnessed the emergence of what is now a multimillion-dollar industry, dedicated to exploring and exploiting this knowledge for commercial use.

Chairman, co-founder, and Director of Research at Mindlab, as well as a Fellow or Associate at numerous professional bodies, including the American Association for the Advancement of Science, David continues to be active in the field. He is also a much sought-after broadcaster, conference speaker, and workshop presenter, and has worked with scores of Fortune 500 and FTSE 100 companies.

A Chartered Psychologist, David has written bestselling books on many aspects of psychology, including *The Soul of the New Consumer: Authenticity—What We Buy and Why in the New Economy* (Nicholas Brealey Publishing, 2000).

Dedication

To Steven Matthews with grateful thanks for all the help and encouragement he has given me over many years

THE BRAIN SELL

When Science Meets Shopping

How the new mind sciences
and the persuasion industry
are reading our thoughts,
influencing our emotions
and stimulating us to shop

Dr. David Lewis

NICHOLAS BREALEY
PUBLISHING

London • Boston

First published in the UK by
Nicholas Brealey Publishing in 2013

3–5 Spafield Street
Clerkenwell, London
EC1R 4QB, UK
Tel: +44 (0)20 7239 0360
Fax: +44 (0)20 7239 0370

20 Park Plaza
Boston
MA 02116, USA
Tel: (888) BREALEY
Fax: (617) 523 3708

www.nicholasbrealey.com
www.thebrainsell.co.uk

ISBN: 978-1-85788-601-6
eISBN: 978-1-85788-942-0

British Library Cataloguing in Publication Data
A catalogue record for this book is available from the British Library.

The views expressed in this book are entirely those of the author and do not,
necessarily, reflect those of the board of Mindlab International Ltd. and its
employees, or of the many industry professionals and academics who have been
kind enough to assist in the research.

Printed in Finland by Bookwell.

Contents

Introduction

The stuff with which we work is the fabric of men's minds.
—Vance Packard, *The Hidden Persuaders*

More than half a century ago, American journalist Vance Packard shocked consumers by revealing the extent to which they were being manipulated for commercial gain. In his bestselling exposé *The Hidden Persuaders*, he revealed "the dark side of advertising," warning: "Large-scale efforts are being made, often with impressive success, to channel our unthinking habits, our purchasing decisions, and our thought processes. Typically these efforts take place beneath our level of awareness; so that the appeals which move us are often, in a sense, 'hidden.'"[1]

That was in 1957. Since then, scientists have learned more about the workings of the human brain than was discovered throughout humankind's entire previous existence. Although these advances do not, at present, allow scientists actually to "read minds," they are not far short of achieving that goal. Already there is a growing understanding of what changes in blood flow to different regions of the brain, or in the electrical signals by which these regions communicate, reveal about our thoughts, emotions, and actions.

Today, every major company in the world is engaged in a race to use advances in neuroscience to develop techniques for influencing (or, as critics would argue, "manipulating") consumers—a race not only to win their hearts, but also to influence their minds.

I know because, for more than 30 years, the focus of my neuroscience research has been the vulnerabilities of the human brain and the various ways in which it can be influenced.

My interest in this now rapidly developing field of study began during the late 1980s while I was working in the Department of Experimental Psychology at the University of Sussex. I attached electrodes to the heads of pioneering volunteers to record the patterns of electrical activity in their brains as they watched television commercials. These very early studies would, over 20 years later, help launch what has become the multimillion-dollar neuromarketing industry.

Since then, I—and my colleagues at Mindlab—have been using increasingly sensitive and complex equipment to analyze what goes on in someone's mind and body as they shop. I have recorded the brain activity, changes in heart rate, respiration, skin temperature, and physical arousal of individuals in retailers from small-town Mom and Pop stores to the marbled halls of luxurious malls. I have seen how spotting a bargain sets the pulse racing, and how the color red stimulates arousal.

I have taken saliva samples to assess stress levels and used eye-tracking equipment to identify how long customers spend studying different displays. More recently, as the internet and social media have become ever more important in their reach and influence, I have examined how consumers shop online. Recording their direction of gaze and level of attention, I have explored the way people surf the internet, scan web pages, and buy online; and how they react to different forms of advertising and participate in social networks such as Facebook and LinkedIn. My purpose has been to put the seemingly mundane activity of shopping—in all its guises—under the microscope, not merely to observe how consumers behave, but to reveal their thoughts and feelings as they search for products ranging from washing-up liquid and floor polish to designer sunglasses and the latest must-have smartphone.

This book offers you an insider's account of the extent to which our rapidly growing understanding of the brain (coupled with advances in neuro/behavioral economics and consumer psychology) is resulting in ever more effective ways of advertising, marketing, and retailing—an ever more powerful "brain sell."

As an advertiser, marketer, or retailer (or indeed a member of the wider "persuasion industry"), you will discover the latest techniques and technologies and how you can exploit them. As a consumer, you will learn how you are increasingly being influenced by this uniquely powerful industry whose techniques, as former advertising executive Robert Heath explains in *Seducing the Subconscious*, profoundly affect choice "without any message, without us attending to or recalling the message, without us attending to or recalling the ad, and regardless of whether we like or hate the ad."[2]

As this book explores, even the environment in which a consumer shops can have an influence on purchasing. For example, lighting in a discount store will be bright and even to show off products to best advantage, while an upmarket cosmetics store may opt for soft lighting to enhance customers' perceptions of their own appearance. The tempo of the music being played can affect the speed with which shoppers move around a store, while in many casinos scented air creates an aroma that relaxes gamers and actually slows the perceived passage of time. These "atmospherics" control behavior and attitudes in imperceptible ways that consumers cannot control. Similarly, the emergence of so-called choice architecture is enabling our decision making to be manipulated in subconscious ways.

Greater knowledge of brain function is only part of the picture, however. The power of the persuasion industry has also been enhanced by the emergence of whole new routes to market, via the internet, social media, mobile devices, and personalized advertising messages. For instance, in Chapter 7 I tell you about earcons, an audible icon on a screen that provides a relevant sound when you click on a particular website—steak sizzling for a restaurant, waves breaking on the beach for a travel agent. Even the television that you—and your children—watch can have a significant effect on your view of the world and your shopping habits, as I detail in Chapter 9.

Another major source of insight and potential influence is the industry's rapidly increasing ability to mine Big Data. I explain in Chapter 11 that this involves using sophisticated mathematics and high-speed computers to unearth buying trends and preferences from social sites such as Facebook and Twitter. The industry claims that this information helps tailor marketing, so your time and attention are taken up only with products and services that have genuine relevance to you. The mining of Big Data is one reason my laboratory, like almost every similar research consultancy, employs not only neuroscientists but also mathematicians, statisticians, and physicists.

The persuasion industry is increasingly powerful, but if you consider yourself immune to its blandishments—if you think that as a consumer, everything you buy is the result of your own free will—take a look around your possessions. I am prepared to take a bet that a fair proportion of these, from the jeans you wear to the car you drive, were purchased for emotional as well as intellectual reasons; that in fact, your choices have been influenced in ways so subtle that you have failed to recognize them.

Consider the following. In one study, a message urging consumers to drink a particular brand of tea was flashed onto their computer screen so briefly as to remain invisible to them. Despite the fact that participants had never consciously seen the message, it caused them to order that particular brand in a free choice. I describe this and other research into what is called subliminal priming in Chapter 8.

But how can this be possible? How can consumers be influenced to buy something without their conscious knowledge? As I explain in Chapter 2, these influences have been part of a consumer's life for so long that they barely even notice them.

The persuasive power of advertising and marketing is hardly surprising given the vast investments of time, talent, and money involved. In the UK and USA alone, more than twice as much, some $313 billion, is spent on advertising than on education ($132 billion). When it comes to developing "must-have" new products, companies employ thousands of highly educated research scientists tasked with developing such useful if unglamorous products as Febreze, Bovril, Pampers, Pot Noodle, Flash, Stork, Duracell, Marmite, Old Spice, PG Tips, Max Factor, and Cup-a-Soup.

A meeting for one fast-moving consumer goods (FMCG) company that I attended recently involved five scientists, all with PhDs from leading British universities. There was a theoretical physicist from Cambridge, an engineer from Bristol, a mathematician from Imperial College, an Oxford-trained biochemist, and myself, a neuropsychologist with a doctorate from the University of Sussex.

Our task? To evaluate the effectiveness of a male grooming product retailing at less than £10 ($15).

Shopping's golden age or an Orwellian nightmare?

Today, the power and sophistication of the persuasion industry have grown to an extent that Packard, even in his most paranoid moments, could scarcely have imagined. For advertisers, marketers, and retailers, advances in neuroscience seem to offer opportunities for achieving a competitive edge in a global marketplace where rival brands fight for consumers' hearts, minds, and wallets.

Take one technique causing concern to many consumers and advocacy groups that has worrying echoes of *Minority Report*, a film predicting a dystopian future filled with covert personalized advertisements. Imagine taking a journey by train or coach and resting your head wearily against the window. Immediately you hear an advertisement that seems to come from inside your head. A voice, which appears to be located behind your eyes and between your ears, is trying to sell you something. What is more, this strange and disembodied voice knows a great deal about your likes and dislikes, about the kind of products or services you often purchase.

A nightmare? An auditory hallucination?

This is merely the latest technique for directing commercials at unsuspecting consumers. An electromechanical transducer fitted to every window converts audio signals into high-frequency vibrations. When a tired traveler leans their head against the glass, the bones of their skull vibrate in sympathy. Even in noisy environments, this produces a crystal-clear sound that appears to originate inside their head. It's a sales message that only they can hear and one that, thanks to data gathered from social media pages and previous purchasing history, can be made uniquely enticing.

Developed by advertising agency BBDO Germany on behalf of broadcaster Sky Deutschland, the system has proved both highly effective and extremely controversial. While welcomed by potential clients as the "next big thing in public transport advertising," many consumers have expressed outrage. A video of the system in action produced comments ranging from anger—"This is a violation of a person's right to rest"—to threats of violence—"I think I'd take a sledgehammer to the window."

With sales techniques like this, and as I shall show in this book even more sophisticated ones on the horizon, it is hardly surprising that for many consumers, these developments raise the specter of their mind being, as they see it, taken over by ruthless commercial interests. They fear the imminent arrival of Orwellian "Big Brother" technologies with the power to dictate their purchasing decisions covertly.

To what extent are these concerns justified? Are the vastly wealthy companies employing these techniques, and the scientists who devise and develop them, out to manipulate consumers or merely to make shopping more productive and less stressful?

How effective are these latest "hidden persuaders" in affecting what shoppers buy and why? And what can you, as an individual consumer, do to protect yourself from their undue influence?

These are some of the questions that I will be answering in the following chapters. But first, let's take a step back in time to 1901, the year that science first met selling.

1

When Science Met Selling

More thought, more effort, and more money go to advertising now than have gone into any other campaign to change the social consciousness.

—Jean Kilbourne (2005)[1]

Advertising is an ancient art. Merchants in the early city-states would verbally extol the virtues of their wares to passers-by, or employ street criers, "chosen for their mellifluous voices and clear elocution,"[2] to sing their products' praises in the streets. There are obvious reasons for the development of advertising—as digital marketing specialists Damian Ryan and Calvin Jones put it in the modern age:

There are few certainties in the world of business, but one thing's for sure: if you don't let your customers know about your business, you won't stay in business for very long.[3]

And for tens of thousands of years, the purpose of advertising was solely promotion—to "keep the client's name in front of the people," in the words of Albert Lasker, about whom more shortly. Success in advertising, so its practitioners firmly believed, merely required creativity, common sense, and practical experience. They saw themselves as artists who neither needed nor wanted any help from science. However, as the twentieth century dawned, all of this began to change.

From promotion to persuasion:
The rise of the subconscious mind

Early in 1901, the organizing committee of Chicago's prestigious Agate Club invited 32-year-old Dr. Walter Dill Scott to give them an after-lunch talk. Scott, an Assistant Professor of Psychology at Northwestern University, chose as his topic "The role of psychology in advertising." After all had enjoyed an excellent lunch and fine wine in the club's elegant, wood-paneled dining room, the president called for silence and introduced the speaker. The audience, including many of the city's most successful advertising executives, settled back in their leather-upholstered seats.

What Scott told them was to spark a growing preoccupation with the consumer's subconscious mind. He explained:

> *Advertisements are sometimes spoken of as the nervous system of the business world. As our nervous system is constructed to give us all the possible sensations from objects, so the advertisement which is comparable to the nervous system must awaken in the reader as many different kinds of images as the object itself can excite.*

He went on to describe how, as advertisers, their efforts were directed toward producing "certain effects on the minds of possible customers. Psychology is, broadly speaking, the science of the mind. Art is the doing and science is the understanding how to do, or the explanation of what has been done. If we are able to find and to express the psychological laws upon which the art of advertising is based, we shall have made a distinct advance, for we shall have added the science to the art of advertising."[4]

Scott's talk and a subsequent bestselling book, *The Psychology of Advertising*, had a profound effect on the way advertisers saw their craft and on the importance they attached to science, especially to psychology. And there was more to come.

"I can tell you what advertising is!"

Three years after Scott's address to the Agate Club, John E. Kennedy, a former Royal Canadian Mounted Policeman, created a second revolution in the advertising world. And he did so with just three words. On a mild spring afternoon in 1904, Albert Lasker, one of advertising's great pioneers, was working in his office when a messenger boy arrived with a scrawled note from a stranger who had walked unannounced into reception. "I am downstairs," the note read, "and I can tell you what advertising is. I know that you don't know. It will mean much to me to have you know what it is and it will mean much to you. If you wish to know what advertising is, send the word 'yes' down by messenger."

Lasker hesitated. A shrewd businessman, who would go on to accumulate a personal fortune in excess of $52 million, he would have been used to being pestered by cranks and charlatans. Nevertheless, the message so intrigued him that he instructed the boy to show the man up. Their meeting, which lasted well into the night, ended with Lasker hiring Kennedy for the then enormous salary of $28,000 a year. Within two years, Kennedy, who had been scraping a living writing advertising copy for Dr. Shoop's Restorative, was earning $75,000 a year—and advertising had a new understanding of its function.

What so impressed Lasker, and would come to revolutionize the approach of the whole industry, was Kennedy's three-word description of advertising: "Salesmanship in print." John O'Toole, a later chairman of Lasker's advertising agency, commented:

It seems so simple and obvious today. But what this definition did in 1904 was to change the course of advertising completely and make possible the enormous role it now plays in our economy. By equating the function of an advertisement with the function of a salesman who calls on the prospect personally, it revealed the true nature of advertising. For the first time, the concept of persuasion, which is a prime role of a salesman, was applied to the creation of advertising.[5]

Two years later, in 1906, Chicago advertising executive John Lee Mahin noted the increasing importance that advertisers were placing on psychology. In his privately published *Lectures on Advertising*, he explained:

> *Advertising is making others think what you desire. It means utilising all those forces which produce impressions and crystallise opinions... The great power of advertisements is of getting into people's minds the ideas that they carry in such a way that people think they always had them... The consumer nearly always purchases in unconscious obedience to what he or she believes to be the dictates of an authority which is anxiously consulted and respected.*[6]

Having woken up to the fact that they were in the business of persuasion as much as promotion, advertising executives began actively to seek out psychologists, whose training, skills, and experience they now considered essential to understanding the consumer's subconscious mind.

Enter the Freudians

By the end of the First World War, an industry that had previously relied mostly on the creativity of copywriters and the imagination of artists was being increasingly influenced by the views of, in the main, psychoanalytically trained psychologists. These experts, a majority of whom were followers of Freud, emphasized the crucial part played by emotions in appealing to the consumer. Desperate to discover new ways of influencing the public mind, many advertising executives sought guidance from Dr. Ernest Dichter.

A sprightly, jovial, balding man who wore a bow tie and horn-rimmed glasses, Dichter liked to describe himself as "Mr. Mass Motivations Himself." On a hilltop overlooking the Hudson River, he set up the Institute for Research in Mass Motivation. Its well-equipped headquarters contained rooms for focus groups and others in which children watched television while being covertly observed from behind two-way mirrors, concealed tape recorders picking up their comments. Dichter also recruited a "psycho-panel" comprising hundreds of families whose emotional makeup had already been psychoanalyzed.

He informed his clients that by employing the methods advocated by Sigmund Freud, he would be able to provide them not only with a deep understanding of the consumer's wants and desires, but also with techniques for "controlling their behavior." Advertising agencies were, he claimed:

One of the most advanced laboratories in psychology... possessing the ability to manipulate human motivations and desires and develop a need for goods with which the public has at one time been unfamiliar—perhaps even undesirous of purchasing.[7]

One such client was a cigar manufacturer that had spent thousands of dollars on an advertisement that failed. It depicted a smiling woman handing out cigars to her husband and his friends. Although attractively painted and widely displayed, the advertisement actually led to a dramatic fall in cigar sales. Dichter explained that men smoked cigars because doing so, subconsciously, made them feel dominant and important. The cigar, he claimed, was a phallic symbol; by showing a woman encouraging men to smoke, the advertisement was psychologically neutering the company's male customers. The illustration was promptly altered, the copy rewritten, and sales improved dramatically; although just what these subtle changes actually were is lost to posterity.

As the Second World War ended, the massive manufacturing capacity that America had built up during hostilities was rapidly switched to civilian production. With the resulting vast inventories to sell, advertisers began listening ever more attentively to the psychologists. According to these experts, society was entering the "psycho-economic" age, in which their challenge was not merely to promote mass-produced products but to mass produce consumers.

In his presidential address to the National Council on Family Relations, sociologist Clark Vincent set out this agenda clearly when he explained that the family was no longer merely a production unit, but a "viable consuming unit."[8] Increasingly, advertising executives came to view the general public not as rational, but as driven by emotion and easily manipulated. The more emotional and the less rational consumers were perceived to be, the more advertisers felt justified in indulging in sensationalist or emotional appeals. This view of the buying public was summed up by one senior advertising executive, quoting approvingly the words of a champion hog caller in Kansas:

The words don't matter, friend, it's feeling that counts. The great thing is feeling. You got to put passion into it. You got to make that hog believe you got something that hog wants.

By the end of the 1950s, an estimated billion dollars a year was being spent on psychological research. It was these techniques, the desire to manipulate and, as he saw it, socially engineer consumers, that led Vance Packard to write his bestselling book *The Hidden Persuaders*.

Among the many examples Packard cited was research conducted on behalf of American Airlines to discover why many businessmen were so afraid of flying that they did so only when no alternative form of transport was available. He used a number of projective experiments, such as the Rorschach inkblot test,[9] before explaining to his clients that what these men feared was not being killed, but embarrassment and guilt at how their family would receive the news of their death. Using this information, American Airlines developed an advertising campaign directed at housewives. They extolled the advantages of flying away on holiday as a family and of the husband being able to get back home faster if he caught a plane. Airlines also went out of their way to create a "psychologically calm environment" in the cabin.[10]

However, it wasn't only advertisers who were attempting to shape public attitudes and opinions. Early in the twentieth century a new profession came into being: the public relations specialist.

Edward Bernays: The King of Spin

In the UK and the US, there are now estimated to be four public relations executives for every journalist. This means that almost every news story you see on television, listen to on the radio, read in print, or peruse on the internet is there only because of public relations, or as some firms now prefer to call it, "corporate communications." Funded by their clients' deep pockets, major public relations companies have more money and resources than most media outlets and are in a unique position to bias stories to the favor of their clients. They also have the power to bury bad news and enhance the reputations of even the most disreputable.

Edward Bernays, the "founding father" of public relations, was a hugely influential figure in his day. He was born in Vienna in 1891, his mother Sigmund Freud's sister and his father Freud's wife's brother, making him a double nephew of the founder of psychoanalysis.

During the First World War, Bernays worked for the US Committee on Public Information (CPI), a government-funded propaganda organization whose mission was to advertise and market the "war to end all wars" as the conflict that would "make the world safe for democracy." After the war, he was instrumental in establishing what his biographer, Stuart Ewen, describes as "a fateful marriage between theories of mass psychology and schemes of corporate and political persuasion."[11]

Bernays developed the strategy, still widely used today, of associating unpopular products with popular causes. During the 1920s, for example, he was commissioned by the American Tobacco Company to increase the number of female smokers by encouraging women to light up in public. He realized that the best way to promote this frowned-on action was to link it to the cause of female emancipation. With this in mind, he persuaded women's rights campaigners to hold up Lucky Strike cigarettes as symbolic "Torches of Freedom" during a protest march down Fifth Avenue in New York. The event made headlines around America and played a significant role in changing public attitudes. Bernays wrote in 1923:

> *A Public Relations man's success depends on his ability to create those symbols to which the public is ready to respond... to find those stereotypes, individual and community, which will bring favorable responses... to appeal to the instincts and universal desires is the most basic method through which he produces his results.*[12]

However, even as Packard's book was flying off the shelves and investment by advertising firms in psychological research had achieved an all-time high, the influence of the Freudians was waning.[13] In their place came a new and super-confident group of experts who called themselves "behaviorists." They dismissed what they considered to be the unscientific hocus-pocus of psychoanalysis and promised to transform psychology into a hard science.

Enter the behaviorists

In 1920, 42-year-old Professor John Broadus Watson was a rising star in the academic world. He had coined the term "behaviorism" in 1912 and the following year had published a widely acclaimed and highly influential paper in the *Psychological Review*. Here, Watson set out his manifesto for behavioral psychology, a "purely objective experimental branch of natural science" whose goal was "the prediction and control of behavior."[14]

The young academic's glittering career at Johns Hopkins University came to an abrupt end, however, when at the age of 42 he was summarily dismissed after leaving his wife to live with Rosalie Rayner, a considerably younger research student. The scandal left him unemployed and, in those socially conservative times, unemployable in academia. Undeterred, Watson set off for New York in search of new and more lucrative employment. His research had already attracted the attention of a number of senior advertising executives, who saw in behaviorism a powerful tool for influencing the masses. Soon after his arrival in the city, Watson got a job with the J. Walter Thompson agency, where he used his psychological knowledge, together with a flair for salesmanship, to mastermind some of the firm's most effective advertising campaigns. For Johnson & Johnson, he persuaded American mothers to use baby powder every time they changed a nappy. For Maxwell House, he established the "coffee break" as a tradition in offices, homes, and factories.

Watson promoted behaviorism in such an "audacious, forceful, and crystallising way" that it became "a sales pitch."[15] It made him a fortune and enabled him to enjoy the life of a gentleman farmer on his extensive Connecticut estate. His new theory of the mind exerted a profound influence over the way advertisers and their clients viewed consumers. From being puzzling, contradictory, and emotional individuals driven by unconscious hopes, fears, dreams, and desires, consumers were transformed in the minds of some advertising executives into an unthinking, anonymous "lumpenproletariat." They were mindless and purposeless, and their behavior could easily be controlled by a series of rewards and punishments, or, to use the behaviorists' term, positive and negative reinforcements.

Within five years, behaviorism had become the dominant psychological paradigm within the US and an important and influential concept throughout Europe. For advertisers and their clients, it seemed like their prayers had been answered. Consumers, they were assured, could be mass produced as easily as cars or typewriters, by means of the powerful new techniques developed in the psychological laboratories. All one needed to do was to provide the right kind of positive reinforcement in the correct amount and at the appropriate time, and people would not be able to prevent themselves from buying.

Not surprisingly, such views shocked and alarmed many people, especially when they were applied to advertising, suggesting both a willingness to control consumer behavior by manipulating the mind and an ability to do so.

Enter the behavioral economists

Advertising was not the only discipline that was becoming interested in psychology. By the end of the 1970s, a number of leading economists were seeking to increase "the explanatory power of economics by providing it with more realistic psychological foundations."[16]

In 1979, the prestigious journal *Econometrics* published an article by a legendary team of Israeli American psychologists, Daniel Kahneman and Amos Tversky, entitled "Prospect theory: An analysis of decision making under risk."[17] The following year, economist Richard Thaler wrote "Toward a positive theory of consumer choice."[18] Between them, these three authors created not only a new, and initially controversial, branch of economics, but a very different way of understanding consumer choices, which became known as behavioral economics.

Kahneman and Tversky also discovered an important factor in decision-making known as the "anchoring" heuristic. What this is and how it crucially affects the way consumers make decisions will be fully explained in Chapter 4.

Enter the neuromarketers

When I was studying psychology at university in the late 1970s, behaviorism was still a powerful force in the academic world. Many eminent psychologists continued to regard the human brain as an impenetrable "black box" and to dismiss any talk of consciousness, let alone of the subconscious, as unscientific. Nevertheless, what some have termed the "long dark age"[19] of psychology was fast drawing to a close.

From the mid-1960s onward, behaviorism began to be replaced by cognitive psychology. This new paradigm focused on the mental processes involved in such crucial skills as memory, language, decision making, and reasoning. Increasingly, psychologists began to perceive the brain as a type of computer. However, since cognitive psychology did not seem to yield much by way of commercially valuable insights, it appeared to be of no great interest or direct importance to advertisers, marketers, and retailers. What did, eventually, cause them to sit up and take notice was the rapidly growing field of neuroscience and the development of technologies that offered a chance to observe the brain in action.

In 2002, Professor Ale Smidts of Erasmus University, Rotterdam, coined the term "neuromarketing"[20] to describe the commercial application of neuroscience and brain-imaging techniques. In his inaugural lecture, Smidts explained that neuromarketing's purpose was to "better understand the customer and his or her response to marketing stimuli, by direct measurement of the processes in the brain," and to increase "the effectiveness of marketing activities by studying the responses of the brain."[21]

When I founded Mindlab in 2001, there was to my knowledge only one other similarly focused company in the world. Today there are more than 250 and academic interest is such that several universities, including Erasmus in the Netherlands, INSEAD in France, Zeppelin in Germany, and Stanford in the US, offer courses in neuromarketing.

The two technologies most frequently used by neuromarketers are quantified electroencephalography (QEEG) and functional magnetic resonance imaging (fMRI). I will describe in detail how these work and what they can tell us about consumer behavior in Chapter 3, but in summary, QEEG measures brain activity by recording and analyzing electrical activity inside the head, and fMRI measures changes in the blood flow to different parts of the brain, enabling researchers to detect the areas that are particularly active when carrying out certain tasks. As we shall see in Chapter 3, however, the technology required for fMRI scanning is large, cumbersome, and costly.

Other tools available to neuromarketers include eye tracking, both in the laboratory and in real-life situations, and devices that record changes in heart rate, breathing, muscle tension, temperature, and skin conductance. By equipping shoppers with GPS devices, or using data from their cell phones, it is possible to track their progress through a store, recording which aisles they visit, what displays they look at, and the length of time they spend in each department.

It would, however, be a mistake to regard these high-tech and high-priced devices as the only tools that neuromarketers can use in their quest to gain a greater understanding of consumer behavior. Rather, they are part of a new and rapidly developing toolkit of methodologies, including many psychological tests, that offer valuable insights into the consumer's subconscious thoughts and how persuasive a brand is being.

To find out what some of these techniques are and how they are being used, we should start by doing what millions of people do every day—go shopping!

2

Hidden Persuaders That Shape the Way We Shop

We are all at the mercy of influences of which we are consciously unaware and over which we have virtually no conscious control.
—*Robert Rosenthal,* Pygmalion in the Classroom

It's a fine spring morning in the Big Apple and I'm on a bargain hunt with a difference. My hunting ground is a fashion discount store on the outskirts of the city. My fellow hunters are half a dozen fashion-conscious New Yorkers with a keen eye for a good deal. The store does not look much: the outside is drab and the inside garishly decorated. No sales staff greet or assist the customers and the in-store music is loud. Receding into the distance of its vast, hangar-like interior are rows and rows of racks. Their garish chromium plating gleams brightly beneath the clinically cold glare of uniformly spaced fluorescent lights.

The racks seem to be buckling beneath lots and lots and lots of dresses, suits, hats, scarves, shoes, boots, handbags, manbags, belts, and fashion accessories. Most of these items are more utilitarian than eye-catching, but I, and my bargain-hunting volunteers, know that squirreled away among the run-of-the-mill are some mouth-watering bargains—designer-label goods, from such icons as Ralph Lauren, Versace, Lanvin, Valentino, Miu Miu, and Prada, that would set any fashionista's pulse racing. What is more, all are being sold at hugely discounted prices.

That a shopper's heart beats faster when a bargain is spotted is not speculation on my part but an established fact. Among the crowds wandering the aisles and searching eagerly through the well-stocked racks are my volunteer shoppers, women who have generously allowed me to record what happens as they track down things to buy.

A young woman wearing a white woolen beret is one of my guinea-pig shoppers. Her beret, the only unfashionable item on this otherwise immaculately turned-out 23-year-old, is something she is only wearing reluctantly and at my request. It conceals multi-colored sensors attached to her scalp by means of gloopy conductive electrogel that will record electrical activity in her brain as she shops. Also hidden from public scrutiny are sensors on her chest that monitor changes in heart rate, and two fastened to the fingers of her left hand that measure her level of physical arousal.

On her nose are perched a pair of spectacles that conceal a tiny video camera and microphone, which record everything she sees and hears during her bargain hunt. All of this equipment is connected, via a spaghetti-like tangle of wires, to a small shoulder bag containing equipment that continuously records what is going on in her brain and body. She has been in the store for 30 minutes and, even in that short space of time, has swooped on a slinky black maxi dress from Theory, a nifty denim vest and jacket from Joe's Jeans, a swish bag from Prada, and a head-turning fringed dress from Free People, all marked down by a significant amount. As I look on, at a discreet distance, she spots a pair of silver Jimmy Choo high heels at less than half price and gives a whoop of delight.

Back in our lab, my colleagues and I will use the video recordings to match the responses of brain and body to her shopping activity. We will be able to tell, precisely, which of her bargains produced the greatest and the least mental and physical excitement.

We will also be able to discover whether these peaks and troughs were linked to any particular location in the store or position on the shelf or clothes rack. In other words, we will be able to ascertain how the store could enhance the thrill of the chase still further, thereby increasing the amount of time people spend on their bargain hunt and thus the profits to be made.

Our research has shown that, for many consumers, the prospect of being able to buy a much-desired fashion item at a bargain price creates a mental buzz equivalent to winning a lottery prize or even snorting a line of coke. We typically observe a burst of high-frequency beta waves in the frontal regions of the brain when a bargain is spotted. This is accompanied by a sharp rise in the shopper's heart rate, which can go from around 70 beats per minute to more than 120. There is also a rise in skin conductance, indicating an increase in sympathetic arousal. This is part of the body's ancient fight, flee, or freeze survival response, the sympathetic branch of what is called the autonomic nervous system. Like the automatic pilot in an aircraft, this "flies" the body by controlling such things as heart rate, blood pressure, and breathing frequency, while our mind is concerned with other things.

Although increased sympathetic arousal can, under some circumstances, be interpreted as a sign of fear or anger, when someone is bargain hunting it is simply perceived as indicating excitement and pleasure. By analyzing precisely how consumers shop for bargains and gaining an understanding of the effects that discovering a deal has on their brain and body, we are able to help retailers make their offerings even more desirable.

Doing the shopping in Portugal

We move from the sunshine and glamor of Manhattan to a cold, damp February morning in the Portuguese coastal town of Porto. Once again, my team have wired up shoppers to monitor their responses as they do their weekly family shop in the vast Continente hypermarket. Like price-conscious consumers the world over, these shoppers keep a watchful eye out for bargains. However, while they eagerly load BOGOFs (Buy One Get One Free), discounted produce, and special offers into their shopping trolleys, what they are really interested in are big brand names. As they maneuver between display shelves stacked with more than 30,000 different items, their attention is mainly directed toward internationally known brands, such as Tide, Persil, and Nestlé, as well as national ones like Xau laundry detergent, Mimosa dairy products, Compal fruit juices, Delta coffee, and Renova's nationally famous black toilet paper.

It is these familiar items that are picked off the shelves first, while lesser-known products tend to be overlooked. Shoppers may glance at them, they may even lift them up for a closer inspection, but they are significantly less likely to put them into their basket or trolley.

Research such as this provides retailers with valuable insights into consumers' subconscious responses to key aspects of a store's layout, signage, and shelf displays. This information enables them to fine-tune their marketing strategy to increase sales. One of our studies, for example, showed that simply changing the position of one product in relation to another boosted sales of both. Other research has revealed that changes in the color or font used in signage, the level or color of lighting, and even the floor covering can exert a powerful influence over buying decisions.

Reading brain waves is not, of course, the only way to gain insights into the brain sell. Other techniques will be described later in the book, but for the moment let us take a closer look at the behavioral aspects of shopping. It is only by understanding the two key motivations underlying shopping that we can start to understand how the hidden persuaders are able to exert their influence.

Going shopping vs. doing the shopping

Going shopping is now the number one leisure activity for consumers in most countries. People go shopping for a wide variety of reasons: for the fun and excitement of acquiring new possessions; for the pleasure of visiting luxuriously appointed malls, gazing at attractive displays, and enjoying the sights and sounds of the bustling crowds; to be flattered and made to feel important by attentive sales staff; as an antidote to boredom or depression; or to meet friends, take exercise, and enjoy a welcome break in routine. Above all, they enjoy the sense of empowerment and control that going shopping provides.

Nevertheless, while *going* shopping is generally considered highly pleasurable, *doing* the shopping is usually regarded—especially by men—as a chore, something to be got over and done with as swiftly and with as little effort as possible. The way some men shop can be likened to a SWAT team rushing in to rescue a hostage, grabbing them and getting out as speedily as they can.

Doing the shopping involves buying things you absolutely need but don't necessarily want. Who, after all, really wants to own washing-up liquid, cat litter, or diapers? They are simply products that people with dirty dishes, cats, or babies have to have.

Consumers *do* the shopping to meet their needs. They *go* shopping to satisfy their wants. The difference between the two motivations may seem clear cut—but it is not, as we shall see.

Transforming needs into want-needs

Once a "want" becomes firmly lodged in a modern shopper's brain, they are not able to focus their mind on much else. The "want" has been transformed into a "want-need." As Jim Pooler, Professor of Urban and Population Geography at the University of Saskatchewan, puts it:

> It can be argued that in our modern economy virtually all purchases, even those that appear to be excessive, reflect real needs on the part of shoppers, and that nothing less will satisfy them. A teenager just doesn't want the latest fashion trend. Rather in his mind it is absolutely essential that you have clothes or accessories that are in style. An adult does not just want that home theatre system. Rather, because all of his friends have one, he just has to have one... This is the essence of shopping in the modern economy, where virtually everything, no matter how superfluous, is perceived not as a want, but as a need.[1]

Want-needs may generate an emotional desire so powerful that, as the following story illustrates, it has to be satisfied, no matter what the cost.

These boots were made for buying

At 19, Catherine has an insatiable want-need for boots and shoes. Her bedroom wardrobe and cupboards are filled to overflowing with every type, design, make, and color of shoe. Dress shoes, low-wedge court shoes, chisel-toe court shoes, slip-on point-toe pumps, stiletto-heel sandals, peeptoe shoes, knee boots, point-toe knee-high boots, ankle boots—Catherine has them all, often several pairs in identical styles and colors.

She gets as great a thrill out of purchasing her hundredth pair of boots or shoes as she did when buying her first. The fact that every purchase adds to her rapidly rising debt never deters her from shopping or diminishes the frisson of pleasure she gets when purchasing a new pair.

My Mindlab team and I recorded Catherine's mental and physical responses while she shopped for shoes at Lakeside, a major shopping mall in the UK. On discovering a pair of boots she desperately want-needed, Catherine's heart rate rose from 85 to 120 beats per second, her skin conductance shot skyward—indicating intense excitement—and her brain waves shifted from a relaxed to a highly aroused state.

"She's going to buy those shoes," I told a colleague as we monitored the young woman's progress from a nearby van. True to my prediction, that's just what she did.

What is important to understand is that want-needs are entirely created—not only by advertisers, marketers, and retailers, but also by public relations firms, internet bloggers, tweeters, and broadcast, print, and social media. Neuromarketing also plays a role, as it helps identify ways of tweaking a product to make it more desirable. In a typical experiment, different versions of a product, in a variety of shapes, colors, and designs, would be shown on a computer screen to volunteers who are wired to record their mental and physical responses. Eye tracking might also be employed to reveal the features that are studied most carefully and those that are paid no attention.

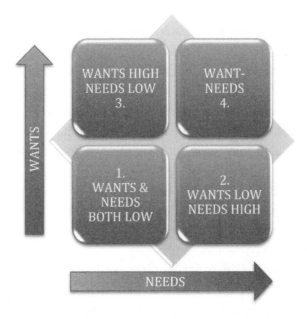

Figure 2.1 The needs, wants, and want-needs matrix

Using digital technology, changes can quickly and easily be made to the virtual product and the experiment run again. The color might be changed slightly, the size enlarged or reduced, the shape subtly altered. By analyzing the subject's subconscious responses, the product version that generated the most powerful want-need can be identified.

The relationship between wants and needs can be illustrated in the form of a matrix (Figure 2.1).

In Box 1 are products or services that consumers neither need nor want at the present time and are, therefore, highly unlikely to buy, at least for the moment. What is included in this box will, however, vary between consumers and contexts. What one shopper dismisses another may value highly, as items sold at yard sales and charity shops often demonstrate. Similarly, something that is seen as valueless in one context may be highly appreciated at another time or in other circumstances. Pottery discarded on the rubbish pile by Greek and Roman citizens, for example, is now displayed in museums and prestigious auction houses.

The products and services located in Box 2 are items people do not generally want, but may urgently need. Hardly anyone, for example, wants to visit the dentist or go to hospital for an operation. They may, however, need to satisfy the secondary want of removing an aching tooth or restoring their health.

Box 3 contains all those products and services that consumers can be persuaded they want, although they do not actually have any need for them.

Finally, in Box 4 are want-needs, those products and services that, once moved into this category in the consumer's brain, will virtually sell themselves.

Moving around the matrix: Creating want-needs

Even low-level wants and needs, those found in Box 1, can be transformed into want-needs through marketing and advertising. Here are six ways in which this can be achieved.

Make shoppers work for their purchases

One of the first to recognize that making customers "work" for their purchases was a great way of persuading them to want-need the product was American marketing guru Dr. Ernest Dichter, whom we met in Chapter 1. During the 1930s, he was approached by General Mills, which owned Betty Crocker, to improve sales of its cake mixes. He advised the company to stop using powdered eggs in its cake recipes; instead, it should instruct housewives to add an egg to the mix themselves. The point was not to make the cake taste any better, but to confer a home-made quality on a factory-made mix. The ploy worked perfectly and helped Betty Crocker become a greatly trusted and commercially successful brand. By giving consumers a role in the cake's creation, however minimal, Dichter enabled women to feel involved in the outcome and, consequently, to value it more highly.

In a fashion discount store, shoppers are obliged to work at discovering bargains. Other retailers encourage customers to achieve a discount by haggling. Allowing them to believe that they have out-smarted the retailer by securing a better price flatters their negotiation skills and makes them desire that item even more.

Occasionally, a shopkeeper may even encourage apparent dishonesty in a customer to close a sale. In his entertaining book *Influence: The Psychology of Persuasion*, Robert B. Cialdini tells the story of two brothers who ran a tailor's shop in New York. On greeting a new customer, one of the brothers would pretend to be hard of hearing. When the customer asked the price of a suit, the "deaf" brother would call out to his sibling, working in the rear of the shop: "How much is this suit?"

The second brother would yell out a price, which might be $190. Claiming not to have heard, the first would again ask the price. Back would come the same reply as before: "I said $190." The "deaf" brother would then tell the customer: "He says $90."

Cialdini recounts that on most occasions the delighted customer would immediately pay the $90 and hurriedly leave the shop, before the pricing "mistake" was discovered.[2]

In studies where we have wired up shoppers and recorded their responses to situations in which they were either offered a discount or encouraged to haggle successfully, we detected an increase in both mental and physical arousal, which peaked at the moment the deal was closed. Not only that, we also found that consumers placed a greater value on that purchase than would otherwise have been the case. This occurs, at least in part, due to what is called the "misattribution effect," which arises when heightened emotions are transferred from the situation that caused them to another object or person. Couples on a first date who ride a scary roller-coaster or watch a horror movie together, for example, may find themselves more attracted to one another because they misattribute the adrenalin buzz caused by the experience to the presence of the other person.[3]

It is the same whenever a shopper gets a bargain. The greater the excitement of the conquest, the greater the importance they attach to ownership. This also applies when people compete with others to buy things in the sales or at an auction.

Create a scarcity

One December afternoon shortly before Christmas, I watched two elegantly dressed, middle-aged women exchange punches in Schwarz's legendary toy store on Fifth Avenue, New York. The cause of this battle of the blue-rinses? The last remaining Cabbage Patch doll—the 1983 must-have Christmas gift from designer Xavier Roberts—which both were determined to buy. When a want-need is in short supply, shoppers may virtually spill blood to get hold of it.

Well aware of this, manufacturers sometimes deliberately ramp up the excitement by restricting the initial supply to retailers. If a buzz gets going on social media, so that shoppers are tweeting about the shortage and bloggers are discussing it, with luck queues will start forming around the block as people clamor to be the first to own the product in question.

Laboratory studies that my company and other researchers have undertaken demonstrate that scarcity, like cutting a deal, exerts a profound effect on physical and mental arousal. The more people are competing for a product, the greater is each individual's eagerness to acquire it.

On another freezing night one January, I started measuring the mental and physical responses of a group of young men queuing outside a major London store whose annual sale was due to start at 7.30 am the next day. Their goal? To get one of a limited number of video game consoles being offered at less than half price.

In addition to monitoring their heart rate, skin conductance, and brain waves, I asked them to complete a paper-and-pencil questionnaire. All of these enabled me to track changes in their attitude to that console as the hours crawled by. Far from their resolve faltering in the cold, they became increasingly passionate in their desire to obtain it. As the moment when the doors were due to open came closer, their heart rate, blood pressure, physiological arousal, and brain activity all increased.

When I asked them how they felt when they emerged from the store clutching their purchase, many describe experiencing a giddy high and feeling more alive than at any other time in their life.

"My heart was racing as I reached the counter," one told me. "I was filled with an overwhelming sensation of excitement. I began to hyperventilate. My hands were sweating. Then I caught sight of the box. It seemed to be beckoning to me!"

These physical changes, and the ever-growing value that those gaming enthusiasts placed on satisfying their want-need, can at least partly be explained by the theory of cognitive dissonance. Developed by American psychologist Leon Festinger in 1957,[4] this has become one of the most influential and intensively studied theories in social psychology.

Cognitive dissonance describes the feeling of discomfort we experience when we attempt to hold two conflicting beliefs simultaneously.

Imagine you are a smoker who wants to quit but finds it hard to break the habit. Being exposed to health messages and dire warnings about the medical consequences of failing to give up while continuing to smoke will create cognitive dissonance. In order to free themselves from these discomforting feelings, smokers have one of two choices: to stop smoking or to rationalize away the risk. Lifelong smokers will often say: "Of course I understand it's a risky habit, but so is driving a car, riding a bike, or even crossing the street." Alternatively, they may point out that their Uncle Charlie smoked 100 cigarettes a day and lived to be a healthy and sprightly 90-year-old. Both of these approaches will remove the dissonance, although only the first actually safeguards health.

In the late 1950s, a study entitled "The effect of severity of initiation on liking for a group" was conducted by Elliot Aronson of Stanford University and Judson Mills from the US Army Leadership Human Research Unit.[5] They persuaded 63 female volunteers to go through one of two initiation ceremonies—one severe and the other mild—in order to join a discussion group. In the severe condition they were obliged to read aloud obscene words, such as fuck, cock, and screw, as well as two vivid descriptions of sexual activity from contemporary novels. This task was probably far more stressful for young women in the late 1950s, when uttering such obscenities was even more of a taboo than it would be today.

The mild condition required them to read out less embarrassing words, such as virgin, petting, and prostitute. There was also a third control group, who were not required to read out any words and were allowed to join the discussion group immediately.

Researchers found that the women who went through the severe initiation found the discussion group significantly more worthwhile and attractive than those in the other two groups. They felt a greater sense of belonging and valued their membership more highly.

The same effect can be found in cults, where members are obliged to go through often strenuous and embarrassing tests before being allowed to join; and among members of US university fraternities, who have to endure hazing and "hell week" in order to be signed up.

The "That's Not All" (TNA) strategy

Although this sales technique predates neuromarketing by many decades, it still offers a fruitful field for research by psychologists and neuroscientists. The TNA strategy comes in two forms. In one, the retailer makes a product more appealing simply by reducing the price. A jar of coffee normally selling for $5 might, for example, be offered at $3.80.

To test experimentally the effectiveness of reducing prices, Carrie Pollock and her colleagues from the University of Arkansas[6] used a gourmet chocolate sale on campus. They set up a table selling large and small boxes of chocolates. Students who asked the price were randomly assigned to one of two groups. In one, the control condition, the salesperson—actually one of the researchers—priced the small box at $1 and the large box at $5. In the second condition, the salesperson initially quoted the higher price of $1.25 for the small box and $6.25 for the large box. At that point a colleague would correct her, saying that the prices were actually $1 and $5. The result of this apparent price reduction was remarkable. When the price appeared to have been reduced, even by as little as 25c, sales increased from 45 to 76 percent of visitors.

The second TNA approach is to include additional items or offer further, even greater savings. In front of me as I write is a magazine with a whole page devoted to just such an offer. A London tailor is advertising shirts, normally £70 to £80, for under £20. But TNA! As a reader of the magazine, I am able to claim a further 15 percent discount. But TNA! If I buy before a specific date, I will also get a free silk tie.

TNA is a widely used and, research shows, highly effective technique for transforming a previously "take it or leave it" product into a must-have item. BOGOFS, three for the price of two, or the free pens, radio-alarm clocks, or dinner services offered by some life assurance companies are all examples of this approach.

TNA works because, as I will explain in Chapter 4, it encourages consumers to adopt a mindless rather than a mindful approach to shopping.

Encourage playfulness

When people are busy playing, they are far more likely to be in a mood for buying. That is why so much money is spent on tacky souvenirs when we're on holiday, or visiting a tourist hot spot, a stately home, or a theme park. In his book *Faith in Fakes*, Italian philosopher Umberto Eco describes how the houses in Disneyland "give the impression of... belonging to a fantastic past that we can grasp with our imagination." However, as he also notes, while these toy houses invite visitors to enter, inside they find a "disguised supermarket, where you buy obsessively, believing that you are still playing."[7] In Chapter 6, I explore in detail the role of fun and fantasy in inducing people to generate want-needs.

Want-needs as distractions

Airports are increasingly being transformed from buildings from which to fly into places in which to buy. These hypermarkets with runways take advantage of the fact that, unlike normal consumers, passengers cannot easily escape their surroundings. They are also likely to be bored and in need of distraction, as well as possibly nervous and in search of reassurance. As a result, they will spend time and money browsing and buying. Often what they are purchasing is a form of friendship rather than a product. The want-need here is for human contact as much as for what is being sold.

An American journalist friend of mine recounted her experience of this "relationship" buying after arriving late and tired at Schiphol airport in Amsterdam. "The flight had been delayed, and I had been traveling alone for more than 10 hours. When we landed I had a couple of hours to kill before my next flight. I felt lonely, bored, and tired," she told me.

Wandering disconsolately around the airport, she came across a good-looking young man selling makeup. He was friendly, helpful, and prepared to devote time to her. As a result, she ended up buying more than $200 worth of cosmetics. "I didn't really need them," she said. "But I felt I owed him a good sale for the time he had spent with me and the way he had lifted my spirits."

Create a sense of inadequacy

At the start of the 1920s, Americans went about their business blissfully unaware that they had a problem that could cost them their chance of forming relationships or holding down a job—a personal inadequacy so severe and potentially life-destroying that even their best friend was too embarrassed to tell them. They had bad breath!

This new condition had been identified by the Lambert pharmaceutical company, which gave it the suitably medical-sounding name chronic halitosis. Having discovered the problem, it offered to sell sufferers what was, literally, the solution: Listerine, a powerful surgical antiseptic invented in the nineteenth century and originally sold as both a floor cleaner and a cure for gonorrhoea. Lambert's advertisements featured sad-looking young men and women, eager for romance, whose path to love was blocked by their apparently foul-smelling exhalations. Identifying this previously little recognized problem certainly paid big dividends for the company. In seven years, its revenues went from $115,000 to over $8 million.

Modern consumers are exposed to some 4,000 commercial messages each and every day, many of which rely on statements of personal inadequacy. We are warned that we are too fat or bald, too pimply or wrinkled, that we risk being bad parents, lousy lovers, inadequate hosts, or ungrateful guests. Our personal relationships may be ruined by body odor, dandruff, skin that is too dry or too oily, indigestion, heartburn, or stained teeth. In short, almost every possible inadequacy that could affect humankind may be inflicted on us unless we purchase the product or service being marketed.

Jonah Sachs, cofounder and creative director of Free Range Studios in New York, points out:

Since the emergence of modern marketing, professional communicators have relied on the "inadequacy approach." Tell your audience that the world is dangerous, that they lack what they need, that they don't quite fit in. Then offer the magic cure—your product.[8]

One way of transforming services like dentistry, surgery, or injections from a need that is not wanted into a want-need would be to market them as an aid to improving appearance and self-confidence. Caps to create perfect teeth, face-lifts for a more youthful appearance, breast implants to enhance sex appeal, and Botox to smooth out sagging skin are all examples.

While inadequacy selling still works, some commentators now believe that such messages are out of step with the more supportive and empowering climate generated by social media. As a result, people are tuning out any advertisements that generate anxiety and tuning in to recommendations from family, friends, and even strangers. The marketing way of the future, according to Jonah Sachs, consists in "messages based on empowerment, which make the audience the hero and remind them of how full of potential they are."[9]

The brain sell of selling

But what precisely are such selling techniques really all about? The *Shorter Oxford English Dictionary* defines the verb "sell" as "giving up or handing over to another person for money." While this is accurate, it does not take us much further in understanding either the psychology or the neuroscience behind the process. A more operationally useful way of understanding selling is as "problem solving." A manufacturer or service provider offers customers neither products nor services, but solutions to problems arising from needs or, as we have seen, want-needs.

No matter how complex a problem is, it will be composed of just three elements. These have been identified by Wayne Wickelgren, Professor of Psychology at the University of Oregon and one of America's most eminent experts on problem solving, as the Givens, the Operations, and the Goals.[10] What exactly these will comprise depends on whether the problem is one confronting the supplier, the marketer, or the consumer.

The supplier

At the manufacturing or service development stage, the Givens are everything the consumer can see, hear, feel, touch, smell, and possibly taste about a product. Neuromarketing can help identify which aspects of the Givens are most likely to appeal and which to appal. By drilling down into the consumer's subconscious through the use of brain imaging, it becomes possible to identify the small and subtle changes that are required. In one case, our research suggested that the color of the cap on a child's plastic bath duck be changed from purple to blue. When tested in the market, this tiny and seemingly insignificant alteration increased sales by more than a third.

Operations comprise the variety of ways the product can be made, and the Goal is in essence to understand precisely what business the company is really in. While this may seem little more than simple common sense, the truth can defeat the finest commercial minds. Nevertheless, the future of most companies depends on the extent to which they get the answer right.

In the *Harvard Business Review* in 1960, Theodore Levitt posed the question of what business nineteenth-century US railroad barons believed themselves to be in. What did they see as their goal? Had this question been put to these men, who were among some of America's wealthiest and most influential business leaders, they would scornfully have replied: "Our goal is to run railroads."

However obvious this answer might seem, it was in fact wrong. The real goal was to transport large numbers of people over great distances as rapidly and as cost-effectively as possible. Had the barons realized this, Levitt comments, they would have invested in roads and air transport—the two modes of transport whose rapidly increasing popularity following the Second World War drove many railroad owners into bankruptcy. Levitt noted:

> *In truth, there is no such thing as a growth industry... There are only companies organized and operated to create and capitalize on growth opportunities. Industries that assume themselves to be riding some automatic growth escalator invariably descend into stagnation. The history of every dead and dying "growth" industry shows a self-deceiving cycle of bountiful expansion and undetected decay.* [11]

McDonald's is a modern example of a company that truly understands its goals. But exactly what business is this exceptionally successful multinational company really in? The answer most people give is "selling fast food and drink." That's true enough—but that's not the company's real business. In reality, it is in the property business. It locates and buys prime sites, which are then rented out to franchisees. It is the latter's job to sell meals in order to pay the rent. Only by understanding the true nature of the solutions they are selling can companies hope to compete in the global marketplace.

As Michael Bevans, Head of Advertising and Publisher Solutions at Yahoo!, says:

> *Too many salespeople are like dogs chasing tennis balls. The customer asks them a question and they race off to retrieve the information. Another question and another ball to chase. So it goes on. A more intelligent approach is to stop being reactive and start to become proactive. They should stop, step back,*

> *and ask customers what they want to achieve. In other words, what are the problems to which they are seeking solutions?*[12]

This is where the insights from neuromarketing can help.

The marketer

When it comes to advertising, marketing, and selling, the Givens are the methods used to communicate information about the product to consumers in the most persuasive way possible. They include not only the item and its packaging, but whereabouts on the shelf it is displayed, how it is lit, the ease with which it can be accessed and evaluated, and what other products are nearby.

One study in which my laboratory was involved concerned advertising movies via billboards, or "out-of-home" advertisements, as they are known in the trade. Because renting sites is costly, companies need to ensure that they provide the right number of posters in the most effective locations. Their problem is how to be sure that this operation is profitable by choosing appropriate sites that will be seen by their prospective audience. Should posters be put on the side of buildings, the back or sides of buses, at bus stops, in railway or subway stations? Getting the location wrong could be an expensive error.

To help solve this problem when it came to advertising in Paris, a major film studio developed an ingenious strategy. It filmed a tour of the city, then digitally superimposed posters for its movies in a wide variety of locations. My lab then took audiences into preview theaters and wired up their brains and bodies to record their responses to the film.

Different audiences were exposed to varying saturation levels of posters, ranging from 15 to 45 percent, in locations that included buses, metro stations, and even the sides of Paris's famous *pissoirs* or public toilets. Our brief was to analyze consumer responses and work out which combination of poster saturation and location worked best at a subconscious rather than merely a conscious level.

Secondly, Operations consist of the different advertising and sales channels available. At the turn of the twentieth century, advertising operations were limited to the various forms of print media. The arrival of radio, then television, significantly increased the range and variety of options. Today, digital and mobile technology have expanded the possibilities still further.

To return to the billboard example, although these are not, perhaps, the most exciting form of advertising, they are in fact one of the few traditional media channels predicted to grow over the next decade. A $6.5 billion business in America alone, revenues are set to increase by more than 4 percent over the next few years, with global spending rising even faster. In part this is due to the fact that consumers who travel by car or rail past a billboard cannot fast forward it, as they might a television advertisement. As a result, they are more likely to attend to and act on the message.

An equally important reason for the rise in popularity is the way technology is transforming the operations this medium can perform. The past few years have seen a move away from print and paper to digital billboards and posters. These enable advertisers to change the image at will and thus make messages more relevant and timely. Commuters might, for example, be tempted by advertisements for cappuccinos while traveling into work, or be persuaded to watch a television show being promoted on the same digital screen on their journey home. Ways in which digital billboards are able to display personalized advertisements will be described in Chapter 11.

For the marketer, the Goal is to explain, in the most persuasive way possible, why the product or service truly offers a better, faster, and more cost-effective solution than those of their rivals. In this task the insights that neuromarketing provides can also prove extremely valuable, by analyzing the ways in which consumers subconsciously react to different types of changes in design, application, or marketing.

The consumer

From the consumer's point of view, the Givens relate to the degree to which a product or service provides the best solution to their problem. In turn, the Operations consist of the range of solutions to which the product or service provides an answer. The greater the range of problems something can solve, or at least appear to solve, the more interested a person will be in buying it.

This is what I term the Swiss Army knife effect. A penknife can cut things and that's about all. A Swiss Army knife can incorporate two different types of screwdriver (flat head and Philips head), a can and bottle opener, a gimlet, tweezers, a toothpick, a corkscrew, a nail file, scissors, a saw, a file, a hook, a ballpoint pen, a magnifying glass, pliers, a keyring, a hex wrench, and a fish scaler, as well as several different-sized blades. These enable it to perform a far wider range of operations.

The cell phone provides an excellent example of a product that started out solving a single problem—communication without a landline—and ended up solving hundreds. My first cell phone was called a Rabbit. Launched in 1992 by Hutchinson, it was a location-specific device, meaning that it could only make outgoing calls when the user was within 100 meters of a Rabbit transmitter. It could be used as a pager, but was not capable of receiving calls. While slightly more useful than a public phone box, the only alternative way of phoning someone when away from office or home, its use was obviously very limited.

The truly handheld cell phone was invented by Motorola researcher Martin Cooper.[13] On April 3, 1973, he used one to make the world's first ever cell-phone call, to Dr. Joel S. Engel of rival Bell Labs. The prototype was slightly larger than a house brick, weighed 2.5 lb, offered just 30 minutes of talk time, and took 10 hours to recharge.

Today's smartphones clearly do so much more. They combine the functions of a still and video camera, sound recorder, calculator, web browser, and music center. With a suitable app, a smartphone can also serve as a radio, a television and video player, a magnifying glass, a barometer, an altimeter, a thermometer, a weather forecaster, a decibel meter, a mirror, and a document scanner, plus a host of other functions.

Nevertheless, simply adding functions to a product is not necessarily going to turn it into a winner. A good many electronic products are engineered to the point where, while providing the user with a wide range of options, they can appear overly complex. Engineers all too readily fall victim to what is termed the "consensual fallacy." This occurs when an expert, whether a computer geek, a medical doctor, or a university lecturer, assumes that everyone possesses the same level of knowledge as they do. The result is that while what they say or write may make perfect sense to anyone with their level of training and experience, it is gobbledegook to everyone else.

Most customers lack either the time or the patience to go up a long learning curve with a new device. For them, the ideal is Kodak's slogan promoting the ease of using its film to take a snap: "You press the button, we do the rest!" Operations that the manufacturer may believe add value can in fact deter the customer. This is not to say that such options should not be present, but merely that they should be hidden from view and capable of being utilized the moment the box is opened. In other words, the best products are plug and play. The insights of neuromarketing can be vital in reaching conclusions such as this.

Finally, for the consumer the Goal is to identify the most satisfactory solution to what is, typically, a divergent problem, one with multiple solutions. It is here that web browsing, price-comparison sites, and specialist blogs, as well as manufacturers' own websites, come into their own, enabling customers to make informed choices about which products will best satisfy their goal. Neuromarketing is playing an increasingly important part in the design of such sites to ensure their appeal at a rational, conscious level while also appealing to subconscious motivations.

The selling power of price

One well-known aspect of marketing is of course price. However, what retailers have long realized is that when it comes to making price judgments, most consumers are fairly clueless.

More than 50 years ago, according to one account,[14] a toothpaste manufacturer was approached by a man who said he could increase its profits by 40 percent at next to no cost to the company. He demanded $100,000 for the secret. Reluctant to pay what was then an enormous sum, the company held urgent meetings with its technical staff to see if they could discover what the man was referring to. When this failed to produce any results, the manufacturer reluctantly signed a cheque for the amount demanded.

In return, it received a slip of paper on which were written four words: "Make the hole bigger."

The company immediately increased the diameter of the hole in its tubes from 5 mm to 6 mm, which meant that the quantity of paste squeezed onto the brush increased by 40 percent. It sold more toothpaste because consumers used it up more quickly. Yet nobody noticed; or if they did, they saw no reason to complain.

This strategy of selling a smaller quantity without reducing the price is one that companies are increasingly using today. By doing so they can hold down the cost to the consumer while maintaining, or even increasing, their profit margins. Such price manipulation succeeds because once consumers have grown familiar with a certain product, they assume that the amount they buy stays the same. MarketWatch.com writer Chuck Jaffe explains:

> *Ask people in the orange juice aisle what, exactly, they are buying, and they will say "a half-gallon of orange juice," even if they are picking up a carton that holds less. That's why people buy a "pint" of ice cream that is really 14 ounces; it may be the same-sized container with more air in the product, or it might just be fancy new packaging that is a tad smaller. The issue is that the manufacturer sets up the unit price in ounces, where the competitor selling a true pint does its unit pricing by the pint. That makes it hard for the average consumer to do a quick-look price comparison and know which is the better deal.*[15]

To squeeze the maximum profit from every sale while giving the impression of providing the best possible value for money, retailers employ highly trained specialists, known as price consultants. One of the strategies that these experts often suggest is to shrink the packaging while keeping the price the same. As Harvard Business School marketing professor John T. Gourville says:

> *Consumers are generally more sensitive to changes in prices than to changes in quantity, and companies try to do it in such a way that you don't notice, maybe keeping the height and width the same, but changing the depth so the silhouette of the package on the shelf looks the same. Or sometimes they add more air to the chips bag or a scoop in the bottom of the peanut butter jar so it looks the same size.* [16]

This is what Kellogg's did when it phased in very slightly thinner boxes for breakfast cereals, including Apple Jacks, Honey Snacks, Cocoa Krispies, and Corn Pops. The differences were so small that shoppers seem not to have spotted them; nevertheless, given the vast quantities of cereals the company sells, the effect on profits was significant. A similar tactic was used by US lavatory paper manufacturer Quilted Northern when it reduced the width of its Ultra Plush paper by half an inch. To give another example, Skippy peanut butter was given a new plastic jar. The old one had a smooth base, while the new one has a dimple in it. Although customers either fail to notice this change or take no account of it if they do, the increase in the bottom line is considerable: the original jar contained 18 ounces of peanut butter, the new version 16.3 ounces.

Donald MacGregor of MacGregor-Bates, an American firm that researches consumer decision making, comments:

> *If a company reduces the price of something by 5% but gives you 10% less, you look at the price and think you are getting a bargain. But they have increased their profit margin by 5%. It looks good to you, but you're really paying more to get less.* [17]

This view can be confirmed using eye tracking and Implicit Association Testing to measure how consumers read labels and what their response is to paying the same amount for smaller quantities. While these packaging differences are usually so small as to be virtually imperceptible to the conscious mind—would you honestly know whether the box containing your favorite cereal has shrunk by a quarter of an inch?—brain scans show that they are detected subconsciously. While this may not, immediately, have any negative effect on shopping habits or product preferences, over time it could well fuel distrust and suspicion among regular users. Although such feelings may always lurk below the level of conscious awareness, they could nonetheless undermine the relationship with that brand. As William Poundstone comments in *Priceless: The Psychology of Hidden Value*:

> *Though price is just a number, it can evoke a complex set of emotions... Depending on context, the same price may be perceived as a bargain or a rip-off; or it may not matter at all.*[18]

Mindless shopping and the left-digit bias
The effect of particular prices can be extremely sophisticated. Imagine visiting your friendly neighborhood coffee shop and finding that your favourite latte has risen in price from £2.20 to £2.42 a cup. Will you still buy it? Now consider a second price hike. This time your brew will set you back not the £2.90 you'd expected but £3.19. Will you pay up or find a cheaper coffee house?

According to Lydia Ashton of the University of California at Berkeley, while the proportional increase in price remains the same, at 10 percent, a majority of consumers will accept the first price increase but walk away from the second.[19] Why is this?

In the first scenario, the left-most digit remains the same, at £2, while in the second it goes from £2 to £3. That is what is striking customers as significant, not the ratio of the price increase.

Although the effect of the left-most digit bias on consumers' readiness to pay has been known for more than 75 years—it was first investigated by Eli Ginzberg at Columbia University in 1936[20]— only more recently has it been subjected to significant academic scrutiny.[21] Something priced at £9.99 or $9.99 will always strike a majority of shoppers as cheaper than something costing £10 or $10, and research has shown that between 30 and 65 percent of all prices end in a nine.[22] And it is not just price, the left-digit bias applies to any transaction involving numbers. After analyzing over 22 million wholesale used-car transactions, for example, Nicola Lacetera of Case Western Reserve University and her colleagues[23] found that sale prices drop discontinuously as the mileage goes above the 10,000-mile threshold. This means that a car with a reading of 28,999 miles will be regarded as more valuable in the eyes of many buyers than one with 30,000 on the clock.

Although the precise neural mechanisms for the left-digit bias have yet to be identified, the most likely psychological explanation is that consumers attend only to the left-most digit and so remain blind to any that follow. Studies of purchases on eBay have found a similar blindness to such additional charges as shipping costs and nonsalient taxes.[24]

Barriers to the brain sell

So far in this chapter, I have outlined some of the ways in which new needs can be identified and then transformed into highly desirable want-needs by the application of consumer psychology and neuroscience. Now let's take a look at some of the barriers to the brain sell, obstacles to purchasing that exist in the consumer's subconscious mind.

The yuck factor

Imagine visiting my laboratory on a hot summer's day to take part in a neuromarketing study. Someone offers you a glass of chilled orange juice, which you accept. As you reach to pick it up, you notice a large cockroach crawling up the outside of the tumbler. An apology is offered and the insect replaced in its container. You are assured that there is no cause for concern: the cockroach was bred for research, is completely clean, and cannot harm you. Despite this assurance, would you still want to drink that previously tempting glass of orange juice?

Eight out of ten of those who took part in this experiment refused to drink the juice. What is more, the moment they set eyes on the insect their heart rate, skin conductance, and brain activity all soared and, in many cases, remained elevated even after the offending creature had been removed from the scene.

Here's an experiment into the effects of the "yuck" factor that you can carry out for yourself. All you have to do is take a sip of water from a tumbler, slosh it around your mouth, and then spit it back into the glass. Repeat the process until you feel unable to continue through your sense of revulsion at drinking a solution containing your own saliva.

For most people, that point comes at around the third or fourth sip. Why are we so repelled by something that can cause no harm to our health?

The answer lies in our innate fear of contamination, combined with a perfectly understandable desire to avoid anything with the potential to be harmful. Most things that disgust us carry such a risk, which is why the yuck factor is an important aid to survival, and why retailers must take it into account when designing shelf displays.

Although you are unlikely to find cockroaches openly crawling along supermarket aisles, there are other sources of in-store "contamination" that can deter you from buying. Certain frequently purchased household items such as rubbish bags, cat litter, cigarettes, feminine napkins, and diapers are subconsciously perceived as so disgusting that the appeal of nearby products is significantly reduced. This is known as the "contagion effect," and shoppers become reluctant to buy food or drink placed on the same shelf. These unconscious fears about contamination are most likely to arise when the "yuck"-related products are displayed in transparent packaging. The negative effect on the sale of other products is lessened by having opaque packaging that makes it harder for the shopper to visualize the product inside.

Summing up their research on the subject, Andrea Morales, Assistant Professor of Marketing at Arizona State University, and Gavan Fitzsimons, Professor of Marketing and Psychology at Duke University, noted that "these effects hold even when actual contact does not take place and that only perceived contact is necessary for contagion to occur. In addition, we find that these effects are not temporary but persist across time and can influence choice, reflecting a meaningful change in evaluations."

They reported that shoppers were "largely unwilling or unable to admit"[25] that such contagion fears had influenced their judgment, suggesting that the effect occurred subconsciously.

Brain imaging studies have identified the regions where these emotions, and their associated expressions of disgust, are generated. One of these, called the amygdala, evokes feelings of nausea and the sensation of being sick when stimulated by a small electric current. According to the researchers, who worked with patients undergoing brain surgery, sensations in the throat and mouth were produced that were "difficult to stand." Such stimulation also caused physical responses, with one patient commenting: "My stomach went up and down like when you vomit." There is more on this important brain region in Chapter 7. The second deep brain structure involved in feeling disgust is the anterior cingulate cortex, which also plays an important role in processing painful stimuli.

Furthermore, these studies have revealed the extent to which disgust is contagious. If we see a fellow shopper expressing even mild disgust, we are likely to experience similar feelings of revulsion. There is, in the words of Bruno Wicker from the Institut de Neurosciences Physiologiques et Cognitives and his colleagues:

a common mechanism for understanding the emotion in others and feeling the same emotions in ourselves. Furthermore, and most importantly, these findings suggest that a similar mechanism allows us to understand both the actions and the emotions of others, therefore providing a unifying perspective on the neural mechanisms underlying our capacity to under-stand the behavior of others.[26]

This is an ancient and basic evolutionary response that, when humankind roamed the earth as hunter-gatherers, safeguarded them against eating rotten or poisonous food. In a retail environment, it means that even a subconscious awareness of another shopper's expressions of disgust is liable to trigger similar feelings of aversion. This negative emotion, again often subconsciously, deters the customer from buying that product or even causes them to leave the store prematurely.

By conducting neuromarketing studies into the effects of contagion fears among consumers, it becomes possible to identify and eliminate many of the triggers for this irrational but still influential barrier to buying.

The subconscious power of the font

The choice of fonts on packaging or labels might seem to be of little, if any, significance. It cannot surely make any difference to consumers whether the lettering on a package or a store sign is in **Arial**, `Courier`, **Verdana**, Times New Roman, or **Comic Sans**—but in fact it does.

The speed and ease with which a customer is able to make sense of any sales message, known as "processing fluency," plays a significant if usually subconscious role in determining whether or not that item will be purchased. This is especially so when the product is unfamiliar to the consumer. A font that is even a little hard to decipher slows shoppers down by increasing the amount of effort and therefore energy that they must expend in making sense of it. As I will explain in Chapter 4, the brain uses energy very frugally and adopts a wide range of mental strategies to conserve it. By making a product seem less familiar, a difficult font also causes shoppers subconsciously to perceive it as less honest. Nathan Novemsky, Associate Professor of Marketing at Yale School of Management, explains:

An effect of processing fluency that is particularly relevant to decision-making is its influence on judgments of truth. People associate familiarity with truth, and high fluency can lead to an inference that a statement is familiar… The more easily a given target can be processed, the more positively it is evaluated.[27]

In one study, Novemsky and his colleagues asked participants whether or not they wanted to purchase one of two cordless telephones, or if they preferred to think about the decision. Information about the phones was printed in either a standard font or one that was difficult to read. When the facts were presented using an easily read font, only 17 percent of people deferred the purchase. When the choice of font made the words harder to read, 41 percent did so.

Researchers have also found that if a photograph is included alongside the text, the brain is able to process the information more easily and swiftly. Strangely, this holds true even when the image used has nothing at all to do with either the product or the printed information.[28]

In a study conducted by my laboratory, these findings were taken one stage further by investigating whether a choice of font that enhanced the attractiveness of a product could actually make food tastier and, consequently, more likely to be purchased again. Astonishingly, under some circumstances this is exactly what happened.

We divided subjects into two groups and asked them to rate a bowl of tomato soup. Each was described on a menu as "rich and creamy." The difference was that one menu was printed using Courier and looked like this:

`Rich and creamy tomato soup`

The second used Lucida Calligraphy and looked like this:

Rich and creamy tomato soup

After eating the soup, participants were asked to rate it for taste, enjoyment, and freshness on a seven-point scale. They were also asked to say how likely they were to buy the soup. Although both groups had soup from the same tin, 64 percent of those whose menu was printed in Lucida Calligraphy rated it as tastier, fresher, and more enjoyable compared to those in the Courier group. Twice as many also said that they would definitely buy the soup for themselves.

In the next chapter, I will explain why this should be, how neuro-marketers set about measuring the thoughts and emotions of consumers, and how advertisers, marketers, and retailers are using these findings to boost sales and increase profits.

3

"I Know What You're Thinking!"

The inviolability of the brain is only a social contract, like nudity.
—*Dr José Delgado*, Physical Manipulation of the Brain, *1973*

"I know what you're thinking," the young man told me. "All I have to do is attach a few electrodes to your head and I can read your mind as easily as I would a book!"

We were chatting while sipping coffee at his company's splashy display stand in the exhibition hall of a New York hotel. A marketing conference was in progress and there was considerable interest among delegates in the new discipline of neuromarketing. Small wonder: Clients were being assured that this revolutionary form of market research would allow them to "eavesdrop" on the minds of their customers, to read their thoughts, probe their subconscious, and locate the "buy button" in their brain. It would, they were assured, soon make every other type of market research obsolete.

This was 2003 and at the time I viewed such claims with great skepticism. If my more than 20 years of experience in consumer neuroscience had taught me just one thing, it was that understanding the brain is a great deal more complex than this enthusiastic young salesman was making out. Indeed, it was evident to me that his pitch owed more to marketing hype than hard scientific fact.

In the 10 years since our meeting, however, advances in brain-imaging technology, combined with an almost exponential growth in our knowledge of brain function, have transformed my views. It is now clear that while neuromarketers cannot read anyone's thoughts, they are able to monitor subconscious responses to brands and products. They can detect changes in interest and attention while people are shopping and predict, with considerable accuracy, which part of a message will be remembered and which forgotten. They can tell whether a consumer's emotional response is positive or negative, the extent of their motivation, and the likelihood of that product being bought.

Before getting into the technical details of how this is done, let's ask a more basic question: Why wire up shoppers' heads to discover what they are thinking or feeling? What is wrong with simply asking them?

The problem with just asking

The traditional way of finding out what consumers think about products and brands is through surveys and focus groups. Unfortunately, even the most carefully constructed and painstakingly conducted such research contains significant sources of error. The main difficulty with this approach is that people will, for a variety of reasons, either lie or put a gloss on the truth. Especially when it comes to sensitive issues, they will provide answers that they think are socially acceptable or that show them in the best possible light. As a result, their explanations are often so far from the truth as to be at best misleading and at worst useless.

The order, manner, and presentation of the questions asked in a survey or focus group can also have a significant influence over the answers received. Even the gender and ethnicity of the person conducting the survey or facilitating the focus group can have a profound, if often extremely subtle, influence.

Daniel Gilbert and J. Gregory Hixon from the University of Texas at Austin demonstrated the power of such aspects in a study that involved asking female students to complete word fragments, such as P_ST, which might be used to form the words POST, PAST, or PEST. Among the fragments they were asked to complete were POLI_E and S_Y. These were presented via a videotape on which either a Caucasian or an Asian female turned over the cards on which they were written. When the assistant was Caucasian, POLI_E and S_Y produced words like POLICE and SKY, but for the Asian female the words were completed as POLITE and SHY. The reason for these differences lay in stereotypical views about the personalities of Caucasian and Asian women, the former being perceived as assertive and dominant, the latter as compliant and passive. The researchers commented:

> *Stereotypic beliefs about women's roles may enable one to see correctly that a woman in a dark room is threading a needle rather than tying a fishing lure, but they may also cause one to mistakenly assume that her goal is embroidery rather than cardiac surgery.*[1]

Unspoken, and often unconscious, assumptions such as this can seriously skew the findings of both focus groups and surveys. While market researchers have developed techniques to minimize these biases, for instance by using well-trained facilitators to run focus groups and statistical methodology to identify anomalous results in surveys, they can do nothing to overcome one serious barrier to understanding what is going on in a consumer's mind: memory. This is not because people are unintelligent or uncooperative, but simply as a result of the way in which mind and memory work.

While we tend to think of memories as offering a more or less accurate record of past events and the emotions they aroused, this is not in fact how they work. Rather, memories are a reconstruction of events, and are built up every time they are accessed, usually with a subtly different result. If there is a gap in our recollection—and there are typically a great many—we fill in these blanks with invention through a process known as confabulation. The extent to which even vivid recollections, which people truly and honestly believe to be true, can actually be works of fiction is illustrated by the strange story of the great New England airship.

The airship that never was

The story begins just six years after Orville and Wilbur Wright had made the first sustained human flight in a powered, heavier-than-air flying machine. On the morning of December 12, 1909, Wallace Tillinghurst, a prominent Worcester businessman, called the *Boston Herald* to inform them that he too had built a heavier-than-air monoplane. Not only that, he and his crew had flown in it for some 300 miles from Boston to New York and circled the Statue of Liberty before returning home.

Tillinghurst's story created a sensation. In the weeks that followed, thousands of New Englanders, among them police and military officers, doctors, lawyers, and respectable businesspeople, reported memories of seeing that historic flight. One eye witness was Alex Randell Revere, MA, an aeronautical engineer. He not only vividly recalled observing Tillinghurst's flight, but gave the following detailed account of the airplane:

> *I saw the frame quite plainly, and it seems to be of unusual size. I should say the wings have a sweep of seventy feet and the tail and propeller seemed about forty-five feet in length. I could plainly hear the engines whirr and from the explosions of the motor I should say it was either a six or eight-cylinder.*[2]

A clear and vivid memory, one might suppose. Yet the airship never existed except in Wallace Tillinghurst's fertile imagination. It was all a hoax.

While this is an extreme example of the way memory can deceive us, such innocently "invented" recollection of events is commonplace and is one of the reasons so little trust can be placed in even the most diligently reported memories.

As I will explain in greater detail in Chapter 4, memories can be divided into two types, explicit and implicit. Explicit memories, those we are able to describe consciously, are often uncertain, inaccurate, and of limited value. Implicit memories are not available to conscious reflection and can only usually be deduced indirectly, by their influence on our behavior. Unfortunately for market researchers, customers only become consciously aware of their buying decisions after they have made them, at which point they often seek to justify them, both to themselves and others, so distorting the true reason for that decision. It is these intellectual justifications that consumers describe during traditional market research interviews.

As the late British advertising guru David Ogilvy put it:

The trouble with market research is that people don't think how they feel, they don't say what they think and they don't do what they say.[3]

However, using "brain-reading" technology, such as QEEG or fMRI, the precise moment at which a memory is laid down or accessed can be accurately determined, as can the regions of the brain most actively involved in those tasks. For instance, neuroscientists at Brighthouse Institute of Thought Sciences, at Emory University Hospital in Atlanta, Georgia, have confirmed a link between activity in the medial prefrontal cortex and attraction to a product. "If it fires," explains Director of Science Clint Kilts, "you are more likely to buy because that product clicks with your self-image."[4]

In a study of decision-making, William Gehring and Adrian Willoughby from the University of Michigan used QEEG to measure the electrical activity in the brains of subjects seated in front of a computer screen on which were displayed two boxes.[5] One represented a bet of 5 cents and the other a bet of 25 cents. The subjects' task was to select either box in the hope of winning a reward. After a box had been selected, it changed color: red denoted a loss of the amount displayed, while green indicated a win. The researchers found that a quarter of a second after the subject had learned of their win or loss, they showed a dip in activity in the area of the brain known as the medial frontal cortex. The more frequent the losses, the greater the dip.

Gehring and Willoughby argued that this was direct evidence of what is known as the "gambler's fallacy," the decision-making error whereby after a string of losses, people increasingly conclude that they must be due for a win. The researchers demonstrated that such decision making must be emotional in nature, since it occurred far too rapidly to be the result of conscious deliberation. Their research also demonstrated the power of QEEG to reveal what is really going on in the brain.

The birth of neuromarketing

Before explaining what QEEG measures and how this form of brain imaging works, let me explain my own involvement in the development of what would, two decades later, come to be called neuromarketing. It all started in the early 1980s, while I was working in the Department of Experimental Psychology at the University of Sussex, conducting research into biofeedback (see Box 3.1).

Box 3.1   How biofeedback works

As its name suggests, biofeedback involves providing—"feeding back"—to individuals information about their mental and physical responses so that they can learn to bring about desired changes. When learning to relax, for example, the person may be attached to a skin resistance monitor. As the tension begins to flow away from their body, the machine in some way indicates the progress toward a more relaxed state. It may produce a buzz that gets lower as the person unwinds more and more deeply, or display a row of lights that extinguish in time with their relaxation.[6]

My interest in using biofeedback for training the brain began when I acquired a newly invented piece of equipment called a Mind Mirror. The world's first easily portable electroencephalogram (EEG), the Mind Mirror had been designed to help train individuals to control their brain. By the standards of today's EEGs, it was a primitive device. Only five electrodes were used (today from 16 to over 200 are employed) and the brain waves could only be stored on a cassette tape. In order to create a viable research tool, my first task was to modify the device so that data was digitized and recorded on a computer. The next challenge was to write the software necessary for analyzing that data.

Using this equipment, I developed a number of therapeutic exercises that trained people to control their brain waves in order to experience deep levels of relaxation and meditation.[7] I also explored ways of using it to enhance mental performance and improve attention, and even undertook some early studies of treating some forms of Attention Deficit Hyperactivity Disorder (ADHD) in children.

What I needed to employ in my research was a suitably attention-grabbing and emotion-arousing stimulus. The answer I found was to use 30-second television commercials. These had the advantage of having been crafted to catch and hold people's attention as well as to arouse a variety of emotions. I contacted several advertising agencies, who sent me over 100 commercials.

My work attracted a certain amount of media interest, including coverage on BBC TV's popular science program *Tomorrow's World*.[8] There were also some articles in the advertising and marketing press, as well as pieces in national newspapers. While some expressed enthusiasm for the technique, others were fearful of what such work implied. One journalist even suggested that I risked creating an Orwellian nightmare.[9] Although some of the companies showed great interest in my findings, advertising and market research firms were either disinterested or dismissive.

Rosi Ware, a spokeswoman for Millward Brown, one of the world's foremost market research companies, could see no purpose in the technology. "It isn't adding anything to what we already do," she told *Tomorrow's World*. "You won't be able to do anything with those results."[10] (The fact that Millward Brown now has an active neuromarketing department suggests that in fact this was not true.)

There the matter rested for more than 20 years. I had little interest in promoting the work commercially and continued my research mainly in the field of stress and anxiety.

Then in 2001, having realized the potential of such techniques, I helped set up what was certainly the UK's, and quite possibly the world's, first neuromarketing company.[11] By 2012, there were some 250 companies worldwide offering various types of neuromarketing to clients including retailers, advertisers, design houses, brand managers, fast-moving consumer goods companies, film and television production houses, marketing consultancies, and even political parties.

Because of my early involvement in this field of consumer research, journalists have sometimes referred to me as the "father of neuromarketing." This is not strictly true. In 1971, 10 years before I began my research, an American psychologist named Herbert Krugman used EEG to discover what went on in a viewer's brain while watching television. His subject was a 22-year-old secretary, onto the back of whose head he taped a single electrode. He then recorded and analyzed her brain activity while she either watched television or read a magazine.

Krugman reported that within 30 seconds of beginning to watch television, the woman's brain waves were no longer fast-moving beta waves, associated with paying attention, and instead were mostly slower alpha waves, indicating a state of inattention. When she began to read the magazine, however, the beta waves once again predominated, showing that alert attentiveness had replaced relaxed daydreaming. In later studies, he also discovered that while she was watching television her right hemisphere, which processes information emotionally and noncritically, showed greater activity than her left hemisphere, whose role is to deal with information logically and analytically. Krugman commented:

It appears that the mode of response to television is more or less constant and very different from the response to print. That is, the basic electrical response of the brain is clearly to the medium and not to content difference. [Television is] a communication medium that effortlessly transmits huge quantities of information not thought about at the time of exposure.[12]

Following Krugman, other US researchers carried out similar research,[13] but it would be more than 30 years before there was any serious commercial interest.

QEEG: A window on the working brain

Communication between brain cells (neurons) involves various chemicals, such as sodium, potassium, chlorine, or calcium. Because these carry an electrical charge, an electrical potential is generated between the inside and outside of the cell. This can be detected from outside the skull as "brain waves." Their frequency is measured in Hertz (Hz), or cycles per second, and power (amplitude). Both vary continually depending on the brain's mental state and the environmental challenges with which it has to deal.

Although there is still no universal agreement on exactly which frequencies belong in which category, most neuroscientists define the frequency ranges associated with each label as follows:

- *Delta waves* (0.5–4 Hz), associated mainly with sleep.
- *Theta waves* (4–6 Hz), associated with a relaxed mental state and daydreaming.
- *Alpha waves* (8–12 Hz), associated with relaxed wakefulness and inattention.
- *Beta waves* (13–40 Hz), irregular, very small-amplitude waves, which are most prevalent when someone is alert and engaged in a task requiring mental effort.
- *Gamma waves* (40–100 Hz), associated with memory formation and consolidation.

What neuroscientists have demonstrated is that every thought we have and every emotion we experience, whether or not we are consciously aware of them, has a corresponding electrical signature that is, at least in theory, capable of detection.

For clinical purposes, the various waves that form part of an EEG trace are read by a specialist trained to make sense of the squiggly

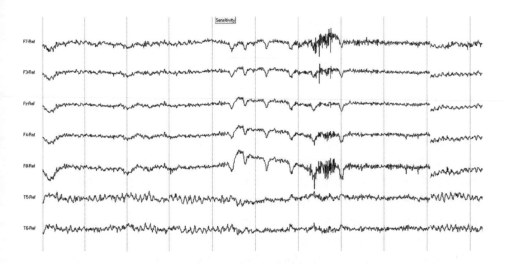

Figure 3.1 An EEG trace—the letters and numbers on the left indicate the position of the electrodes on the scalp.

Courtesy Mindlab International.

lines of raw data on a computer screen or long paper strips. From EEG traces such as the one illustrated in Figure 3.1, doctors are able to identify neurological disorders, such as epilepsy or a tumor, by the characteristic patterns they produce.

For neuromarketing and other nonclinical purposes, the outcome is digitized (which is where the "quantified" in QEEG comes from), making it easier to understand. Neuromarketing researchers employ their knowledge of the location of different frequencies to answer such questions as: How did viewers respond to that television commercial? What emotions did that new brand design arouse? How much attention did shoppers pay to different shelf displays?

In the course of our work, my colleagues and I have analyzed recordings from people who were going shopping, watching movies at the cinema, reading bestselling books, driving cars, piloting light aircraft, and even from police officers undergoing riot control training. When combined with other specialist equipment, such as eye-tracking devices that record precisely where the person is looking on a second-by-second basis, it is also possible to discover precisely what that individual was seeing and hearing at the moment specific brain activity was being recorded.

The strength of EEG recordings is that they show events unfolding in the brain in real time. When analyzing a television commercial, for example, time frames can be selected corresponding to the length of individual scenes. This enables the impact generated by each scene, together with its relationship to the rest of the commercial, to be evaluated and compared. Similarly, a shopper's gaze and brain activity can be monitored while they are walking up and down the aisles of a supermarket and scanning products on the shelves.

If, for example, there was a surge of beta waves at 1 minute 37 seconds into a television commercial, this would be the precise moment at which something happened on screen to trigger an increase in interest and attention. Greater activity in the frontal regions on the left side of the brain, at another point in the reading, would show that the individual was experiencing positive emotions. The same increase on the right side of their brain would, however, indicate a more negative emotional reaction.

However, QEEG is only one technique used to explore the workings of the brain. The second, more complex and costly approach is functional magnetic resonance imaging, or fMRI.

fMRI: Seeing into the consumer's mind

Whenever any part of the brain becomes especially active, the small blood vessels in that region dilate, causing more blood to flood in, bringing extra supplies of oxygen and fuel (glucose) for the neurons.

This oxygen-rich blood reduces the amount of oxygen-free hemoglobin and causes a small change in the magnetic field and, consequently, in the MRI signal. The scanner is able to detect these changes and identify which brain regions have been activated. If, for example, a subject sees a sudden flash of light, the visual regions at the back of their brain are activated, blood flow increases, and the MRI signal changes accordingly.

The power of fMRI to reveal the secret workings of the brain is immense. Since the early 1990s, when this type of noninvasive brain scanning first became possible, the technology has led to enormous medical advances. It has provided a window on the way people reason, make decisions, form memories, and experience emotions. It has also resulted in some remarkable and commercially valuable insights into the workings of the consumer's mind.

In one of the first demonstrations of brain scanning's potential as a neuromarketing tool, a team at Baylor College of Medicine in Houston, Texas, led by Read Montague, recreated the famous Pepsi blind taste challenge. While they were inside the scanner, volunteers were asked to sip some cola. When they were not told whether they were drinking Pepsi or Coca-Cola, a region of the brain associated with experiencing rewards—the ventral putamen—was five times more active with those tasting Pepsi than with Coke. When they were told what they were drinking, however, the results were very different. Dr. Montague explains:

Not only did the subjects nearly all say they preferred Coke but another area at the front of the brain, the medial prefrontal cortex, which is linked with thinking and judging, lit up as well as the ventral putamen. This showed that subjects were allowing their memories and other impressions of the drink— in other words its brand image—to shape their preferences.[14]

Brain scans can also reveal other details of potential commercial value. For example, when an area known as the somatosensory cortex is active, it indicates that the person is imagining owning and using that product. "[Brain scans] show that preferences have measurable correlates in the brain; you can see it," says Justine Meaux, a Brighthouse neuroscientist. "We can use this difference to guide our decisions about how we market to people."[15]

While both QEEG and fMRI—and, in some laboratories, the two combined—have proved themselves to be powerful neuromarketing technologies, they are not without their problems. The most important are that QEEG tells you precisely *when* a brain event occurred but not exactly *where* in the brain it took place, while with fMRI you know fairly precisely *where* but not *when*. There are more details in Box 3.2.

Box 3.2 Brain imaging problems

QEEG

- QEEG only detects electrical signals close to the surface of the brain. It is relatively insensitive to activity in the deeper structures, where emotions are generated.
- While it shows the precise moment a signal was produced, it cannot accurately determine its location.
- Pressures of time and cost limit the number of people involved—there are seldom more than 40 in a study and often considerably fewer.
- Brain signals recorded in the real world are likely to be contaminated by "noise." A major source is the 50 Hz (UK) and 60 Hz (US) alternating current produced by almost every type of electric or electronic equipment, such as fluorescent lights, air conditioning, elevator motors, and so on. The recording equipment itself can also generate unwanted noise.
- Other artifacts—false signals generated by interference from inside the person's body, the equipment itself, and the surroundings in which it is being operated—include eye movements and so-called myogenic artifacts, produced by the muscles underlying the scalp and some muscles in the neck.

fMRI

- A brain scanner is noisy, subjects must remain motionless, and claustrophobia can pose a problem.
- fMRI is not a cheap technology. Scanners cost around $2 million (£1.5 million) to purchase and hundreds of thousands of dollars a year to run. They also depreciate like crazy: a scanner becomes more or less obsolete within five years.

- Scanners require skilled technicians to make and interpret the scans.
- Subjects must travel to a scanning center for testing and only one person can be recorded at a time.
- While commercial messages can be sent to the volunteers lying flat on their backs in a scanner, either by means of a mirror or a miniature television screen, these are scarcely the most natural surroundings in which to evaluate brands or compare products.
- The length of time taken to record the image means that it is a snapshot of how the brain was responding over a period of some ten minutes. It is not possible, for instance, to analyze the rapidly changing images in a television commercial.

The difficulties with artifacts can be especially acute when making readings under real-life conditions, such as when out shopping. As Jon Ward, Director of Acuity Intelligence, told me:

> *If you go in with an EEG system in a university, you'll be in a sterile room, with blank colored walls, controlled lighting, no windows, no sound (in most cases). And then you try going into a supermarket and do an EEG study, where you've got a hundred kids, you've got music, you've got your mobile phone ringing: you've got all this other stimulus around you and you'll never get clean data.*[16]

The scientific credibility of neuromarketing

In its early years neuromarketing faced a barrage of criticism, some entirely justified. A 2004 editorial entitled "Brain Scam?" in the prestigious journal *Nature Neuroscience*, for example, described neuromarketing as "little more than a new fad, exploited by scientists and marketing consultants to blind corporate clients with science."[17]

One source of difficulty arises from the need to protect client confidentiality. This makes neuromarketing companies unable to offer their data and, often, their methodology for peer review, something academics consider essential to validate an approach and prevent fraud.[18]

Roger Dooley, author of the widely read *Brainfluence*, told me one further reason for companies' reticence:

> *It may be the data is not all that good in some cases, or it's conflicting or it requires too much human judgment to really be publishable. I think there is also a tendency, if you're a neuromarketing firm, and if you feel you have cracked the code for interpreting the data, you would prefer to keep that as your own secret sauce, rather than exposing it to outside scrutiny and allowing your competitors to piggy-back on your work.*[19]

However justified such secrecy may be from a commercial viewpoint, it leaves many scientists skeptical about the industry's claims. In 2008, a blogger writing under the name Tzramsoy summed up the situation when he complained:

> *Trying to get to grips with what neuromarketing really is, must be a frustrating task. Because wherever you turn, companies flash their brain brand logos, fancy phrases and selling points. Neuromarketing does indeed seem to be a phrase for the commercial (and VERY rarely validated) use of neuroimaging tools to test consumer's preference.*[20]

Nevertheless, steps are now being taken to increase the scientific credibility of these approaches.

In 2011, the American Research Foundation set up an initiative to evaluate the credibility and commercial value of neuromarketing. It invited eight of the world's leading neuromarketing companies, including my own, to analyze the same eight television commercials. The reports produced were reviewed by a panel comprising some of the most eminent QEEG and fMRI specialists. After lengthy deliberations, these experts concluded:

> *Some of the methods and constructs used are scientifi-*
> *cally well validated in terms of the existing neuroscience*
> *literature and peer reviewed publications... Other vendors*
> *demonstrated proprietary measures with a high correlation*
> *with marketplace outcomes even though science may not*
> *yet provide a clear foundation for the interpretation of such*
> *measures.*[21]

Their recommendation, which all of us at Mindlab fully endorse, was that the industry must "undertake more scientific research and validation of neuromarketing research methods and findings."[22]

Other neuromarketing techniques

Although QEEG and fMRI are the technologies with which people interested in the brain sell are most familiar, these are not the only ways in which neuromarketers can investigate the subconscious mind.

Eye tracking

Using infra-red beams to detect eye movements, eye-tracking devices reveal not only the direction a person's eyes took while studying, for example, a magazine advertisement, but how long they spent examining a particular aspect of the ad. Participants can either sit in front of an eye tracker and view images on a screen, or carry a portable device with them as they pursue a wide range of activities, from going shopping to driving a car. One way in which this information can be presented is shown in Figure 3.2.

Heart rate

Changes in heart rate, due to increases in physical arousal, can easily be detected using sensors placed on the chest or by means of a finger pulse meter. This can provide a useful indication of physical excitement.

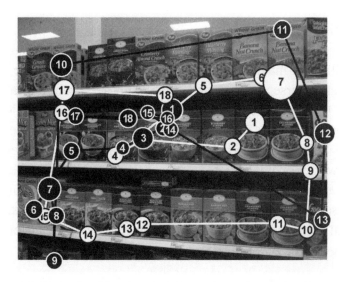

Figure 3.2 Gaze plot. Numbers in the circles indicate the direction of gaze of male (white circles) and female (black circles).The size of the circles shows how long the part of the image was attended to.The larger the circle, the greater the attention paid.

Courtesy Mindlab International.

Skin conductance

As we become more physiologically aroused, changes occur in our body's ability to conduct a small electrical current. These changes may be measured by means of electrodes attached to the fingers and can provide a very sensitive indication of subconscious responses.

In one study, we recorded our subjects' memories of different types of loss, from losing their keys or cell phone to the death of a fictional character in a book or film. In addition to measuring changes in skin conductance, we also asked them to rate their emotions on a scale. One of the losses explored was the shooting of baby deer Bambi's mother in the Disney cartoon of the same name. All our subjects remembered watching the film and some of the women said they had been moved by the slaying. None of the men admitted to feeling in the least upset, but their skin readings told a different story. As they recalled this memory, all of them showed a significant spike of emotional arousal.

Implicit Association Test

In addition to making physiological measurements, some neuro-marketers, ourselves included, also employ psychological tests. One of the most commonly used is the Implicit Association Test (IAT), which enables an individual's subconscious responses to be studied without the need for brain imaging. In an IAT, the speed with which words or images are sorted into different categories, such as "Accepted" and "Rejected," is measured precisely. Because the responses are made too rapidly for the conscious mind to intervene, the final sorting provides important insights into the subconscious workings of the brain.

Tracking the subconscious online
At Mindlab we have developed software that enables subconscious decisions and emotions to be tracked over the internet. In this way, thousands of consumers can be tested, rather than the very limited number of participants whose responses can be analyzed in a laboratory setting.

One of the techniques we employ involves very gradually exposing images of a well-known brand and asking the participant to indicate the moment it becomes recognizable. This enables different brands to be compared and the effectiveness of a particular advertising campaign to be evaluated.

All of these approaches are enabling advertisers, marketers, and retailers to develop ever more refined and sophisticated methods of selling, both in the high street and online.

The future of neuromarketing

Over a decade ago, Professor Uttal, a pioneer of brain-imaging research, warned:

More imaginative applications of EEG produce "conclusions" that usually turn out to be little more than science fiction fantasies… No psychologist has yet been able to demonstrate a solid association between specific thoughts and these errati- cally changing scalp potentials.[23]

Since he made that pronouncement, the tremendous advances in our understanding of brain function have, as I made clear at the start of this chapter, helped transform those "science fiction fantasies" into science facts. While we are still only at the frontiers of truly understanding the brain or of being able to make complete sense of those "erratically changing scalp potentials," progress is being achieved.

In this chapter I have presented a "warts and all" portrait of neuromarketing to highlight some of the problems currently facing this newly emerging discipline. It may be a long way from that young neuromarketing salesman's confident boast that "All we have to do is attach a few electrodes to your head and we can read your mind as easily as we could a book!"

Nevertheless, neuromarketing has established itself as a commercially valuable technique that can provide insights into consumers' subconscious minds—insights that simply could not be obtained in any other way. The rest of this book looks at some of these discoveries in more depth.

4

Why Shopping Isn't "All in the Mind"

The relationship between the mind and the body is more complex than has previously been presumed... evidence on embodied cognition is starting to establish that the body too might be influencing the mind to a greater degree than has previously been recognized.

—Iris Hung & Aparna Labroo[1]

Could your brain survive outside of your body? If it was placed in a vat of life-sustaining fluid, could it go on functioning as normal long after the rest of you had perished?

The first time this intriguing idea crossed my mind was when, as a student, I attended my first post mortem. The body to be opened up by the pathologist's knife for medical examination was that of a 22-year-old man, who had been killed after his motorbike skidded on a patch of spilled oil and he crashed into a parked lorry.

Pathologists learn to objectivize the human body, to regard it not as a person but as a collection of organs, an intellectual puzzle whose solution, the cause of death, they are tasked with discovering. As a 20-year-old student attending his first autopsy, I had no such defenses. Perhaps that is why, decades later, I can still vividly recall the sights, sounds, and smells of that old-fashioned basement mortuary.

The first stage of the autopsy process involved slicing through first skin, then subcutaneous tissue, and finally the thick fibrous tissue, the galea aponeurotica, that attaches scalp to bone. The pathologist began his incision behind the young man's left ear, cutting firmly and deeply as he extended his cut around to the top of the head, finishing behind the right ear. Now he was able to drag hair, skin, and tissue away from the bone as one might remove peel from an orange. Using a bone saw, he next cut through the skull, taking great care not to slice too deeply and so risk damaging the brain. Having deftly sawed through the cranium, he was able to remove the top of the head and reveal a large blood clot between the brain and the outer protective layer of tissue, the dura. It was this trauma, known medically as a subdural hematoma, that had killed the motorcyclist. All that remained before the brain could be removed from the skull was to slice through the optic and third cranial nerves, which control eye movements, and the brain stem. The blood-covered organ could then be lifted from the head and placed in the scales.

Staring down at the slimy, convoluted organ in the scoop, I could well understand why Egyptian embalmers mashed the brain with hooked bronze needles before extracting it in globules through the nose. They saw its sole function as a sort of radiator to cool the blood. Only one organ would be left inside the mummified body, the heart. This, they believed, possessed the individual's essence or *ka*, and this was all that was necessary for a person to take with them into the afterlife. I remember asking myself in wonder: "Can this unprepossessing lump of fat, protein, and water truly be everything that makes us human?"

In this chapter, I want to try to answer such a question from the point of view of a neuroscientist, and explain why it is a mistake to view the brain as a separate organ, rather than as part of our body, our immediate surroundings, our society, and our culture.

Science and the disembodied brain

The concept of the brain surviving outside of the body is an idea that has long fascinated novelists, philosophers, and scientists. In *William and Mary*, Roald Dahl tells the story of a philosopher named William who leaves instructions for his brain to be removed after death and kept alive. An artificial heart supplies the blood and one eye is left floating on the surface of the vat to allow William literally to keep an eye on his surroundings—on a world that, of course, he can now only observe but never interact with. If you want to know what happens to William and his wife Mary, you'll have to read this engrossing short story, which appeared in Dahl's 1960 collection *Kiss, Kiss*.

American philosopher Hilary Putnam famously created the "brain in a vat" thought experiment as an attack on metaphysical realism, the view that the world is composed of objects that are independent of the mind. He asked people to imagine the possibility that they were merely a brain connected to a computer program capable of perfectly simulating real-life experiences. A skeptic could argue that if we cannot be certain that we are *not* a brain in a vat, we are unable to exclude the possibility that all our beliefs about the outside world are false. Putnam's argument, which "centres on the possibility of an evil demon who systematically deceives us,"[2] formed the basis for the science fiction film *The Matrix*.

Although for obvious ethical reasons no doctor today would ever consider conducting such a grisly experiment, attempts to preserve the human brain after death were made during the late nineteenth century. In 1884, a French researcher, Jean Baptiste Vincent Laborde, made what seems to have been the first ever attempt to revive criminals who had just been guillotined. A century before, the inventor of this method of execution, Dr. Joseph Ignace Guillotin, had claimed that the "decapitation machine" offered a more humane and merciful death than hanging. Over subsequent years, increasing numbers of doctors and anatomists disputed this assertion, reporting that the victim's brain remained alert and active for several agonizing minutes after being separated from the body. As early as 1795, German anatomist Samuel Thomas von Sömmering noted, in a letter to Parisian journal *Moniteur*: "For as long as the brain retains its vital force the victim is aware of his existence."[3]

In an effort to resolve the controversy and calm concerns, the French government commissioned Laborde, a physician, to undertake a study, for which they supplied the heads of several recently guillotined prisoners. Some of what he referred to as *restes frais* (fresh remains) he attempted to revive with injections of oxygenated cow's blood. On another occasion, he connected the carotid artery of a severed head to that of a dog and reported partial restoration of brain function. The head's eyes opened and closed, appearing to attend to what was going on around it.

Another physician, Gabriel Beaurieux, reported how the "eyelids and lips" of a decapitated murderer named Languille "moved in irregularly rhythmic contractions for about five or six seconds." He went on to describe how, when the face started to relax and the eyelids began to close, he had bawled out the prisoner's name:

> *I called in a strong, sharp voice, "Languille!" I saw the eyelids slowly lift up without any spasmodic contractions... but with an even movement, quite distinct and normal, such as happens in everyday life, with people awakened or torn from their thoughts... Languille's eyes very definitely fixed themselves on mine... I was dealing with undeniably living eyes which were looking at me.*[4]

It was not until the twentieth century that medical science was sufficiently advanced to give such a macabre project any chance of success. During the 1960s Robert White, a neurosurgeon at Cleveland Metropolitan Hospital, undertook a series of studies in which he removed the brain of one monkey and attached it to the circulatory system of a second. In an account of his work,[5] White described how the monkey's eyes "tracked the movement of individuals and objects in the room." When food was placed in its mouth, it "chewed it and attempted to swallow it." Despite the fact that all his monkeys died within three days, White had no hesitation, when asked whether he would consider carrying out such an experiment with a human brain, in replying: "Of course. I see no reason why it wouldn't be successful with a man."[6]

No brain is an island

If the brain could survive physically outside the body, could it also survive psychologically? According to Lawrence Shapiro, Professor of Philosophy at the University of Wisconsin-Madison, many scientists are committed to a computational theory of mind, according to which "Cognition begins with an input to the brain and ends with an output from the brain." As a result, they believe that they can limit their investigations to "processes within the head, without regard for the world outside the organism."[7]

If this view is correct and our senses are merely devices for "inputting" information and our skeletal muscles the means of "outputting" actions, then a brain could indeed continue to function, at least after a fashion, as a biological computer uninfluenced by its surroundings.

However, this "standard cognitive model" is being strongly challenged by a relatively new approach known as "embodied cognition." Proponents of this view argue that the brain's workings can only be understood in terms of its relationship to the body. For instance, Bram Van den Bergh and his colleagues at Erasmus University, Rotterdam argue:

Cognitive activity is fundamentally grounded in a physical context. Cognition is both supported and constrained by the architecture of bodies and brains. As a consequence, our body is capable of influencing consumer behaviour.[8]

Other neuroscientists take this argument still further by suggesting that the brain is not only embodied but also extended. It stretches out beyond its immediate surroundings of home, family, and friends into society and the wider culture. All of these are intimately interconnected and function as a dynamic and tightly integrated whole. Communications specialist Dr. Wilson Bryan Key observes:

We are an integral part of the reality we perceive. No known way has been discovered whereby humans can detach themselves from their perceptions and their myriad of inherent biases. The realities perceived are products of unconscious socio-economic–political conditioning. Over time, these perceptions aggregate into cultural perspectives.[9]

So what does this mean in terms of the brain sell? If this view is correct, then consumers' thoughts and emotions will be influenced, to varying degrees, by everything in their surroundings. From this it follows that, by subtly altering the environment (or for that matter the culture), it becomes possible to change the way shoppers think and feel in any direction one wishes—to influence, consciously and subconsciously, how consumers relate to brands and how they can be persuaded to buy.

We can illustrate this by looking first at the relationship between our selves and our brains. Note the plural. It comes as a surprise to many people to discover that we possess not one but two brains.

The influence of our second brain

The first brain is located inside our head and the second inside our guts. Both profoundly influence the way we think and feel.

The enteric nervous system (ENS) comprises around 100 million neurons, about the same number as one finds in the brain of a cat.[10] Although this is thousands of times fewer than are present in the cerebral cortex, there are good reasons for describing it as a second brain. For one thing, the ENS is able to operate autonomously, continually monitoring mechanical and chemical conditions in the digestive tract. It controls the churning of the guts and the secretion of enzymes, making use of in excess of 30 neurotransmitters, most of them identical to those in the central nervous system.

Our two brains have extensive connections and work together to control digestion in order to meet the body's varying energy demands. As a result, anything that affects our "gut" brain also influences our "head" brain, and vice versa. Anyone who has experienced acute anxiety over an exam or a job interview will be only too well aware of the extent to which this decreases performance and increases the urgent need for a toilet!

What this means for anyone in the business of selling products or services is that the consumer may be swayed by an appeal to either of their two brains. However, for greatest effect, the influence should be extended not so much to hearts and minds, but to both the brain in the head and the one in the guts.

The influence of our second body

Just as surprising for most people is the discovery that we are really not one but two different organisms who happen to share the same skin.

This "second self" is composed of some 100 trillion bacteria that live inside the guts of every healthy adult. At approximately a kilogram, or a little over 2 lb, this microbiome weighs as much as many of our organs. It also contains around ten times as many cells as those formed by our father's sperm and our mother's egg. While the latter provide about 23,000 different genes, the microbiome contributes around 3 million.

Both of these organisms coexist in a state of intimate mutual dependency, with the wellbeing of each dependent on the health of the other. In exchange for warmth, protection, and nourishment, the microbiome provides the ability to digest many of the complex carbohydrates that we would be unable to process in its absence. Up to 15 percent of the energy used by the average adult is generated in this way. Our second self also plays an important role in weight gain or loss. While those who pile on the pounds are often blamed for greed, the answer may lie not in their head but in their guts.

In 2006, Dr. Ruth Ley and her colleagues at the Washington University School of Medicine in St. Louis, Missouri, published the results of a study into the differences in gut bacteria of overweight and undernourished Americans.[11] There were, they reported, significant differences between these two groups, which could help account for their variations in weight.

The powerful influence of bodily needs over consumer choice is demonstrated every time we go shopping for food, when whether or not we have eaten recently has a significant impact on the quantity and type of food we purchase. In a study designed to measure the extent of this influence, I gave two groups of volunteers £10 each to buy food for lunch in a supermarket. The only difference between them was that one group had been denied anything to eat all morning, while the second was supplied with 370 calories of healthy snacks. Each was allowed to choose at will from the supermarket shelves.

When their baskets were examined, substantial differences in food choices were found. The "hungry" group bought mostly junk foods, those high in fat and sugar that would provide a rapid energy boost. Their purchases totaled an average of 2,840 calories per person, of which 141 grams were fat and 118 grams sugar. Those allowed to consume the healthy snacks made far more nourishing and less fattening choices. Their purchases provided an average of 715 calories, of which only 28 grams were fat and 48 grams sugar. In other words, shopping for food while hungry caused people to consume 300 percent more calories, 400 percent more fat, and 146 percent more sugar compared to the nonhungry shoppers.

That brain and body are an indivisible unity becomes all too painfully apparent to us any time we try to concentrate on a task with a raging toothache, make decisions while suffering from a splitting headache, or remain cheerful and optimistic during a dose of flu. Similarly, thoughts can influence our health in a wide variety of ways: by producing psychosomatic aches and pains, causing us to self-neglect or self-harm, leading us to over- or under-eat, or weakening our immune system and rendering us more vulnerable to infection. No less influential than this constant interplay between our two brains and our two selves are the ways we stand, sit, move, and behave. Even the slightest physical movement on our part can have a significant impact on how we think and feel. And there are many ways in which customers can be subtly and subconsciously influenced by sales appeals that take account of the embodied brain.

Attitudes, motion, and emotion

Shoppers' attitudes toward the products they buy, the brands they favor, and the ways they shop play a key role in determining which producers and retailers will flourish and which will fail. What is the relationship between what may seem, at first sight, to be two distinctly different things: attitude and emotion?

The word "attitude" comes from the Latin *apto* (aptitude or fitness) and *acto* (postures of the body), both having their root in the Sanskrit word *ag*, meaning to do or to act. The term was first introduced into psychology in the mid-nineteenth century when it was used to refer to an internal state of preparation for action. One of the first psychologists to propose a link between posture and attitude was Sir Francis Galton,[12] who suggested that the attitudes of dinner-party guests to one another could be gauged by observing how they oriented their body. Since that time, the close intimate relationship between movements, attitudes, and behaviors has been demonstrated in numerous studies.

Researchers have found, for example, that simply clenching our fists can make us feel more altruistic.[13] Extending one's thumb, a gesture of approval in many countries, while reading an ambiguous description of a fictional character causes women, though not men, to rate that person more positively. Those reading the same extract while extending their middle finger, a hostile gesture in Western cultures, rated the same character as more hostile than those who extended their index finger.[14]

When it comes to consumers, one study reported that customers who relaxed in a soft cushioned chair were more willing to be flexible when negotiating the purchase of a car than those who did so while seated on a hard wooden seat.[15]

Even fairly minor changes in posture can influence how much attention customers pay to spoken sales messages as well as how likely they are to remember them. In one study, volunteers listened to information while turning their heads either to the right or the left. You might reasonably suppose that the direction would make little or no difference either to what they heard or the accuracy of

Figure 4.1 Low-power pose

Based on illustrations in Power posing: Brief nonverbal displays affect
neuroendocrine levels and risk tolerance by Dana Carney, Amy Cuddy, and Andy Yap,
with permission.

their later recall, but in fact it did. Those who listened with their head turned to the right paid greater attention and recalled the message more precisely than those whose head was turned to the left.[16]

Dr. Dana Carney of Columbia University and her colleagues randomly assigned participants to either a low- or a high-power pose.[17] In the low-power pose (Figure 4.1), participants either sat in a chair with head bowed and hands folded in their lap, or stood with the lower part of one leg crossed over the other and their arms folded across their chest.

The high-power pose (Figure 4.2) involved either leaning back in a chair, legs outstretched, feet on a table and hands clasped behind the head, or leaning forward with arms spread wide and resting on the table.

Both poses were held for exactly 60 seconds. Saliva was collected from both groups, and they were then tested on a gambling task and questioned about their feelings of power.

Among those who had adopted the high-power pose, 86 percent were prepared to take a risk, with 14 percent being risk averse when

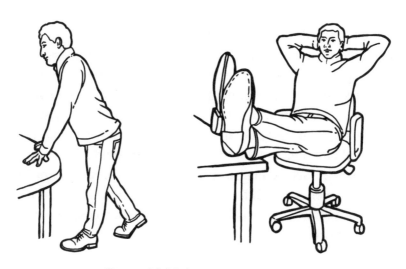

Figure 4.2 High-power pose

Based on illustrations in Power posing: Brief nonverbal displays affect
neuroendocrine levels and risk tolerance by Dana Carney, Amy Cuddy, and Andy Yap,
with permission.

gambling. This compared with 60 percent of those in the low-power pose group being prepared to take a risk and 40 percent who were risk averse. Those in the high-power group reported feeling significantly more "powerful" and "in charge" than those in the low-power group. When their saliva was analyzed for the dominance hormone testosterone and the stress hormone cortisol, participants empowered by their posture were found to have higher levels of the former and lower levels of the latter.

As the authors noted, this simple manipulation of different power poses was "enough to significantly alter the physiological, mental and feeling states of our participants." Remarkably, the same effect can be found when we merely watch people adopting such postures. If, for example, the spokesperson in a television commercial has a high-power stance, they are likely to be viewed as overly assertive, perhaps even aggressive. When they are depicted in a low-power pose, by contrast, their message may be seen as more relaxed and friendly.

Which of these two is the more appropriate depends, of course, on the nature of the message and the purpose of the campaign. The point is that this nonverbal persuader will, subconsciously, have a significant impact on how the advertisement comes across. The same applies to sales representatives. A consumer entering a store who sees the assistant leaning forward across a counter with hands resting on the top will subconsciously associate that stance with dominance and be reluctant to approach. By the same token, an assistant standing in a low-power posture could be subconsciously dismissed as lacking in power, authority, and product knowledge. In this way, even small differences in body language might make the difference between a satisfied and a dissatisfied customer and a sale or lack of sale.

Head nods make customers view products more favorably

Jens Förster, from the University of Würzburg, Germany, carried out an experiment in which well-known products were presented moving horizontally or vertically on a computer screen. This obliged participants either to shake (horizontal movement) or nod (vertical movement) their head while watching the products move past their line of vision. In the control conditions, the products were presented without any movement. Dr. Förster found that those obliged to nod (vertical movement of product) displayed more positive emotions toward the items shown and were more likely to purchase them. Those compelled to shake their head (horizontal movement of product), by contrast, made less favorable evaluations and were less likely to be interested in buying these products.[18]

The subconscious association between head nods and positive emotions may originate in infancy. Charles Darwin observed that babies typically move their heads up and down when seeking the mother's breast and from side to side after they have finished feeding. This may also explain why, in the majority of human cultures, people nod to indicate agreement and shake their head in disagreement.

These findings suggest that choreographing a sales situation in which the consumer is encouraged to nod frequently will significantly increase their desire to purchase a product, just as having them shake their head, for whatever reason, makes the sale less likely.

Shopping and the invariant right

Everyone's body is lopsided. Because the majority of us have a dominant hand, usually our right one, we interact more easily with things on one side of our body than the other. This leads us subconsciously to associate our dominant side with positive emotions and our nondominant side with negative ones. In a largely right-handed world, this means that the right side is seen as good and the left as bad.

This association can be found across virtually every language and culture. In English, for example, left-handed people are described as *sinistral*, a Latin word from which we also get "sinister" or evil. Right-handed people are *dexter*, from which we get dexterous or skillful. Similarly, being told by your boss that you are "out in left field" or "have two left feet" does not bode well for the future, while being congratulated for being "right on target" or being a "right-hand man" suggests imminent promotion.

When shopping, we favor the displays to our right over those on the left; indeed, so pronounced is this preference that it is referred to as the "invariant right." Nevertheless, this can vary depending on whether the shopper is right or left handed. In one study, people were asked to judge which of two products to buy based on brief descriptions printed on either the left or the right side of a page. Those who were right handed chose the product described on the right more often than the one featured on the left of the page, while left-handed people did the exact opposite.[19]

The majority of people are right handed, so retailers often design their store layout to accommodate them. To prevent shoppers, especially newcomers to the store, from automatically turning right after entering, the designer may block their way with a display of low-cost items that they are likely to add to their trolley or basket. Not only does this obstacle slow the shopper down, so encouraging them to view more products, it can also direct them down aisles with high-margin items. There will be more on store design in the next chapter.

The subconscious influence of fluency

To understand why being right or left handed exerts such a powerful influence over the way the brain works, we need to explore the concept of mental *fluency*, the subjective ease or difficulty of making sense of incoming information. As Daniel Oppenheimer of Princeton University explains it:

> *Fluency isn't the process itself but, rather, information about how efficient or easy that process feels. Objects are fluent, for example, when they have been seen frequently, have been seen recently and/or have been seen for a long period of time.*[20]

As I will explain in the next chapter, the brain seeks always to maximize its use of energy. Clearly, activities that can be performed easily require less investment of energy than those that demand greater time, effort, and thought. One study found that in the initial weeks after a company went public, stocks from firms with easily pronounced names were judged to have higher values than those from companies with names that were harder to pronounce. This perception of enhanced value drives purchasing decisions, which, in turn, inflates the actual value of the stock and causes it to outperform its rivals.[21]

At the Yale School of Management, Nathan Novemsky and his colleagues have shown that when a consumer product is made harder to understand, for instance when the packaging uses a font that is difficult to read or consumers are asked to come up with many reasons for choosing the product, shoppers are much less likely to buy.[22] It is this need for fluency that causes people to dislike, and often avoid, making a choice when a great many different options are possible. Having a hundred shampoos or a choice of two dozen toothpastes on offer might seem like a positive benefit to the shopper, but research suggests that the opposite is usually true. Consumers rely on familiar brand names to restore fluency to the situation.

Bending arms increases desire

When taking a product off the shelf, a customer will bend their arm; to replace it, they extend their arm outward. So far, so obvious. However, due to the embedded nature of the brain, these simple actions lead to significant subconscious influences over the product's emotional appeal; and, of course, over the likelihood of wanting to purchase it. As a result of repeating these actions many thousands of times, we quickly learn to associate bending the arm (arm flexion) with a desire to acquire, while reaching out (arm extension) is likened to rejection. When we are attracted to another person, for example, we draw them close to us (arm flexion), while those we dislike are pushed away (arm extension).

The same applies to possessions. Over a lifetime, countless repetitions of the pairing of physical movements with either the wish to acquire or a lack of interest in doing so creates a subconscious link between these simple movements and our desire to possess or reject a product. Findings like this could mean that shoppers carrying a basket (arms flexing) around the supermarket are in a more acquisitive mood than those pushing a trolley (arms extending). Furthermore, when consumers flex their arms in order to examine a product, they are more likely to buy it than are those obliged to extend their arms, for example by reaching up to a high shelf.

This was exactly what Bram Van den Bergh, Assistant Professor at Erasmus University, Rotterdam School of Management, and his colleagues found when studying shopping behavior in supermarkets. In one of a number of studies, they observed 136 customers in a hypermarket and found that those who carried a basket were more likely to buy products offering immediate benefits (e.g., chocolates) than were those pushing a cart.[23] Research has also shown that simply *watching* another person either flex or extend their arms can lead to a similar reaction.

In a fascinating study of this powerful effect, female under-graduates were asked to drink glasses of water until they no longer felt thirsty. They were then handed a glass containing a measured amount of what was described as a new high-energy sports drink, and invited to drink as much as they wanted while watching one of two videos. These depicted an athlete exercising with a bell bar. In the arm bend (approach) condition, the athlete was standing upright and pulling the weight from his waist to his chest, by flexing his arms. In the second, arm stretch (avoidance) condition, he was seen lying on his back and pushing the weight up from his chest by extending his arms. As the researchers had hypothesized, those watching the "arms bending" video consumed *more* of the drink than those viewing the "arms stretching" version.[24]

This suggests that the way actors are told to perform even simple actions in television commercials may exert a significant if seldom recognized influence over the way viewers evaluate the products being shown. It has been argued, furthermore, that corporations like Nintendo and Microsoft are using consumers' body movements to hack into their embedded brains. Games consoles controlled by physical gestures, such as the Nintendo Wii, Microsoft Kinect, and Playstation Move, may owe some of their tremendous com-mercial success to the positive emotions triggered by specific body movements.[25]

The persuasive power of sex

The power of sexual imagery has long been used to influence con-sumer behavior. The importance that retailers and advertisers attach to using scantily clad female (and less often male) models is appar-ent at almost any motor show or product promotion.

On some occasions, as I will explain in Chapter 8, these sexu-ally arousing images are presented subliminally and are intended to influence consumers subconsciously. The extent to which such sex-ual arousal influences a man's decision making was explored by Dan Ariely from the Massachusetts Institute of Technology and George Loewenstein from Carnegie Mellon University. Their study, which must have raised not a few academic eyebrows, involved persuading male undergraduates to complete a survey while masturbating to "a high but sub-orgasmic level of arousal."[26] The responses were then compared with a control group of males who had answered in a nonaroused state.

Ariely and Loewenstein found that sexual arousal not only led to riskier sexual decisions, for example having unprotected intercourse, but to a narrowing focus of motivation, "creating a kind of tunnel-vision where goals other than sexual fulfillment become eclipsed by the motivation to have sex." They also reported that their subjects had very limited insight into the "impact of sexual arousal on their own judgments and behavior."

This lack of appreciation for the ways in which arousal influences judgment and biases decision making could, they point out, have important implications for both individuals and society. They claim:

> *The current study shows that sexual arousal influences people in profound ways. This should come as no surprise to most people who have personal experience with sexual arousal, but the magnitude of the effects is nevertheless striking. Efforts at self-control that involve raw willpower are likely to be ineffective in the face of the dramatic cognitive and motivational changes caused by arousal.*

For retailers especially, the implication of this study is that even a moderate level of sexual arousal is likely to make male shoppers more impulsive and less rational in their purchasing decisions. Does the same apply to women shoppers faced, for example, by a semi-naked and muscular male model?

While to the best of my knowledge no research has been conducted into this, studies have shown that the sex drive is more intense and uncompromising in men than in women.[27] This suggests, say Ariely and Loewenstein, that "at least, in principle... the lesser intensity of the female sex drive entails that women would not be (or not as much) affected by sexual arousal in their decisions."

Customers have been known to exploit their own sex appeal in the hope, often justified, of striking a better deal. A study by Laura Kray[28] and her colleagues at the Haas School of Business, University of California, concluded that men regard women who flirt during a business negotiation as being more confident than those adopting a serious approach. "Women are uniquely confronted with a trade-off in terms of being perceived as strong versus warm," explains Kray. "Using feminine charm in negotiation is a technique that combines both."

To find out just how effective what she and her researchers termed "feminine charm" could prove to be, 44 men and 49 women read a hypothetical scenario in which they were asked to imagine selling a car, worth $1,200, to a potential buyer named Sue. In what the researchers called their "charm" version, Sue's behavior was described as follows:

> *As you meet and shake hands, Sue smiles at you warmly and says, "What a pleasure to meet you." You chat about the weather as Sue takes off her coat and sits down. Looking you up and down, Sue leans forward, briefly touches your arm and says, "You're even more charming in person than over email." Then, somewhat playfully, she winks at you and says, "What's your best price?"*

In the second, "neutral" scenario, Sue is far less playful and a great deal more businesslike:

> *As you meet and shake hands, Sue smiles and says, "It's a pleasure to meet you." You chat about the weather as Sue takes off her coat and sits down. Looking you directly in the eye, Sue says, "I'm looking forward to talking over the financials with you and hopefully working out a deal today. Let's get down to business." Then, somewhat seriously, she says, "What's your best price?"*

When dealing with a male seller, Flirtatious Sue negotiated an average sale price of just $1,077. The best price offered to Serious Sue was $1,279. Unsurprisingly, perhaps, flirting cut no ice when the seller was female; indeed, it actually added a few dollars to the price, with Serious Sue being offered the car for $1,189 and Flirtatious Sue $1,205.

"The key is to flirt with your own natural personality in mind," advises Kray. "Be authentic. Have fun. That will translate into confidence, which is a strong predictor of negotiation performance."

The persuasive power of touch

Personal space can sometimes be deliberately invaded to enhance the consumer's experience and encourage repeat business from female customers. If a sales agent, of either gender, lightly, unobtrusively, and apparently accidentally touches the customer's hand while serving her, she will feel more positive about both the purchase and the store.

This was demonstrated in a landmark 1976 study by Jeffrey Fisher from the University of Connecticut and his colleagues, which involved students using the campus library.[29] When handing out books to some of the students, the librarian was asked to brush her hand gently against theirs. It was found that the female students, although unaware of the touch, evaluated the library service far more positively than those whose hand had not been touched. Male students' response to touch was, however, more ambivalent.

It must also be stressed that this study was conducted in the US. Cultural differences with regard to any form of touching in other parts of the world could produce a very different result.

Weather affects whether we buy

Finally, let's look at something over which high-street retailers, at least, have no control: the weather. As every retailer knows to their cost, a shopper's readiness to spend declines when the weather is bad. Cold, wet days—especially in summer—spread financial as well as meteorological gloom. By the same token, sunny weather not only encourages people into the shops, but makes them more likely to spend.

In a paper entitled "Stock prices and Wall Street weather," Edward Saunders Jr. from Massachusetts University's Department of Accounting and Finance compared the rise and fall of stock prices in New York City and found a significant link between the amount of cloud cover and mean returns. He reported:

> *The mean returns on the 0–20% cloud-cover groups are always higher than the mean returns on the 30% cloud-cover groups. The mean returns on the 100% cloud-cover groups are always lower than the mean returns on the 80–90% cloud-cover groups.*[30]

While retailers cannot do anything, at least for the moment, about levels of cloud cover, within the controlled environments of their stores they are able to manipulate shoppers' surroundings to create precisely the right mental and physical state for enjoyable (and of course highly profitable) shopping. Key factors here are heat and humidity. Both need to be carefully controlled in order to create surroundings that will maximize consumer comfort in order to extend their stay and boost their spend. How this is done forms one of the topics of Chapter 6.

Our life narrative

In their attempts to make sense of the brain, philosophers and scientists have long resorted to metaphors. During the seventeenth century, French mathematician and writer René Descartes likened it to the elaborate fountains and hydraulically operated automata at the Palace of Versailles. He believed that fluid, stored in hollow spaces within the brain, the ventricles, was pumped along the tubes of the nerves to move muscles. During the 1940s, researchers compared the brain to the then most complex piece of technology, the telephone switchboard. By the early 1960s, the metaphor of choice was the digital computer, a piece of equipment that was starting to be more widely used.

Today, this view of the brain is coming under increasing challenge from neuroscientists. As we have seen in this chapter, they argue that our thoughts and emotions are not solely generated between our ears and behind our eyes. This embodied cognition model of mental functioning proposes that the environment in which the brain operates—which includes the body in which the brain resides, as well as cultural, social, and familial factors—significantly influences those mental processes.

Clearly, this way of conceptualizing human thoughts and emotions has important implications for neuromarketing. A comprehensive understanding of shoppers' thoughts and feelings must take into account the workings not only of their brains but also their bodies. The narrative by which we live our lives is dictated by parents, siblings, relatives, friends and neighbors, teachers, and preachers, as well as by advertising, marketing, retailing, public relations, and the media, the whole panoply of the persuasion industry.

As I will explain further in the next chapter, the ability to dictate the narrative of someone's life for commercial gain is becoming ever easier as a result of our rapidly growing knowledge of the rules that run the buying brain.

5

Inside the Buying Brain

The brain costs about a penny every 5 hours to operate, less than a nickel a day—now that's an efficient machine!
　　　　　　　　—*Read Montague,* Why Choose this Book?[1]

Your brain, fine-tuned over millions of years of evolution, responds swiftly and usually effectively to virtually any situation. And it does so using a third of the energy needed to power the average household light bulb.

On this meager amount of energy, the brain reasons, makes decisions and solves problems, executes plans, dreams dreams, experiences emotions, and constantly monitors its surroundings by evaluating the billions of bits of data that arrive, every second, from over 20 different senses.[2] It regulates blood flow and pressure, monitors its chemical constituents, controls the speed and depth of breathing, supervises digestion (with the aid of the second brain described in Chapter 4), maintains balance, and interacts with the outside world via the body's 642 pairs of skeletal muscles.

Brain versus computer

If we compare the human brain with the world's most advanced computer, the verdict is a clear no contest. The brain operates at a speed of 2.2 petaflops (10,000,000,000,000,000 operations) per second, uses 20 watts of power, and fits inside the average shoe box. While the IBM Sequoia supercomputer, currently the world's fastest, has an operating speed of 16.325 petaflops, it requires 7.9 megawatts of power and is roughly the size of a large refrigerator.

As computational neuroscientist Reed Montague points out:

> *No matter how one divides this energy consumption among ongoing neural computations, one arrives at an unavoidable conclusion: evolved nervous systems compute with almost freakish efficiency.*[3]

The brain achieves this astonishing economy of energy by carrying out the vast majority of its operations via the automation of many thought processes in one of three main ways—all of which have significant implications for the way people shop.

The first way is by making most purchasing decisions subconsciously; the second by categorization; and the third by utilizing speedy but simple rules of thought, known as heuristics. In this chapter I explore how making sense of the world in this way influences shopping choices and why it makes consumers so vulnerable to outside influences and commercial persuasion.

In two minds about shopping

Chris, a 37-year-old company lawyer, is a rational shopper who thinks long and hard before purchasing any high-priced item. She uses the internet to compare prices, check quality, and review the various deals on offer. It usually takes her around three weeks between thinking about buying a product and closing the deal, but when she does make up her mind it is with the comforting certainty that she has spent her money wisely and well. While most people do, on some occasions, choose to shop in this rational, reasoned, and reflective manner, far more frequently they purchase on the basis of intuition and emotion.

Stevie, aged 27, is a typically impulsive and emotional shopper. The moment she sees a product she likes, she wants to possess it right away. Her approach to shopping is see it, want it, buy it— sometimes followed swiftly by "regret it." While Chris remains cool and detached when researching her purchases, Stevie becomes very emotional about them. When measuring the physiological responses of shoppers like Stevie, I find a sharp increase in heart rate and skin conductance at the moment a "must have" product is spotted. This excitement remains high until the moment the purchase has been made, often within less than ten minutes after spotting the item online or in the shop.

With thoughtful, reflective shoppers such as Chris, however, the initial excitement is far more muted and rapidly decreases as the research and comparison stage of the buying process begins. While this reflective approach to shopping usually leads to a more satisfactory outcome, the investment of both time and mental energy is much higher than for the impulsive shopper. The rational consumer uses abstract, logical reasoning to plan their purchase and calculate the value they will derive from it. As a result, having made the buying decision they are able to explain and justify the motivation for their purchase. Emotion-driven shoppers, by contrast, often find it very hard to explain the logic behind what they have bought.

Brain-imaging studies have shown that rational shopping decisions occur mainly in the cerebral cortex, a layer of neurons only a few millimeters thick that comprise the brain's outer covering, what many people refer to as their "little gray cells." More intuitive purchasing decisions are made deep within the brain, in an area located between the cortex and brain stem known as the limbic system. The oldest part of the brain, this is not only responsible for generating emotions but also, in a region called the thalamus, for processing data from our senses, muscles, circulatory, digestive, and immune systems. These are integrated with information stored in the memory and colored with emotions before being expressed as utterances and actions.

Understanding dual-process thinking

Answer the following questions as quickly as you can:

- What is a common abbreviation for Coca-Cola?
- What do we call the sound a frog makes?
- What is a comedian's funny story called?
- What do we call the white of an egg?

When asked these questions, most people reply, rapidly and effortlessly, coke, croak, joke, and yolk. Maybe you did the same. If so, your final answer was, of course, wrong. For the record, egg white is called albumin. This party trick demonstrates that much of our thinking is rapid, automatic, and occurs outside of our conscious awareness. Had people who fell into the trap of the final answer paused for rational thought, most would have come up with the right response.

As nineteenth-century German philosopher Arthur Schopenhauer remarked:

> *One might almost believe that half of our thinking takes place unconsciously. I have familiarised myself with the factual data of a theoretical and practical problem; I do not think about it again, yet often a few days later the answer to the problem will come into my mind entirely from its own accord; the operation which has produced it, however, remains as much a mystery to me as that of an adding-machine: what has occurred is, again, unconscious rumination.*[4]

This perceptive comment is very much in line with one of neuroscience's most remarkable and startling findings: Most of our everyday thinking happens without us even being aware of the fact, and we perform many, perhaps the majority, of our everyday actions without pausing for thought, in an automatic and mindless rather than a deliberate and mindful way.

In 1975, two of the first modern psychologists to study dual-process thinking, Michael Posner and C.R.R. Snyder, named the fast, nonconscious kind "automatic activation"[5] and the slower, reflective kind "conscious processing." I employ the terms System I (for Impulsive) and System R (for Reflective) to describe the two.[6]

Unconscious, System I thinking, which we have in common with other animals, comprises a set of subsystems operating with some degree of autonomy. It forms associations, develops categories, and then automatically places events, people, actions, and situations into them. As the name suggests, it is fast, energy efficient, and can never be turned off. It is also extremely gullible and very easily fooled.

Conscious, System R thinking is rational, logical, and skeptical. It is constantly asking questions and seeking answers. It strives, often without much success, to control the words and actions initiated by System I. System R operates slowly and analytically. Its processing capacity is low, it makes considerable demands on memory, and it has a far higher energy requirement. However, it also, and uniquely, endows us with the ability to think about the way we think and to analyze the mental processes by which decisions are made and problems solved.

As Nobel Prize–winning psychologist Daniel Kahneman points out in his book *Thinking, Fast and Slow*, the diverse mental operations performed by reflective thinking have two features in common: They all require attention and they are disrupted when attention is withdrawn. He comments:

> *The often-used phrase "pay attention" is apt. You dispose of a limited budget of attention that you can allocate to activities, and if you try to go beyond your budget, you will fail. It is the mark of effortful activities that they interfere with each other, which is why it is difficult or impossible to conduct several at once.*[7]

Sometimes System I and System R thinking work together; at other times they may be in conflict; and on yet other occasions they blend seamlessly into one. What starts as an impulse-driven idea may segue into profound reflective thought. What seems at first sight to be the outcome of reflective thinking may turn out, on closer inspection, to be based on an impulse.

These two modes of thought can be compared with the two different ways we breathe. Most of the time our breathing, like our thinking, occurs automatically and effortlessly. Our ribs expand and contract, our diaphragm rises and falls, our lungs take in and expel air, all without our ever needing to think about the actions necessary for sustaining life. We can, however, very easily and at any moment we choose, consciously control our breathing, in several ways. We can change the depth, breadth, length, texture, rate, and quality of each breath.

In the same way, although most of our thinking is subconscious and automatic, we can, at almost any time we choose, take control of our thoughts and direct them along a particular path, using whichever mode of thought—abstract reasoning, logical inference, creativity—seems most appropriate.

Two minds, two memories

The choices we make when buying depend on two different types of memory. An early but largely forgotten pioneer in thinking about this field was French philosopher François-Pierre-Gonthier Maine de Biran, born in Bergerac in 1766.[8] In his writings he distinguished between conscious and unconscious memory systems: implicit, "sensitive memories" that were responsible for emotional responses; and explicit, "habit-based memories" that took care of physical movements. Since that time, hundreds of studies have confirmed that we can remember without being aware we are remembering, and that even memories we are unable to recall consciously are capable of exerting a measurable influence over our behavior.

Explicit memories are the ones we are able to describe. They are what we draw on when asked to explain why we chose a particular brand or bought a specific product. Explicit memories are highly malleable and often of limited validity. For example, the order, manner, and presentation of questions can significantly influence the answers that we give. Research has also demonstrated that explicit memories are unreliable, liable to change over time, and vulnerable to confabulation, the invention of incidents to fill in gaps in the memory and make for a more coherent narrative.

In contrast, implicit memories are subconscious and cannot therefore be expressed in words. They can only be detected indirectly through their influence on our behavior. They are open to persuasion techniques operating below the level of conscious awareness, so-called subliminal messages, the role of which I will discuss in Chapter 8.

Implicit memories play a major role in determining which brands consumers will pick up from supermarket shelves. They can also provide far more accurate insights into shopping behavior than can more readily accessible explicit memories. One of the tasks of neuro-marketers is to drill down into this rich layer of subconscious memory in order to discover what consumers really think about brands, products, and the whole experience of shopping. Psychologist John Bargh, who believes that System I thinking pervades all aspects of mental and social life, comments that just as Galileo "removed the earth from its privileged position at the centre of the universe," so should we too banish "consciousness from its privileged position."[9]

The pattern-seeking brain

Take a look at the illustration in Figure 5.1. What does it depict?

Figure 5.1

Provided you have never seen it before, this will probably look like a series of meaningless black and white blobs. If you have, or once you have read the description that comes next, it will never appear that way again. The image is that of a leopard sniffing the ground with its head pointed to the left of the picture.

Because our brain is composed of massive parallel processors with a vast number of interconnected neural networks, we have an astonishing ability to see patterns. One of the brain's strengths is its capacity for making connections between objects, words, events, visual patterns, and different ideas. This involves the process of categorization. Compulsively, continuously, and effortlessly, the brain transforms sensory data into meaningful impressions and files them away in their own little "box" in the memory.

"Categorization functions like a chisel," says Lisa Feldman Barrett of Harvard Medical School, "dividing up the sensory world... leading us to attend to certain features and ignore others," adding, "to categorize something is to render it meaningful."[10]

While this helps us make sense of the world by placing new experiences, people, or products in context, it also makes us far more vulnerable to external influences. Because our brain operates in this pattern-seeking and pattern-matching way, we can all too easily find nonexistent causal relationships between events.

In one study, people were briefly shown one of two photographs of the same school-aged girl. The first depicted her standing in a clearly prosperous, middle-class neighborhood, the second in a rundown, socially deprived part of town.

Participants were then handed the results of a test the girl was supposed to have completed. Exactly half of the questions in this test had been answered correctly and half incorrectly. The subjects were asked to assess the girl's IQ. Although the photograph was never mentioned, those who had seen her pictured against the middle-class background intuitively rated her as having above-average intelligence and predicted a bright future for her. Those who believed she had come from a deprived background judged her to be of below-average intelligence and unlikely to enjoy much success in life.

Such illusionary correlations seriously bias our thinking when we shop. Not surprisingly, therefore, they have been widely employed for more than a century in advertising and marketing. Consumers may, for example, favor one brand of energy drink over another because it is endorsed by a sporting legend, or decide to spend more than $3,000 on a Louis Vuitton bag because they remember an advertisement in which a celebrity, such as U2 front man Bono, was carrying one. Other notable examples include Givenchy's use of Justin Timberlake to promote its perfume Play for Her, Roger Federer endorsing Rolex, and Penélope Cruz L'Oréal.

Advertisers know that in the minds of many consumers, such associations will, if only subconsciously, evoke a belief that they too can enjoy that level of success by simply purchasing the products. Categorization helps make the unfamiliar familiar, so increasing the degree of control we believe we have over our behavior and reducing any anxiety or stress. Categorizing products enables shoppers to exercise choice more quickly and effortlessly.

It is important to understand that all categories are bipolar, since it is impossible to conceive of one without also, if only subconsciously, having a notion of its opposite. Suppose, for example, that we have a mental folder labeled "Healthy" into which all produce that we regard as good for us is automatically consigned. This implies that we also have another folder labeled "Unhealthy," even though we may not be consciously aware of this second category. One result of this is that manufacturers, marketers, advertisers, and retailers can use simple tactics to persuade us to place their product in the "Healthy" category.

In a study looking at the way in which words and images can bias consumer choice, I offered two groups identically made low-fat carrot cakes that were labeled differently, although not dishonestly. The first label, illustrated by attractive countryside pictures subtly suggesting good health, read:

Low-Fat Carrot Cake—Enjoy a healthier eating option with this organic carrot cake, containing freshly grated carrots, sun-ripened sultanas, tasty pecan nuts, refreshing spices and new-laid eggs. 370 calories per 100g.

The second avoided any reference to the cake being low fat and focused instead on the pleasures of eating it:

So naughty but oh so nice. Treat yourself to a generous slice of this taste-tempting carrot cake. Sweetly delicious and simply irresistible with brown sugar, eggs and pecan nuts topped with soft cheese and icing sugar. 370 calories per 100g.

While the calories were equal in both cases, the first description was designed to ensure that participants instantly categorized the cake under the heading "Healthy Eating," while those offered the second cake were being led toward the heading "Indulgence Eating."

The results were intriguing. Those offered the specifically stated low-fat option ate 40 percent more cake than those who were provided with no information regarding fat content. Why? Because having categorized the cake as healthy, they felt able to indulge in a guilt-free binge, despite the fact that the number of additional calories every further slice would provide was clearly stated. The phrase "enjoy a healthier eating option," while never explained or qualified (healthier than what—botulism?), bestowed a feeling of control over consumption and so empowered them to eat more.

Ena Inesi, from the London Business School, comments:

Power and choice represent two important forces that govern many aspects of human behaviour. Possessing power—control over other individuals or over valued resources in social relations—has been shown to affect individuals' decision making, ability to take action, focus on personal goals and resistance to persuasion and conformity. Similarly, having choice—the ability to select a preferred course of action—also fundamentally affects individuals' psychology, from increasing positive affect and satisfaction to improving task persistence and cognitive performance.[11]

This deep-rooted need to control events in our lives plays a major, if seldom recognized, role in almost all aspects of consumption. Recognizing this basic human need, manufacturers and retailers take steps to ensure that customers are, or at least perceive themselves to be, in control of every aspect of their shopping. whether online or in the high street.

The belief that they are able to exercise control over events when shopping is essential if consumers are to experience the "processing fluency" I discussed in Chapter 2. To enhance sales and ensure satisfaction, retailers must seek to keep shoppers relaxed yet excited, calm but engaged, and attentive rather than distracted. These ideal mental and physical states – which are easily monitored using modern technology – are significantly disrupted by the negative emotions, such as irritation, anger, frustration, sadness, or a sense of personal inadequacy, typically associated with stress and anxiety.

Going shopping as an antidote to stress

When *going* shopping as opposed to *doing* the shopping, we are buying far more than just products. We are also purchasing power and control. During the time we are in the retail environment with cash or credit cards at hand, we feel, perhaps for the first time that day or that week, fully in charge of our lives. We believe, although often mistakenly, that in making our purchasing choices we are exercising free will: deciding objectively which items to buy, which parts of the store to visit, what displays to look at or pass by, how long to shop, and when to leave. These heady feelings of control and empowerment are ones that will lure us back to shopping time and again.

The shopper's sense of agency is, however, normally illusory. As we shall see in the next chapter, in a modern retail environment almost every move shoppers take and every buying decision they make will have been dictated, both covertly and overtly. Just as a magician is able to "force" a card on a member of the audience while apparently allowing them free choice, so too are advertisers, marketers, and retailers able to persuade consumers that they are in control even when the opposite is true.

However, the need for shoppers to *feel* that they are in control of events is something retailers ignore at their peril. They are likely to lack such a feeling when, for example, they come across a product that is either unfamiliar, and therefore does not fall into any predetermined category, or known to them but in some way different from what they expected. Supermarkets are often criticized for rejecting fruit that falls outside their tightly drawn specifications regarding color, shape, and size. While certainly wasteful, this policy reflects a clear understanding of how unwilling some consumers are to accept produce that cannot be easily categorized. The narrower the attributes that are used to categorize such items, the more likely shoppers are to refuse to accept something outside these bounds, a refusal often based on a fear of losing control.

Another way in which retailers can inadvertently challenge the shopper's sense of control and empowerment is by obliging them to stand in line for a second longer than is necessary. Delays at checkouts or when seeking assistance from a sales agent trigger the feelings of powerlessness that many consumers go shopping to avoid. (The role of shopping as a form of stress control is an important one, which I will discuss in greater detail in the final chapter.) While such a challenge may not be something of which the shopper is consciously aware, it will certainly exert a subconscious influence over their behavior, mood, and appraisal of the shopping experience.

What applies in the world of bricks is no less relevant in the world of clicks. One reason for Amazon's remarkable commercial success has been its ability to make all transactions on its sites as quick, easy, and intuitive as possible. The results speak for themselves. Set up in 1995, the company took two years to sell its millionth book. Six months after that it had sold two million. Within six years it had become the first internet business to demonstrate that serious money could be made online. Although Amazon executives are unwilling to say just how much revenue is generated by its personalization algorithm, they often point to this engine as key to the company's success. By innovating "One Click" shopping, enabling its customers to complete a transaction in record time, Amazon also demonstrated an understanding of the need to empower online purchasers.

While offering ample choice is regarded as essential by many retailers, this too can prove disempowering when it obliges shoppers to invest an excessive amount of cognitive energy in reaching a decision. It causes them to shift from shopping on subconscious autopilot and compels them to engage in rational, conscious thought processes.

Rules of thumb that shape our shopping

The brain also saves energy by employing subconscious rules of thumb known as heuristics. This term for a shortcut to decision making comes from the Greek for "find" or "discover."

Some of these shortcuts are learned through experience; others are genetically programmed into the brain and reflect the survival demands of our earliest ancestors. When humans were evolving on the savannas of eastern Africa, there were so many physical threats to survival that the brain developed strategies that enable very rapid judgments to be made and choices taken. One example is the "startle response," which instantly transforms us from a state of relaxation into one of maximum alertness. This could spell the difference between life and death in an environment where danger lurked behind every bush. As a result of their origins, such decision-making rules tend to be fast, frugal, and sufficiently effective to work on most, if not all, occasions.

Although widely used, and often regarded as little more than common sense, heuristics can also lead to errors. For example, if you had just tossed a coin 30 times and it had landed heads up on every occasion, you might be tempted to think that the probability of it coming down tails up on the next throw would be higher than at the start. In fact, of course, the odds (provided the coin is a fair one and fairly tossed) remain precisely the same on the millionth toss as on the first, at 50/50. Known as the gambler's fallacy, this is one of the reasons that, in the long run, casinos will always win and punters always lose.

According to Daniel Kahneman and Amos Tversky, people are especially likely to resort to heuristics when making decisions in situations where a great deal of information has to be considered, there is uncertainty, and time is short. That is why in today's fast-paced world they continue to exert a profound influence over consumer choices.

Here are six widely used mental shortcuts that consumers employ when making buying decisions.

If warm then secure

Every infant requires food, warmth, comfort, and safety in order to survive and grow. Since such needs are typically met by clinging to the mother's body, this creates an association that develops into two rules of thought: "If I am close to mother then I feel warm and if I am warm then I feel secure" and "If away from mother then I feel cold and if I am cold then I am also insecure." As we mature, these rules of thought are simplified into:

- If warm then secure. If secure then relaxed.
- If cold then insecure. If insecure then tense.

By the age of 5, concepts of warmth and social inclusion versus cold and loneliness become so tightly intertwined that we no longer distinguish between emotions and physical sensations. We speak, for example, of having warm feelings for one person while giving someone we dislike the cold shoulder. Such an individual might be dismissed as a cold fish and given a frosty reception. Someone we fancy could be described as hot stuff and given a very warm welcome. We may feel lukewarm about a proposal or say we have gone cold on one we have rejected. We may start our first job burning with ambition and end up frozen out by colleagues and left in the cold. These links between physical and emotional warmth are not restricted to English. The French might give a friend *un accueil chaleureux* and Italians *una dimostrazione calorosa*—or a warm welcome. The French describe a less than welcoming smile as *un sourire froid*, while Italians refer to *una fredda accoglienza*. A German who feels comfortable in someone's presence might talk about *mit jemandem warm werden*; the German description for a cynical individual is *kalt lächelnd*, literally someone with a cold smile.

Studies have shown that every language expresses this psychological association between warmth, closeness, and security.[12] It has also been found that we judge others not merely on how emotionally warm they seem, but how physically warm we feel.[13] In other words, we like people better at first meeting if the encounter takes place in a warm rather than a cold room. Even holding a warm or cold beverage, however briefly, increases immediate liking between strangers.[14]

Retailers who spend large sums of money to ensure that their stores are held at a constant, comfortable temperature reap the benefits by ensuring that customers remain sufficiently cool to be calm yet energetic, but sufficiently warm to have a good feeling about the shopping experience.[15] I will examine the importance of temperature and humidity while shopping in the next chapter.

Finally, it should be noted that although inclusion within a group makes us feel physically warm, exclusion leaves us feeling physically colder.[16] This is a major reason people follow fashion and are attracted to specific brands: to identify themselves with, and therefore be accepted by, a particular social group that they see as especially desirable. In this sense, they "are" what brands they wear and display. This is especially true for luxury goods. John Lanchester, author of the 2012 novel *Capital* dealing with the moral climate underlying the financial crash of 2008, says:

> *The whole thing about luxury goods is that they are an international language. The prices... are for the super-rich, who don't really care what things cost. In fact, they want them to*

cost more, because the price signifies only that most people can't afford them.

It is partly these feelings of having gained entry to an exclusive club, at an affordable price, that so physically excite the bargain hunters I describe in Chapter 2.

Shopping from habit

Habit plays a major role in determining how we shop. We tend to move around familiar stores in a predictable pattern, which is why most of us hate it when displays change and departments move. We also select products with which we are familiar and often show great reluctance to deviate from a well-established shopping list.

The heuristic mainly in use here is the recognition rule, relating to the ease, or fluency, with which information can be processed. We encountered it previously in relation to Nathan Novemsky's work on fonts. If we are presented with two products, one familiar and the other unfamiliar, then this rule persuades us to regard the former as suiting our needs better than the latter. While shopping for a washing-up liquid, for example, you spot a familiar brand next to the store's new own brand. The recognition rule will cause you to place the instantly identifiable brand into your shopping basket while ignoring, or perhaps not even seeing, a cheaper and better but less familiar product. This rule represents the default mode for System I thinking, since shopping from habit offers a far more energy-saving option than rationally weighing up the pros and cons of unfamiliar items. The less mental energy we have to expend when understanding and evaluating a product, the more likely we are to choose it.

This explains why constant repetition of a brand name in television advertising, something that most viewers find intensely irritating, is actually a very effective way of boosting sales. So too is the use of jingles, "ear worms" that burrow their way into our brain and are extremely difficult to evict. I shall have more to say in later chapters about both television advertising and the potency of cheap music from a neuromarketing viewpoint.

Monkey see, monkey do

Put simply, this heuristic states: "Watch what other people are doing and do the same." Hard-wired into our brain, it derives from an innate need to be accepted and viewed by others as normal.

From our earliest years, we define ourselves as a member of various social groups. At first this comprises our immediate family, where we acquire and perfect tactics for winning attention and gaining approval such as smiling, laughing, crying, or even having temper tantrums. As we grow up, our social group expands to teachers and our peer group, employers and colleagues at work, friends and neighbors. We tend to want to be like those people. "Monkey see, monkey do," otherwise known as the mimicry heuristic, explains our desire to follow fads and adopt the latest fashions. Being in step with others makes us feel stronger, bolder, and more confident than acting alone.

Employing this heuristic reduces stress and anxiety, increases the appetite for consumption, and leads us to make riskier decisions because we feel safe. It also fosters a "groupthink" mentality, in which individuals can both surrender individual responsibility for their actions and feel more certain that they are doing the "right thing." That is one reason that, over two centuries since soldiers last marched into battle, the military still expends a tremendous amount of time and effort in training new recruits to march in step; or religions incorporate chanting and singing into their rituals; or shoppers queue overnight to buy the latest video game, tablet, or cell phone.

In studies designed to explore the reasons behind the widespread popularity of cultural rituals involving synchrony, Scott Wiltermuth and Chip Heath of the Department of Organizational Behavior at Stanford University put some volunteers through activities designed to enhance synchrony. These included walking in step around the campus and singing in chorus while beating time to the music.[17] Other participants performed the same activities but without synchronizing their actions with one another, for example by strolling around the campus or listening silently to the music.

The researchers found that the synchrony group cooperated more effectively and thought more similarly than those whose previous actions had not been synchronized. Wiltermuth explains:

> *This physical synchrony, which occurs when people move in time with one another, has been argued to produce positive emotions that weaken the boundaries between the self and the group, leading to feelings of collective effervescence that enable groups to remain cohesive.*

The mimicry heuristic is of great importance to advertisers, marketers, and retailers. When a critical mass of consumers has been persuaded—or at least appears to have been persuaded—to buy a product, read a book, go to a movie, download a music track, see a show, favorite a Tweet, or register a liking for something or someone on Facebook, then many more will follow.

However, there is a subtle catch here. Those who buy and use the product must be viewed by fellow consumers as PLU, "people like us." If the "wrong" kind of people are seen to be using the product, sales could be hit. Those managing high-end brands seek to direct sales to the desired demographic by their choice of advertising media and retail outlets. At the same time, they take steps to restrict availability to consumers considered not to be PLU.

The extent to which some companies actively seek to manage their customer base was brought home to me many years ago. The manufacturer of a luxury fashion accessory commissioned a study designed to find what was least attractive, in terms of image, words, and music, to blue-collar workers. The brand manager explained that they would use this information to create a series of advertisements deliberately designed to deter consumers in this social group from purchasing their products. We duly came up with a list of "turn-offs," which included black-and-white photography, lengthy shots with slow-paced editing, and atonal music. Whether or not this information was ever used to create the world's first noncommercial commercial, I never found out.

A journalist friend of mine came across an example of sales management while visiting friends in an unfashionable and somewhat impoverished seaside resort on Britain's East Coast. She went into the high-street branch of a well-known retail chemist to try to purchase a bottle of expensive designer-label perfume. "I'm afraid we aren't able to stock it," the sales assistant apologized. "We get quite a few customers asking for it, but the manufacturers won't supply this branch."

"We two form a multitude," wrote Ovid in *Metamorphoses*. Today, thanks to social media, endorsement by a single individual can sometimes "form a multitude" and propel a person to stardom or ensure that a new product flies off the shelf.

Anchoring

As I mentioned in Chapter 1, the important and unexpected rule of thumb known as anchoring was discovered by Daniel Kahneman and Amos Tversky in the late 1970s. To understand how it works, try this simple but insightful experiment next time you are with a group of friends. Ask half of them to multiply together all the numbers from 1 to 8 in ascending order (i.e., $1 \times 2 \times 3 \times 4$... etc.) and the other half to do so in descending order (i.e., $8 \times 7 \times 6 \times 5$... etc.). Allow them just 5 seconds to come up with an answer.

Clearly, in such a brief amount of time, both groups must take a guess. What is curious is that estimates made by those given the sequence in ascending order will tend to be significantly lower than those given it in descending order. In one study, the average when people were told to multiply the numbers in ascending order was 512. When they were asked to do so in descending order, the average was 2,250. The correct answer (in both cases) is 40,320.

Why the major difference in the two guesses? The answer can be found in the anchoring heuristic. When instructed to come up with an answer in the few seconds allowed, people must guesstimate the result. Since the first few steps of multiplication, carried out from left to right, will clearly be lower in the first case (e.g., $1 \times 2 \times 3 = 6$) than the second (e.g., $8 \times 7 \times 6 = 336$), those given the numbers in ascending order will produce a lower guesstimate than those calculating them in descending order.

A remarkable illustration of the way this mental shortcut biases the judgment of even experienced professionals comes from a study by Birte Englich from the University of Würzburg.[18] He asked a group of trial judges with more than 15 years' experience to pass sentence in a hypothetical case. All the judges read the same evidence and were provided with identical background information about the accused. The judges were then instructed to roll a die. Unbeknown to them, this was loaded to produce either a high or a low number. The effect on their sentence was remarkable. When a judge rolled a low number they ordered that the man spend significantly less time behind bars then when they rolled a high number.[19] Even when a number has absolutely no connection with the decision being made, it influences the outcome.

Retailers use the anchoring heuristic as a hidden persuader to influence shoppers' judgment about whether or not a store offers value for money. One way of doing this is by what are called "destination goods" or "known value items" (KVIs). KVIs include such core grocery lines and weekly staples as milk, bread, baked beans, and bananas. Supermarkets call these "traffic generators" because they have to be purchased frequently and are the most price sensitive.

While the average consumer's awareness of prices tends to be limited, a majority of shoppers do know the prices of these regularly bought items and so are able to make comparisons between rival stores. By ensuring that the price of benchmarked KVIs is kept artificially low, by selling them at or even below cost, supermarkets are able to use anchoring to persuade shoppers that all of their products are similar value for money. It helps convince consumers that the store is on their side in the struggle to keep down the cost of living.

One of the best demonstrations of this promise is supermarket Tesco's "Every little helps" slogan. These three words are viewed by both retailers and advertisers as having had a major influence in transforming a "pile 'em high and sell 'em cheap" store into one that was, for many years, the most trusted in Britain.

Availability

Many purchasing decisions are based on how available either the product or information about it is to the shopper. This arises from the fact that consumers assume that what they are able to bring to mind most easily must also be important and significant. The old truism among salespeople that the easiest customer to sell to is an existing customer provides an example of this rule in action. The more readily a brand name can be recalled, the more likely it is not only that the product will be chosen, but that it will be more highly regarded and valued than a less easily remembered rival.

We are social animals programmed to respond to stories, particularly those that arouse strong emotions. By creating an emotionally arousing narrative around their product and then encapsulating that story in an easily recalled phrase—"A Mars a day helps you work, rest, and play," "Go to work on an egg," "Guinness is good for you," "The Esso sign means happy motoring"—advertisers make bringing their product to mind easy and effortless.

Expended effort

Would you feel differently about spending £100 you had taken several hours to earn or spending the same sum that someone had given you as a present? Research suggests that while most people want to ensure that their hard-earned cash is spent wisely, most are happy to blow a something-for-nothing windfall on a more trivial and self-indulgent purchase.

While, as I mentioned at the start of this chapter, some consumers take a great deal of thought and care when doing even routine shopping, most have neither the time nor the inclination to do so. Although some customers may possess specialist knowledge that guides some purchasing choices, for example when buying cars, cameras, or computers, most buy in relative ignorance. Only a minority know enough about chemistry to evaluate different brands of soap or toothpaste, or have sufficient nutritional expertise to differentiate between various processed food options. As a result, most shoppers have little choice but to depend on the expended effort heuristic, or some of the other mental shortcuts described here.

In the next chapter, I will explain how, by utilizing and manipulating these subconscious rules of thought, retailers encourage shoppers to spend more time in their stores and, of course, to part with more money in the process.

6

The Persuasive Power of
Atmospherics

Customers always get more than they bargain for, because a
product or service always comes with an experience.
— *Lou Carbone and Stephan H. Haeckel,*
"Engineering customer experiences"[1]

A mid-July day in sun-baked Istanbul and I'm about to go shopping in the world-famous Grand Bazaar. Before doing so, however,
I pause for refreshment in a traditional coffee shop. Its dimly lit,
smoke-filled interior is perfumed with the fragrant aromas of shee-
sha tobacco and sweet coffee. Waiters weave expertly between the
low, closely packed tables. In their hands are ornate brass trays,
laden with small cups of intensely black Turkish coffee, and hook-
ahs, water-cooled pipes.

As we lounge in comfortable armchairs sipping our scalding
hot drinks, my friends and Mindlab Istanbul colleagues, Yavuz
Bayraktar and Dr. Ugur Erdogan, provide a potted guide to the
long history of Istanbul's Grand Bazaar. Built between 1455 and
1461, the Kapalıçarşi, as it is known in Turkish, is one of the
world's largest and oldest indoor markets. It was constructed on
the orders of Sultan Mehmed the Conqueror, to store and sell
produce arriving each day by mule and camel train from all over
Europe and the Middle East. A bewildering maze of 61 narrow
streets, 4,000 shops, four fountains, and two mosques as well
as countless cafés, bars, and restaurants, the Kapalıçarşı today
employs 26,000 people and on a busy day has over half a million
visitors.

Entering through one of its many vaulted gateways, you take a step back in time. Sunlight filters in through narrow arched windows set in the high roofs and the air is heady with exotic scents and spices. The bewildering labyrinth of narrow streets and twisting alleys, many decorated with intricate Islamic mosaics in blue, white, and ocher, intersect haphazardly. Most of the small stores, opening directly onto the crowded thoroughfares, are crammed from floor to ceiling with brilliantly colorful carpets, silks, embroidery, pottery, and jewelry. A Phoenician merchant, transported in a time machine from 2,500 BCE, could start a business in the Grand Bazaar without any sense of being in a different era. The atmosphere is a mixture of interest, surprise, mystery, and discovery.

A few hours later I experience a very different kind of retailer in downtown Istanbul. The Cevahir mall, the name meaning diamonds or precious stones, opened in 2005, at a cost of $250 million, and is one of Europe's largest and most lavishly decorated shopping malls. With a total floor area of some 4.5 million square feet, it has 343 shops, 34 fast-food restaurants, 14 world-class restaurants, 12 cinemas, including one catering exclusively for children, a bowling hall, a roller-coaster, a stage for theatrical entertainment, a themed play area, and parking for 2,500 cars. The glass roof is topped by the world's second-biggest clock with hands 10 feet high. The floor of the atrium, designed to resemble an oasis, boasts fully grown palm trees and flowing water. Beyond are white marble floors, broad thoroughfares supported on gilded columns, and wide, glass-fronted balconies.

The atmosphere here is very different to that of the Grand Bazaar. The air is pleasantly cool and lacks the heady fragrance of the old market. This cathedral to consumerism smells of scented air conditioning and reeks of expensive luxury and money. While it's certainly a place for the public, the Cevahir is no public place. Here the bustling chaos of the Grand Bazaar gives way to order and control. To enter the mall, all shoppers must first pass through an airport-like security zone. Bags and packages are X-rayed, while metal detectors and armed security guards scrutinize every visitor. The same level of security extends throughout the mall. Within moments of my taking some photographs, a uniformed security guard was at my side warning that photography was forbidden and that my camera must be put away or it would be taken away.

I love the unique atmosphere of the Grand Bazaar with its heat, noise, and bustle; its pungent aromas, pools of darkness, and shafts of brilliant sunlight; its carved stone arches, intricate mosaics, vaulted ceilings, and displays of brilliantly colorful produce. I have often shopped in similar markets and souks in the Middle and Far East and found the unique, unpredictable, sometimes anarchic shopping experiences they provide to be part of their charm. Sadly, they also seem destined to become part of retailing history.

The Cevahir, like modern shopping malls anywhere in the world, probably represents retailing's future, in which the consumer experience has been minutely planned and meticulously engineered to mass produce a sort of hyper-reality. Through the use of architecture, design, lighting, sound, and aroma, an atmosphere is created that positively encourages spending—a retail environment in which shopping is made as easy, relaxed, comfortable, safe, predictable, and, from the retailer's point of view, profitable as possible.

The birth of atmospherics

The term "atmospherics" was coined more than 30 years ago by Philip Kotler, Professor of Marketing at Northwestern University in the US. He defined it as: "The conscious designing of space to... produce specific emotional effects in the buyer that enhance his purchase probability."[2]

Kotler's vision was to replace the haphazard and idiosyncratic spontaneity of markets like Istanbul's Grand Bazaar with scientifically designed multisensory shopping experiences. While his ideas provoked some interest among some retailers, they failed to change the way most went about their business. It was not until the last years of the twentieth century that retailers came to realize that, as L.W. Turley and Ronald Milliman of Western Kentucky University put it:

If consumers are influenced by physical stimuli experienced at the point of purchase, then, the practice of creating influential atmospheres should be an important marketing strategy for most exchange environments... particular elements of the atmosphere do not always have to be blatant to have an effect on consumers. Sometimes, understated and subtle changes to the retail environment are all that is required to change how shoppers behave inside a store.[3]

What finally began to change attitudes was partly the need felt by major retailers to attract more customers by standing out from the crowd, and partly the growing realization by scientists that, far from consumers making rational choices, their choices were mainly driven by subconscious thoughts and emotions. Increasingly, the major players recognized that to develop customer loyalty and keep the tills ringing, shopping had to be transformed from an unavoidable chore into a rewarding and entertaining experience.

Shopping as fantasy and fun

As far back as the 1980s, some researchers suggested that what consumers really wanted from a shopping trip was pleasure and excitement. In 1982, Morris Holbrook from Columbia University and Elizabeth Hirschman from New York University made the point that what shoppers really wanted were "playful leisure activities, sensory pleasures, daydreams, aesthetic enjoyment, and emotional responses... a steady flow of fantasies, feelings, and fun encompassed by what we call the 'experiential view.'"[4] However, it was not until the start of the new millennium that Kotler's ideas about atmospherics and notions of shopping as an emotion-enhancing entertainment experience finally began to coalesce in the minds of many major retailers.

The idea of creating surroundings in which shoppers feel both relaxed and excited, secure yet stimulated, at ease but also engaged was very much in the minds of those designing the Bluewater shopping and entertainment mall, some 23 miles south of London. One of those was retail specialist Nick Thornton, who is vastly experienced in developing shopping malls in many parts of the world. He explains:

> *All great retail places in the world are a function of three things. These are the offer, the environment and the experience. In the past the industry saw offer and environment as the key components and experience almost as a function of happenstance. If you got the offer and the environment right, then the experience would just follow along.*[5]

Because both the offer and the environment continued to improve over the years, it became ever more difficult for shopping malls to stand out from the competition. As Thornton was quick to point out, this meant that "Experience suddenly became much more important."

Experiences and experience clues

"'Experience clues' are impressions that can be very subtle—even subliminal—or extremely obvious," explain Lou Carbone and Stephan H. Haeckel. "They may occur by happenstance or by purposeful design. They may exist as isolated episodes or as managed suites. Collectively, they become an experience."[6] In traditional stores, experience clues present themselves in a largely haphazard and disorganized fashion. In modern shopping malls, they are precision engineered. Carbone and Haeckel categorize experience clues under two headings: humanics and mechanics.

Humanics refer to the people, both sales staff and other customers, whom shoppers encounter and the interactions between them. Mechanics include all the sights, sounds, smells, tastes, and textures within the retail premises, the way buildings are landscaped, the layout of stores within a mall, and the arrangement of displays within those individual retailers.

Let's start by considering the trickiest part of the atmospherics to control: the attitudes and behavior of people.

The brain sell power of humanics

When it comes to customer service, the acknowledged world master is the Disney Corporation, the US's biggest single-site employer. On my many professional visits to various Disney parks in Florida and California, I have never failed to be impressed by the friendly help-fulness of its employees. Given that Walt Disney World has more than 55,000 of them, the consistency of the service they provide is astonishing. The secret of their success lies in careful recruitment and intensive training. Indeed, this training is so detailed and thor-ough that one former employee described it to me as a sophisti-cated form of "behavioral manipulation."

Known within the company as "cast members" rather than employees, Disney's staff do not so much go to work as go on stage. Like actors in a play, they audition for their parts, wear costumes, work with props, and are carefully rehearsed in their roles. To ensure that they always stay in character, many—those playing the roles of maids and butlers in the Haunted Mansion, for example—learn not only a script but also detailed back stories of the various Disney characters involved. To avoid spoiling the illusion by visitors seeing cast members in their everyday clothes, the Magic Kingdoms are served by a tunnel complex almost two miles long. This ena-bles staff to reach their positions in the vast attraction without ever coming into contact with the public while they are out of character.

Another retailing giant that takes employee training extremely seriously is Apple. In a way it is lucky since, at least at the time of writing, bright, articulate people of all ages are prepared to stand in line for a chance to work with the company. One told me, only half jokingly, that it was harder to get a job on the shop floor at Apple than to be accepted by Harvard.

Before they can put on the blue shirt and receive the job title of "Genius," those who make it through the rigorous vetting procedures are sent on a two-week course, a sort of psychological boot camp dedicated to teaching them how to ensure that every consumer who enters the store really does feel like they are having a "nice day." The Genius Training manual provides a comprehensive list of Apple's dos and don'ts, including prohibited words as well as lessons on how to identify and capitalize on customers' emotions. The words that should never be used include "crash" and "bug." An Apple computer never crashes, it just stops responding, and it never has a bug in the software, it has an issue, a condition, or a situation.

Writing in Gizmodo.com, Sam Biddle described Genius Training as "An exhaustive manual to understanding customers and making them happy." He went on to point out that almost the entire volume

> is dedicated to empathizing, consoling, cheering up, and correcting various Genius Bar confrontations. The assumption, it seems, is that a happy customer is a customer who will buy things. And no matter how much the Apple Store comes off as some kind of smiling likeminded computer commune, it's still a store above all—just one that puts an enormous amount of effort behind getting inside your head.[7]

The basic idea, according to Biddle, is to be strong while appearing compassionate, to use persuasion while seeming passive, and to sell through empathy. The sales process begins when a Genius initiates a five-step sales plan, summarized in the manual as (A)pproach, (P)robe, (P)resent, (L)isten, (E)nd. After the initial greeting (Approach) the sales agent discusses, in a relaxed and friendly manner, the customer's needs and concerns (Probe). Suggestions are offered (Present) and any problems or concerns carefully listened to (Listen). When these arise they are often dealt with, according to the version of the manual I saw, using a very old but extremely effective sales technique known as Feel—Felt—Found. This exchange illustrates how it works:

Customer: "I love the new tablet, but I've always worked with a mouse on my computer and I'd miss not having one."

Genius: "I know how you *feel*, I *felt* the same when I started working with it. But within a very short time I *found* that I didn't miss it at all."

At that point a sale is usually made and the process ends (End). "Every Apple customer should feel empowered," says Biddle, "when it's really the Genius pulling strings."

Silent selling: The persuasive power of body talk

All salespeople possess the power to transform a good service into a great one by quite small pieces of nonverbal behavior. A friendly look, open body language, under the appropriate circumstances a light touch, or even something as basic as a cheerful smile can all transform the customer experience. This makes people feel included, accepted, and consequently subconsciously empowered. Such empathic gestures can usually, although by no means inevitably, trigger an equally positive and receptive response.

In a study of the interactions between customers and sales staff in a large shopping mall in Seoul, South Korea, Eugene Kim and David Yoon found that the more positive the employee, the more positive the customer. And when a shop assistant acted positively, the customer responded in kind, causing both to feel good about their exchange.[8]

As the world becomes ever smaller and customers increasingly international, it is essential for retailers to understand different cultural demands, expectations, and requirements. To see what this means for humanics in the twenty-first century, I spoke with two of the world's leading experts in this specialist retail area, Dag Rasmussen and Vincent Romet of Lagardère Services.[9] With an annual turnover in excess of €5 billion, this group that specializes in catering to the traveling public has a presence in more than twenty countries on four continents. In the boardroom of Lagardère's Paris headquarters at 2 Rue Lord Byron, not far from the Champs-Élysées,

Dag and Vincent told me about the challenges of dealing with customers from all parts of the world while ensuring that every one of their airport retailers stocks local products and creates an authentic local atmosphere. As Vincent explained:

> *It's a whole lot of different initiatives. Some of them are very structural, like working hard with the airport to make sure that the location of our stores is the best. A very good example of this is what we have achieved recently, in one terminal where we created a walkthrough store. Which means that, basically, you are making sure that 100 percent of the passenger flows will be directly in touch with the products... so that's a very structural initiative. But it is mainly through the training of our personal staff that we are able to create this capacity to convert the passenger into a customer. You need to know exactly how a Japanese customer reacts and how an American feels when they are approached by a salesperson... so that is a significant part of the training we are giving to our staff.*

Dag took up the story, outlining how the company caters to a great number of Chinese customers:

> *They're not exactly the same customers as they are in China, and they're definitely not the same customers as French customers or Italian customers. An Asian customer wants more service, whereas a European one often wants to be left alone, and doesn't want to have a very active sales staff on them— they want the staff to be available, when he or she wants it, but the Asian wants much more proximity, so we train our staff in a very specific way, in order to embrace all different types of customers.*

These differences in approach are reflected in the extent to which staff take the initiative or allow customers space in which to shop unattended. Dag continued:

If it's an Asian, you would be much more on the person, because they want this advice and so on, but many French or European people, if they know what they want, don't care about having somebody walking in the store with them. Asians would not accept coming in the store and not having people walking with them.

Vincent nodded in agreement and pointed out the importance of attending to the details of how to say hello and goodbye, how the salespeople present themselves. "With all things, it is very, very specific by nationality. These are very specific behaviors," he said.

While the company takes great care to give each of its airport stores a strong sense of being rooted in the national culture, it also knows that its customers prefer to be served by a fellow countryman. Dag pointed out:

Our high spenders are Asians, Russian, and the Brits, so we hire staff from these countries. If you have a Russian, the Russian staff would interact with them. If it's Chinese, our Chinese staff would interact. So we staff in order to have the demographics which go best with our customer flow.

This attention to detail can pay big dividends. Dag recalled with a smile how Chinese staff selling to one Chinese customer made the highest ever single sale: 24 bottles of vintage wine valued at €150,000.

The brain sell power of mechanics

Walt Disney is also good at mechanics. For instance, from the moment visitors exit Interstate 4 and enter Disney's Magic Kingdom in Orlando, Florida, every aspect of their experience will be controlled down to the smallest detail. On entering the park, and usually without being aware of the fact, they find themselves walking into a three-dimensional illusion. Leading up from the entrance, the street has the appearance of a long, bustling avenue flanked on either side by colorful, eye-catching attractions. Nevertheless, appearances are deceptive. Bustling it may be, long it is not.

Although it appears level, Main Street actually slopes gently upward. Together with building façades that have a slight lean, this creates what is termed a forced perspective. Also known as Hollywood perspective due to its widespread use in films, this artificially creates an illusion of depth and distance, causing objects to be seen as further away, closer, larger, or smaller than they really are.[10] The illusion makes Main Street look longer when visitors first arrive, but shorter as they leave at the end of a long and tiring visit. Cinderella Castle also employs forced perspective to make its already impressive 189-feet height look even taller. The top spire is only half as big as it seems and other key parts of the building are angled and scaled to produce an illusion of greater distance and height.

Crowd management, another key feature of ensuring an enjoyable consumer experience, is also expertly handled within the Kingdoms. Queuing times, posted on signs at every attraction, are deliberately made slightly longer than the actual wait. If a sign says you will have to stand in line for 15 minutes, it means you will probably be there within 10. If it said 10 minutes and you had not reached the end of the line for a quarter of an hour, many customers—or "guests," as Disney likes to refer to them—would feel aggrieved. Thanks to this simple piece of crowd psychology, everybody is happy.

Although only a limited number of shopping malls and superstores can match either Disney's huge investments of time and money or the skill and expertise of its "imagineers," the people who dream up and design the attractions, many do use the corporation as a role model when developing their own mechanics. Effective mechanics enhance the fluency of the shopping experience and they come into play the moment a customer arrives.

Just as we judge a product by its packaging, retailers know that what their premises look like on the outside provides shoppers with their first clue as to what they can expect to find on the inside. At

Bluewater, Nick Thornton directed my attention to the greenery flanking the massive car parks. More than a million shrubs, bushes, and trees were planted when the site was developed. He explained:

We wanted to ensure there was color all the year around. But we also wanted to create a green environment that is safe and secure, where a woman with children can feel secure and relaxed while walking to and from her car after dark. The shrubs will never grow higher than your waist and the tree canopy will never be lower than around six feet. This means that everywhere people look, at any time of the year, they see greenery and color without providing any opportunity for people to hide from view.

In the mind to shop

For a combination of humanics and mechanics to exert their persuasive effect over sales, members of the public must first be put in the right frame of mind. This transformation starts at the moment they enter the premises and is typically completed in less than 30 seconds. Known as the Gruen transfer, it is named after Austrian architect Victor David Gruen,[11] the man who invented the modern shopping mall. It refers to the subtle mental and physical changes that occur as you walk into a shopping center.

During the transfer, a customer's walking pace falls from a brisk walk to a slow wander. The pupils of their eyes expand or contract as they adapt to changing light levels. Their noses are assaulted by different aromas, their ears by a wide variety of different sounds, and their entire body by changes in temperature and humidity. Using equipment to monitor changes in brain and body as shoppers pass through the transfer, we have found a general slowing in heart rate and skin conductance, together with brain activity indicating a more relaxed and less alert frame of mind.

This suggests a switch from rational and attentive thinking to a more impulsive and automatic mode of thought. The reasons for such changes are not hard to fathom. While navigating their way to the mall, either along a congested pavement or across a busy car park, shoppers had little option but to remain alert and be consciously aware of their surroundings. Once inside the mall, by contrast, they are able to change gear cognitively. They can, and do, safely switch to mental autopilot as their brisk stride slows to a saunter and their gaze is caught by enticingly dressed window displays. From being at the mercy of the elements outside the shopping mall they are now in "Goldilocks" country, neither too hot nor too cold, too damp or too dry, but just right. In the many shopping centers I have visited in northern Europe, the temperature averaged 72 °F with 45 percent humidity.

For the reasons I gave in Chapter 3, this is a combination that generates subconscious feelings of relaxation and security—a state of mind that encourages customers to shop for longer and buy more products.

Lighting and eye appeal

In addition to architecture and design, the two aspects with the greatest eye appeal are lighting and color. Their power to influence mood and behavior is familiar to anyone who has hosted an intimate, candlelit dinner for two or taken the family to a fast-food outlet. Restaurants designed for romance have soft lighting and subdued colors, while fast-food eateries typically have bright lights and decor based on primary colors.

Similarly, a retailer seeking to communicate luxury, refinement, and exclusivity will employ a number of prestige clues: smartly dressed and well-groomed staff, subdued pastel or natural colors, soft classical music, and carefully selected aromas. However, one of the key clues is the level of illumination. To create an immediate impression of exclusivity, this should always be subdued rather than bright. The atmosphere should nevertheless be closer to Gothic cathedral than nightclub. In other types of store, such as a discount fashion retailer, bright, even illumination shows off products to their best advantage. In supermarkets, lighting is used in more subtle ways to create a specific response from the shopper: warmer lights in the bakery and cooler ones in butchery, for example. In a cosmetics department, soft lighting that flatters the face by smoothing out lines and wrinkles will do more for sales than harsh fluorescent lamps that emphasize every blemish.

As I explained in the previous chapter, customers depend on the appearance of the product when deciding how to categorize it and whether or not to buy. Color is important here too. Tomatoes must look really red, bananas a rich yellow, lettuce a crisp green, meat a healthy pink. While the freshness of the products themselves is obviously important, these features can be discreetly enhanced by the use of appropriate lighting.

At Bluewater, as in many sophisticated modern shopping malls, the lighting is adjusted several times a day to create different moods designed to appeal to changing customer profiles and the natural environment. For instance, it is brighter in the morning and in stores catering for younger people, and more subdued toward evening and where the need is to attract a more mature customer.

Yet lighting does more than merely create a desired mood. It can also have a significant influence over customer behavior and the resulting sales. Dim lighting has been shown to calm customers, encouraging them to walk around the store more slowly, spend more time shopping, and examine merchandise more carefully.[12]

In one experiment, psychologists installed additional lighting, which they were able to control independently, in two stores. They found that it was possible to control the time customers spent examining products and the number of items they looked at purely by adjusting the level of brightness. In general, the brighter the lights, the greater the interest and the higher the sales.[13]

Light and color are, of course, intimately related. When scientists tested two shops, one painted blue and the second orange, they found that if the lighting was bright, customers were more willing to spend money in the blue shop. However, when it was softly lit, customer liking for and sales in the orange shop increased.

Color me profitable

One of the first psychologists to realize the influence of color on shoppers was Ukrainian Louis Cheskin. During the 1930s and 1940s, he advised major companies on how it can be used to increase the appeal of their products. His pioneering work clearly showed that color makes a significant contribution to customers' moods, making them feel energized or relaxed, excited or calm, inspired or uninterested. Today these early studies have been advanced still further through the use of techniques that directly measure the effects of color on brain and body.

In my own laboratory, we have measured the extent to which different shades of red increase mental and physical arousal and the depth of relaxation produced by greens and blues. Our work has confirmed the findings of other researchers that these changes can exert a significant influence over consumer behavior. These have shown the following, for example:

- Cool colors, such as blue and green, make customers feel more relaxed, while those with a long wavelength, such as orange and red, are stimulating.[14]
- Shoppers evaluate retail premises that use cool colors more positively than those with warm (e.g., orange) interiors.[15]
- While saturated colors are experienced as being more pleasant, they are also more easily associated with fear than are cool colors.
- Dark colors, which are perceived as dominant, have been found to trigger feelings of hostility and aggression.
- Red and yellowish green, together with bright and dark colors, increase stress and tension, producing negative emotions and a desire to leave the premises concerned.

Joseph Bellizzi of Arizona State University and Robert Hite from Kansas University compared sales in two stores, one predominantly red and the other predominantly blue.[16] They found that in the blue environment, customers made more purchases, more rapid buying decisions, and had a stronger inclination to shop or browse than in the red store. This difference they attributed almost entirely to the color scheme, with red creating a mood that was negative and tense, if physically arousing, while blue led to a calmer, more relaxed, and more positive shopping experience.

The response to color is, however, very subjective and varies according to both the age and gender of the customer. Women are more sensitive than men to the brightness of colors, regarding vivid colors as more arousing and dominant. Nancy Puccinelli of Saïd Business School, Oxford University, and her colleagues found that the color in which promotional advertisements were printed influenced male but not female shoppers. When discounts offered on items like toasters and microwaves were printed in red, men were far more likely to believe they would save "a lot of money" than if the same discounts were in black (4.26 versus 2.56 on a seven-point scale). The effect persisted when several different items were being advertised.

However, red only swayed men's judgment so long as they were not paying much attention to the offer. The bias disappeared the moment they were asked to think about the price. Women remained unaffected by the color, possibly because they tend to shop in a more focused and systematic way than men. As the researchers put it: "Women appeared to be naturally inclined toward greater elaboration of the ad and showed greater price recall."[17]

The context in which a color is used is also important. Using red in a cinema foyer, for example, helps create a warm and festive atmosphere. The same color in an airport departure lounge would be likely to increase anxiety in nervous flyers. The colors of choice here, and for aircraft interiors, are natural hues in dark blue, green, and brown.

Color also affects customers' perceptions of the passage of time. Under red light time appears to pass more slowly and objects seem bigger and heavier, whereas under blue light time seems to pass more quickly and objects look smaller and lighter. Casinos use red as a basic color not only to make customers more aroused, but also to slow their perception of time passing.[18]

What works with color in bricks-and-mortar retailers also produces similar effects when shopping online. Studies of the way computer users respond to internet pages have shown that they feel most relaxed and that time is passing more quickly when the web page is brightly colored with a predominance of blue. Stress and tension, together with a perception that information was downloading more slowly, tended to increase when the screens displayed a large amount of red or yellow.[19] I shall be discussing other hidden persuaders in online shopping in Chapter 9, and have more to say about how color engineers different emotions in Chapter 7.

How music boosts sales

The music played in stores can significantly influence shopper behavior, not only encouraging spending but even directing people toward products to purchase. This effect occurs even when the customers are not consciously aware of it. Charles Gulas at Wright State University and Charles Schewe at the University of Michigan found that baby boomers were more likely to buy things when classic rock was being played, despite the fact that two-thirds of them were unable to say what music had been on while they were shopping.[20]

Studies have linked music to a wide variety of consumer behaviors, including perceptions of the time actually spent in a store, walking speed, and the way customers attend to the visual aspects of their surroundings. While many shoppers, especially older ones, claim to dislike loud music, this may in fact make little difference to the time they pass in a store or the amount of money they spend.

The tempo of the music does, however, affect both the speed with which customers move around a store and how much they outlay. In one study, the daily sales in a department where slow music was played were 38 percent higher than in another when the tempo was faster.[21] When wine buyers listened to classical music as opposed to songs from the Top 40, they spent more money, buying not more wine but more expensive wine.[22]

As important as the sound itself is the means by which it is delivered. Two sound systems specifically designed for this purpose are currently being introduced into US shopping malls and will shortly be coming to a supermarket near you. The first beams sales messages at individual shoppers by means of a narrowly focused signal. Promotions and special offers are also "hidden" behind music to act subliminally on their targets as they walk past sales hot spots. These messages can also be concealed within music so that they act on a target shopper walking past. (There is more on subliminal priming in Chapter 8.)

While subliminal voice commands on their own prove powerfully effective, if they are combined with what are termed cloned emotional signatures, the result has been described as "simply overwhelming." This is the promised claim for a second, even more high-tech approach being developed by Dr. Oliver Lowery of Norcross, Georgia. His Silent Sound Spread Spectrum (sometimes called S-quad or Squad) transmits sales pitches directly into the consumer's brain, bypassing their ears. It has been reported that this system can be linked to computers capable of identifying human emotions by detecting and analyzing electrical activity in the brain. According to Lowery, when transmitted alongside sales messages these "emotional signature clusters" will "silently induce and change the emotional state in a human being."

The smell of sales success

A further key component of retailing success, and one whose persuasive influence also often works subliminally, is aroma. This can be used to evoke memories, stimulate appetites, make shoppers feel more relaxed or excited, increase the time they spend in the store, and boost sales.

A wide range of retailers now use aromas as a routine element of their engineered environments, as the following examples show:

- In South Korea, Dunkin Donuts increased awareness of its coffee by injecting coffee aroma into public buses at the same time as its advertisement was played on the radio. This resulted in 16 percent more people visiting its stores and a 29 percent increase in sales.[23]

- McCain utilized multisensory advertisements for its microwave baked potato range. The bus shelter advertisements comprised a 2-feet-wide fiberglass jacket potato, which people could push to activate heaters in the bus shelters (given the February start date in the UK, this saw a lot of use). As the heaters came on, the scent of freshly baked potatoes was released into the air.[24]

- In the US, Bloomingdales has been scenting its stores differently by department: you may now find the soft scent of baby powder in the infant department, the tropical scent of coconut in the swimsuit department, the sensual smell of lilac in the lingerie department; during festive shopping periods, the smell of sugar cookie, chocolate, and evergreen creates a warm and cheerful experience.[25]

- At a Net Cost grocery store in New York, various culinary smells are being artificially pumped into the aisles in a bid to stimulate customers' appetites and encourage them to spend more. Scents like chocolate in the sweet snacks aisle, grapefruit in the produce aisle, and rosemary focaccia near the bread aisle have all been strategically chosen and positioned. According to early reports, the strategy appears to be working: sales rose by 7 percent after the system was installed.[26]

- The Hard Rock Hotel at Universal Resort in Orlando, Florida used artificial sugar cookie and waffle cone scents as a billboard to lead guests downstairs to an Emack and Bolio ice-cream outlet. The shop was previously going unnoticed due to its out-of-the-way location, but the "aroma billboard" helped increase sales by 30 percent.[27]

- Finally, a finding close to the heart of any author or publisher. Researchers at Belgium's Hasselt University report that the aroma of chocolate helps boost book sales. During a ten-day study, Lieve Doucé and her colleagues infused a bookshop with the scent of chocolate for half of its opening hours. Despite the aroma being too subtle to be immediately noticeable, they found that it still exerted a significant influence over the amount of time customers spent browsing, the number of titles they reviewed, and the books they bought. The greatest effect was on sales of books about food or drink together with romantic novels, all of which increased by an impressive 40 percent during the hours the store was perfused with the chocolate scent.[28]

In Charlotte, North Carolina, I discussed the scope and influence of aromas with Ed Burke, Marketing Director of ScentAir, a global leader in scent marketing. His company offers clients in the retailing, hospitality, and gaming industries a catalog of nearly 2,000 different aromas in addition to those it creates especially for a company or brand. Currently operating in 109 countries and with 50,000 customers worldwide, it claims to produce some 5 billion "enduring impressions" each year.

Burke told me how the company designs a bespoke scent to match the mood a client wants to achieve:

> We sit down and we figure out, number one what is the business you are trying to accomplish? At the end of the day our whole solution is set on driving toward that goal. Everything from the choice of the fragrance, where we scent within that space, is it one scent or several different scents. There is an element of science and an element of art. What are they doing in other realms of the sensory experience? We use all that information and then we go into a very creative design process because the scent has to fit in with all the other sensory elements.[29]

He cites as an example work undertaken for the high-end fashion retailer Hugo Boss. Here ScentAir started out by defining the meaning of the brand:

We asked questions like: Why does a customer choose HB? Why would they walk in through the door versus another brand? What does it represent to them? What are the elements of the store and the clothing and the experience which deliver that promise?

The answers they came up with were that the brand was typified by "luxury, style, discerning quality and exclusivity."

To create part of the atmospherics needed to communicate that message, the company realized that the chosen scent couldn't be "some very simple fragrance note that you could walk into the grocery store and get. It needed to be discerning, interesting, unique, rich, almost sensual, to match the brand. We needed a scent that had some character, some depth, some style. It needed to be unique, but perhaps also very familiar, very classically grounded."

With this in mind, they began to narrow down fragrances, rejecting anything bright and citrusy as not being sufficiently sexy and anything too floral as too much like perfume. "We looked at a lot of rich woods and some spices and some notes along those lines, and we finally came up with Pamboti wood from Africa. It is a very rich, clean, almost decadent fragrance, unique, luxurious, and very interesting," Burke explained. When this scent was introduced into Hugo Boss stores worldwide, the response of customers was almost universally positive; so much so that the store now proposes to sell it in the form of scented candles.

In most casinos around the world, ScentAir creates an aroma that induces players to relax and spend longer in the gaming rooms by helping to slow the passage of time. Research has shown that by introducing certain scents into the atmosphere, owners can significantly increase the amount gambled. Furthermore, this effect occurs even if the players, or the shoppers, remain unaware of the way in which scents are controlling their actions and emotions.[30]

In oxytocin we trust

One of the most widely produced subliminal aromas is oxytocin, a naturally occurring hormone that enhances the bond between mother and baby immediately after birth. To test its effects on adults, Michael Kosfeld of the University of Zurich asked subjects to inhale a nasal spray containing the hormone before playing a game using real money. In this game one player, the "investor," had to decide how much money to entrust to a second player, the "trustee." The trustee was then allowed to choose how much of that money they would give back.

Players who had received a whiff of oxytocin were prepared to risk more money than those who had inhaled a placebo. This willingness to put more of their money in jeopardy did not arise from a greater readiness to gamble, but from an increase in readiness to trust the other player.[31]

Oxytocin is produced naturally and normally during our everyday interactions with other people. It can be released by our conscious or unconscious response to someone else when meeting them for the first time. While we are shopping, it could be triggered if a member of the sales staff gives us a friendly smile, by their relaxed and approachable body language, or by the way they shake our hand.

As I shall explain in the next chapter, brands are also able to trigger the release of oxytocin and so make consumers trust them more. This may have worrying consequences, as neuroscientist Antonio Damasio commented in connection with the Zurich study:

> *Current marketing techniques, for politics or products, may well exert their effects through the natural release of molecules such as oxytocin in response to well-crafted stimulae. Civic alarm at the prospect of such abuses should have started long before this study.*[32]

The selling power of awe

Before leaving this account of the power of atmospherics to control shoppers' behavior and spend, we need to consider a further persuasive if seldom recognized element of some modern building design. This is the ability of giant malls to generate a sense of awe.

In my experience the three most likely malls to do this are:

- The Dubai Mall in the UAE, which is the world's largest and includes a 22-screen cinema, a giant aquarium, an Olympic-sized ice rink, and a replica of London's Regent Street.
- The SM Mall of Asia in Manila, the world's fourth largest at 4.2 million square feet, which boasts the biggest ice rink in Southeast Asia, a planetarium, an open-air music hall, and the world's largest 3D IMAX screens. This mall is so large that you travel around inside it by tram!
- The West Edmonton Mall in Alberta, Canada, with its huge water park, three radio stations, and almost life-sized replica of Columbus's ship the *Santa Maria*.

Creating a mall that inspires awe is a matter not of vanity but of sound commercial sense. It is a way of overcoming the modern shopper's greatest scarcity: a shortage of time. Surveys have shown that most consumers are time starved. In a recent poll of more than 1,000 Americans, for example, almost half (47 percent) said that they were too hard pressed to meet the many demands made on them in their daily lives.[33] As a result of this "time famine," shopping is often simply one more chore to be shoehorned into an already overly busy schedule, something to get over and done with as soon as possible.

As I explained in Chapter 2, there is a considerable difference in the attitude, motivation, and brain patterns of people who are doing the shopping rather than going shopping. So far as retailers are concerned, the former activity, while obviously desirable, is much less profitable than the latter. The more time people spend shopping, the greater their expenditure and the higher the profits.

I have already indicated that casino owners manipulate time very efficiently. Visit a Las Vegas casino and you will find that time appears to stand still. Day and night no longer have any meaning; there are no clocks to alert players to the passage of time. The majority of casinos have no windows, so the artificial lighting is moved up and down to simulate day and night—except that daylight starts around

4 am to further distort and disorient players. The air in some Vegas casinos is also supercharged with oxygen to help people stay awake longer and, if drinking alcohol, as most players do, become intoxicated faster.

Retailers cannot suspend time to quite the same extent and in the same way as casino operators, but there are other ways of persuading people that time has slowed down. If you have the budget, you can create an environment that is so grand, so overwhelming, that shoppers can only stand and stare in amazement. Research has clearly shown that when customers consider an environment awe inspiring, they shop for longer and spend far more.

In a series of experiments, Melanie Rudd and her colleagues at the Universities of Stanford and Minnesota studied how feelings of awe change people's perception of time while also making them feel happier and, therefore, more willing to buy. One study involved subjects watching one of two videos. The first, designed to create a sense of awe, showed people "interacting with vast, mentally overwhelming, and seemingly realistic images, such as waterfalls, whales, and astronauts in space." The second, intended to induce happiness, showed a "parade of joyful people... wearing brightly colored outfits and face paint." After watching these two advertisements, participants answered questions about how swiftly or slowly they felt time to be passing. The researchers reported that "awe... led to the perception that time is more plentiful and expansive."[34]

Research conducted in my own laboratory has confirmed the potency of awe-inspiring imagery to increase feelings of happiness, make customers more patient, and exert a positive influence over their buying decisions and readiness to spend.

Many consumers fail to appreciate the extent to which when they shop, they are subjected to a vast array of hidden persuaders created by an army of scientists, engineers, and architects, many of which I have discussed in these pages. Furthermore, as it is with retailers, so with brands. Multinational corporations don't only produce products—they also engineer emotions, which is where we turn in the next chapter.

7

Brand Love: The Engineering of Emotions

A great brand raises the bar, it adds a greater sense of purpose to the experience, whether it's the challenge to do your best in sports and fitness or the affirmation that the cup of coffee you're drinking really matters.
—Scott Bedbury, Head of Marketing, Nike[1]

The notion that consumers "fall in love" with or even form deep and lasting attachments to brands will strike many people as absurd. Yet a host of studies, by consumer psychologists and neuromarketers alike, confirm that such emotionally charged relationships not only occur but are commonplace. Researchers speak of brand devotion,[2] brand love,[3] brand attachment,[4] and brand commitment.[5] Psychologists have even compared consumers' affection for brands with the love they feel for family and close friends.[6]

In this chapter I will describe some of the advertising and marketing techniques used to engineer these powerful emotions and explain the role of neuromarketing technology in determining whereabouts in the brain they are generated.

Shelfspace or mindspace?

According to US marketing expert Jack Trout, over a million products now fight for consumers' attention. A major supermarket might have shelf space for around 60,000, or just 6 percent of the relevant products potentially available.[7] Even so, this leaves customers with a bewildering array of choices. In his medium-sized neighborhood supermarket, Barry Schwartz, Professor of Social Theory and Social Action at Swarthmore College, Pennsylvania, counted

> *85 different varieties and brands of crackers... 285 varieties of cookies... 13 "sports drinks," 65 "box drinks" for kids, 85 other flavors and brands of juices... 61 varieties of suntan oil and sun-block, 80 different pain relievers... 40 options for toothpaste, 150 lipsticks, 75 eyeliners, and 90 colors of nail polish... 116 kinds of skin cream and 360 types of shampoo, conditioner, gel, and mousse.... 29 different chicken soups... 16 varieties of mash potatoes... 120 different pasta sauces... 275 varieties of cereal... and 175 types of tea bags.*[8]

Brand managers are painfully aware that an average family can satisfy three-quarters of their needs with only 150 products. That means, as Trout points out, "There's a good chance they'll ignore 39,850 items in that store... In this global killer economy you have to find a way to differentiate yourself."[9]

Ensuring that their own brand not only holds its own on ever more congested supermarket shelves but continually expands its market share has always preoccupied brand managers. Today, as the result of recent discoveries in psychology and neuroscience, they have another challenge to keep them awake at night: how best to engineer the consumer's emotions. In the words of author Geoffrey Miller, modern brand marketing has become the place "where the wild frontiers of human nature meet the wild powers of technology."[10]

When emotions began to matter

Fifty years ago, people in marketing, advertising, and retailing shared the widely held view that emotions were the consequence rather than the cause of rational thought. It was not that they were unaware of the importance of emotions or that they did not try to generate positive feelings as well as supplying hard facts. The concern of their research, conducted mainly through surveys and focus groups, was to discover what customers were *thinking*, not what they were feeling. Such companies firmly believed that consumers could best be persuaded to buy their products through an appeal to reason.

Most consumers of the day felt the same way. They held to the view that, in the words of marketing guru Rosser Reeves, advertisements worked "openly and honestly in the bare and pitiless sunlight."[11]

Psychological and neuroscientific research over the past 30 years has shown these confident beliefs to be profoundly mistaken. The work of pioneering psychologists like Robert Zajonc[12] and Robert Bornstein[13] has demonstrated not only that emotions are more important than thoughts in influencing shopping behavior, but also that emotions can be successfully engineered without consumers ever becoming consciously aware of how their minds are being manipulated.

Today, every company strives to manufacture a deep emotional connection between its brand and some desirable personal goal or worthy aspiration. For example, Starbucks recognizes that for its customers coffee is coffee and there is not any great difference between various brands, so it set about engineering an emotional attachment to its own brand through what its founder Howard Schultz calls "the romance of the coffee experience, the feeling of warmth and community people get in Starbucks stores."[14] In the UK, however, such efforts were significantly damaged by the revelation that the coffee chain was using sophisticated strategies to avoid paying billions of pounds worth of tax, which illustrates the fragility of this kind of connection.

Nike, which began life as a small-time distributor of Japanese track shoes and rose to become one of the world's leading athletic shoe and apparel retailers, built its business on the passions aroused by sport. Phil Knight, its founder, Chairman, and CEO, claimed:

> *For years... we put all our emphasis on designing and manu-*
> *facturing products. But now we understand the most important*
> *thing we do is market the product... Nike is a marketing-oriented*
> *company, and the product is our most important marketing tool.* [15]

Nike has used catchy slogans and fast-paced television commercials to engineer emotions associated with physical prowess and competitive success. "You can't explain much in 60 seconds," admitted Knight, "but when you show Michael Jordan, you don't have to. It's that simple."

Branded from birth

Emotional attachment to a brand can occur very early in life. Juliet B. Schor, Professor of Sociology at Boston College, claims that "Contemporary American 'tweens and teens have emerged as the most brand-orientated, consumer-involved, and materialistic generations in history."[16] A significant number of children in the US believe that their clothes and brands describe who they are and define their social status. American kids display more brand affinity than their counterparts anywhere else in the world; indeed, experts describe them as increasingly "bonded to brands."

According to a 2001 study by Nickelodeon, the average American 10-year-old knows between 300 and 400 brands; by the age of 14, nine out of ten requests are brand specific. A survey of parents found that two-thirds of mothers considered their children to have been aware of brands from the age of 3 and one-third by the age of 2.

From playground to playing field and schoolroom to boardroom, brands are increasingly being perceived as the outward and visible signs of personal accomplishment and social inclusion. Thanks to emotional engineering, their ownership has come to symbolize everything that represents, especially for the young, the concept of sophistication and financial success. By the same token, a failure to possess and flaunt such brands speaks to many of failure and social exclusion.

Given these pressures, it is little wonder that decoding brands is one of the first lessons children learn once they are old enough to turn on a television. Long before they hit puberty, they use brand names to make judgments about other people. They know which brands are fashionable and which ones no self-respecting child should ever be seen with. And this is not only occurring in America. A study of British adolescents by psychologist Helga Dittmar found that teenagers effortlessly use brands to separate the very well-off from the moderately well-to-do and to make sweeping judgments based on these distinctions. They believe that brands not only indicate income levels, but also how intelligent, successful, educated, and in control of their lives people are. The higher the social class of the child, the more brand conscious they are.[17]

Given such powerful emotions, branding is a race in which the winner takes all and the prize for breasting the tape first can be astronomical (Box 7.1).

Box 7.1 The billion-dollar brand

What is the cash value of a brand? If that brand is Kraft, the answer is $12.6 billion—or around $2.5 billion per letter. This huge sum, six times the book value, was paid by Philip Morris when it bought the company in 1988. What it was buying was the name. As anti-globalization activist Naomi Klein pointed out in her bestselling book *No Logo*, "With the Kraft purchase, a huge dollar value had been assigned to something that had previously been abstract and unquantifiable."[18]

In 2010 Kraft paid $19.6 billion to purchase the British company Cadbury. Analysts saw this, at least in part, as the price of acquiring a prestigious and highly respected brand name.

To understand how a brand can acquire such a value, consider the case of Ivory Soap. This was launched in 1879 by Harley Procter, one of the founders of Procter and Gamble, after he had listened to a church sermon taken from Psalm 45: "All thy garments smell of myrrh, and aloes, and cassia, out of ivory palaces." The word "ivory" stuck with him as he walked back from the service. It became what I shall describe shortly as a "brain worm" that he could not get out of his head. Instead, he used it as the name for his new soap, the first white soap from P&G, which was advertised as 99 percent pure. "The brand promise of Ivory hasn't changed in 118 years," reported marketing expert David Aaker in 1991, and it has "contributed profits to P&G somewhere in the neighborhood of $2 billion–$3 billion over its lifetime."[19]

If you can successfully engineer the emotions that a brand generates so that it will appeal to consumers across their lifetime, then you have a license to print money. However, beware of making changes in the brand that alter its emotional appeal or, even worse, generate negative feelings toward the product. There is a graveyard of once-mighty brands that were done to death in precisely this way (Box 7.2).

Box 7.2 The man who made snot beer

Brands, like people, have a birth, a life, and a death. Some can go on for decades, a tiny minority for more than a century, while others suffer a premature demise for a wide variety of reasons. Around 80 percent of all brands are stillborn, failing even as they are introduced, while a further 10 percent perish within five years.

The reasons for the decline or collapse of established brands include a failure to change with the times (Kodak and Polaroid), gaining a bad reputation in the marketplace (Rover), changes in public tastes (Ovaltine), and not meeting high public expectations (boo.com). However, the following case history illustrates the way in which a combination of cost cutting and managerial incompetence together with the creation of a "yuck" factor, as described in Chapter 2, can cause even a well-established and highly popular brand to fade and die.

Schlitz, for many years America's bestselling beer, had been brewed since 1902 by the Joseph Schlitz Brewing Company. Known as "The beer that made Milwaukee famous," it was advertised with the slogan "When you're out of Schlitz, you're out of beer." It was a nationally renowned brand name that generated the positive emotions associated with tradition, integrity, and wholesomeness. By the early 1970s, however, it had dropped from first to second place behind Budweiser.

To restore profitability, the company's boss Robert Uihlein, Jr. decided to reduce the cost of ingredients and speed up the brewing process. Unfortunately, while the new beer made more money, it also made its customers feel nauseous. The taste was horrible and the cheaper ingredients clumped together, looking, in the words of one critic, "disconcertingly like mucus." Disgusted drinkers termed it "snot beer" and sales collapsed. Robert Uihlein had to recall 10 million cans and watch his company's once highly prized brand name become synonymous with disgust. The Milwaukee brewing plant closed in 1981 and the company was bought out by a rival the following year.

Creatives or researchers?

While engineering an emotion and attaching it to a brand can prove a long, complex, and costly process—involving a wide range of factors from celebrity endorsements and sponsorships to the support of suitable good causes, extensive public relations, advertising, marketing, and packaging—at the heart of any brand is almost always a mixture of three key elements:

- Images
- Words
- Music

Aroma, taste, and feel also play a role with some brands, but the three listed above are those most usually employed in emotional engineering. Until quite recently, the choice of these elements was largely a matter of the imagination and experience of creatives, the men and women who earn their living dreaming up advertising campaigns. Although these are sometimes guided by the findings of focus groups and surveys, ultimately what appears on the printed page, the television set, and the cinema screen is a product of their creativity. It is a freedom they have long cherished, which, in my experience, makes many of them highly resistant to any research that pours cold water on their inspirations. An advertising insider once confided to me:

> *What creatives really want is to be given a million dollars to produce a campaign that wins them an award. Whether it actually sells any product is much less important to them!*

There are, of course, occasions in which creatives are perfectly correct to stick to their campaign in the face of adverse findings by surveys, focus groups, and even the clients themselves. In 1984, Apple's now famous one-minute "1984" commercial,[20] made to introduce the Macintosh personal computer, was viewed by its board and every one of them, including Steve Jobs, rejected it out of hand. In their collective opinion, it utterly failed to present the Apple Macintosh as a serious business computer. They were concerned that if the commercial ever aired, their company would look "insane" and "out of control" to employees, stockholders, investors, their rivals, and consumers. Focus groups were equally dismissive, rating the commercial as well below average for "effectiveness" and scoring it only 5 against the normal average of 29 for business-directed commercials.

Apple's plan had been to air the commercial in a million-dollar advertising slot during the third quarter of Super Bowl XVIII. It was only after he had failed to sell this slot on and was faced with having to write off $1 million that Steve Jobs reluctantly, and in the face of strenuous opposition from his fellow directors, gave his approval. The commercial aired and history was made. Recall of the advert the following day ran at an unprecedented 78 percent. The next morning, in just six hours, Apple sold $3.5 million worth of computers; it achieved $155 million in sales over the next 100 days.[21]

In the end, it was not Apple's expensive investment in research that led to the commercial being aired, but one man's change of mind when confronted with the loss of the investment the company had already made. Today, the mood is somewhat different: Research is no longer a dirty word but an economic necessity. Much of the most cutting-edge research is being conducted in neuromarketing and neuroscience laboratories around the world.

In the laboratory of US neuromarketing company Sands Research, nestling in the foothills of the North Franklin Mountains, director Ron Wright described the company's most recent annual Super Bowl Ad Neuro Ranking. To achieve this, EEG is used to measure not what people *say* about a television commercial but how they *feel* about it. In 2011, one of the ads the company tested was the story of a miniature Darth Vader who comes to believe in the power of the "force" after his dad uses the remote-start feature of a Volkswagen. It was a commercial that, like Apple's "1984," might never have seen the light of day had the auto company relied on traditional tests and measures. According to Douglas Van Praet, Volkswagen Planning Director, these indicated that "the spot generated a below-average persuasion score—the measure of stated purchase intent that has achieved exalted status in the industry despite its weak correlation to actual sales."

The neuromarketing study, however, told a very different tale. As Dr. Stephen Sands, Chair and Chief Science Officer at Sands Research, explained, "The Darth Vader advertisement elicited such a strong emotional response, it ranks as the highest we have ever tested."

Reassured by these findings, Volkswagen ran the advertisement, with spectacular results. "The Force" became one of the most admired and shared Super Bowl ads ever, amassing a staggering 56 million views on YouTube, earning a reported 6.8 billion impressions worldwide and more than $100 million in earned media. It also helped the VW brand achieve its best market share in the US in 30 years.

Brands in the brain

Can knowledge of where emotions are found in the brain be used to engineer them more effectively? As we have seen in previous chapters, scientists seek answers to these questions by sliding volunteers into million-dollar brain scanners and attaching arrays of electrodes to their scalps. By comparing the way a brain responds to slightly different versions of, for example, a television commercial, they can suggest ways to improve the emotional impact produced. Even minor changes to the images used, the way they are edited, the choice of background music, the words spoken or written, even the speed, intonation, and accents of the speakers can make a significant difference to the emotional impact on viewers.

Which brain regions are of greatest interest to neuromarketers? The first is the amygdala (its name comes from the Greek for almond because of its shape), which processes incoming information, and the hippocampus (from the Greek for seahorse, again due to its shape), which is concerned with short-term memory. Both are located in the limbic system, which is responsible for emotions, both pleasurable and disagreeable. Their location in the brain is shown in Figure 7.1.

According to neuroscientist Joseph Ledoux of New York University, incoming information can reach the amygdala by what he calls a "low" or a "high" road.[22] To translate this to the retail environment, when a shopper spots a familiar brand on the supermarket shelf, this information is initially sent to a part of the brain known as the sensory thalamus. From there it can either travel directly to the amygdala, producing an immediate response, or it can take a slightly different and slower route, enabling memories to be attached to it. This ensures a more considered response based on what the person already knows, or thinks they know, about what their senses are telling them.

George Loewenstein of Carnegie Mellon University explains:

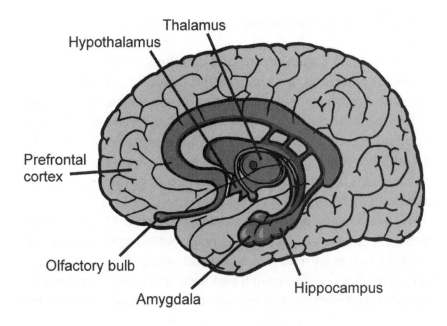

Figure 7.1 Image of the brain showing areas of greatest interest to neuromarketers: the amygdala, the hippocampus, the thalamus, and the prefrontal cortex

Emotions can flood consciousness, because the wiring of the brain at this point in our evolutionary history is such that connections from the emotional systems to the cognitive systems are stronger than connections from the cognitive systems to the emotional systems.[23]

When a bargain is spotted, signals travel by the fast "low" road and produce an immediate emotional response. This leads to some of the bodily changes among my fashion hunters in New York, described in Chapter 1. The heart beats more rapidly and there is an increase in both respiration and sweating. The way the brain is working also changes, and these effects are detected both by brain scans and from the electrical activity. It is only after the signal has reached the amygdala and triggered this immediate "excitement" emotion that it uses the "high" road to access memory, before returning to the amygdala with a more informed response to the situation.

Another brain region involved in emotions is the insula cortex or lobe. The name is derived from the Latin for "island" and it is sometimes known as Island of Reil, with some anatomists regarding it as the fifth lobe of the brain. Its task is to receive and integrate information from inside the body, including processing of emotion and self-awareness. Seeing an expression of happiness or sadness on someone's face, for example, can trigger bodily responses associated with increased insula activity.

This brain region is divided into two main parts. The part toward the back (posterior) of the brain is responsible for integrating sensory information with muscle movement, while the anterior region (toward the front of the brain) transforms information arriving from the body into emotions and actions. The insula has close, two-way connections to other regions deep in the brain, such as the amygdala and prefrontal cortex.

What does all of this mean for a brand? As Martin Reimann of the University of Southern California and his colleagues have discovered:

> *Based on these insights, we expect that established close brand relationships, when compared with neutral brand relationships, should be associated with increased activation in the insula because the insula integrates bodily information (e.g., an urge to possess the loved brand) into emotional and motivational functions. Indeed, in the context of interpersonal relationships, several fMRI studies have provided neurophysiological evidence that increased insula activation is strongly associated with romantic love, maternal love and unconditional love... adopting the perspective of a loved one [also] increases insula activation.*[24]

Because these regions lie deep within the brain, their activities can only be indirectly measured using QEEG, whose sensors, as we have seen, are placed on the outside of the head. They can, however, be closely monitored using fMRI, which provides a picture of all parts of the brain and can easily and accurately detect changes in blood to, say, the amygdala or hippocampus.

I have already discussed the role of the frontal regions of the brain, which are responsible for making purchasing decisions based on information arriving from many different regions, but especially from the emotionally driven limbic system. Because activity in these areas occurs in the cortex, or outer layer of the brain, the signals can be recorded using electrodes attached to the scalp.

"Understanding this process has many implications towards research methods prominently used today in advertising research," points out neuroscientist Annette Kortovna Simson, "since all of them are based on cognitive and not emotional processes."[25]

What brand managers and advertisers seek to do is implant an emotional memory, what I term a "brand worm," in the consumer's brain. Once lodged there, it triggers the same feelings and memories whenever the brand is seen. The more people who share this response, the greater will be the impact on your purchasing decisions. Termed the "bandwagon" effect, this was demonstrated in an fMRI study by neuroscientist Gregory S. Berns at Emory University, Atlanta. In his study, 30 volunteers were asked to compare over 50 pairs of abstract three-dimensional images and decide whether they were alike or different.[26] During the test, participants were also provided with the responses given by other subjects. Berns found that most people went along with the view of the majority, even if it was wrong. By measuring relative degrees of activation in the parietal lobe, an area involved in integrating visual images, and in the prefrontal cortex, where decision making takes place, he was able to identify brain changes that occurred in response to peer-group pressure.

"There is probably some reward or kick in conforming to a group," says Berns, who believes that his research can help explain the emotions behind fads and trends ranging from the popularity of Burberry plaids to the feeding frenzy of internet and property bubbles.

The persuasive power of emotional engineering was confirmed by Dr. Christine Born and her colleagues at Ludwig-Maximilians University in Munich.[27] They conducted a study in which the brains of 20 well-educated young men and women were scanned while they looked at well-known and lesser-known brands of cars and insurance companies. Her team found that strong brands activated regions of the brain involved in processing positive emotions, as well as those linked to self-identification and rewards. Furthermore, strong brands were processed with far less effort than weaker ones. The latter also produced higher levels of activation in regions concerned with working memory and negative emotional response. This effect was independent of the type of product or service offered.

"This is the first functional magnetic resonance imaging test examining the power of brands," Born told delegates attending the annual meeting of the Radiological Society of North America. "We found that strong brands activate certain areas of the brain independent of product categories."

This novel, interdisciplinary approach to understanding how the mind perceives and processes brand information is a further example of the insights being gained through modern brain imaging technologies. Born added:

> *The vision of this research is to better understand the needs of people and to create markets which are more oriented towards satisfaction of those needs. Research aimed at finding ways to address individual needs may contribute to a higher quality of life.*

With this background in mind, let's look at how some, often fairly minor changes to the images, words, or music used in advertising can enhance a brand's emotional potency.

Engineering emotions through picture power

As we saw in the previous chapter, emotions can be engineered in retail premises via all the senses. Eyes can be dazzled, ears bombarded, and nostrils assaulted by a vast assortment of visual, auditory, and olfactory techniques and technologies.

When devising ways of engineering an emotion via a brand alone, marketers are more usually limited to pictures, words, and, with some products, touch, taste, and smell. A picture is often claimed to be worth a thousand words. In fact, pictures can express in an instant far more information and emotion than would ever be conveyed as speedily using words. What is more, images are far more likely to stick in the memory and be brought to mind more easily. This is because, despite the fact that words are essential to the way most people—mathematicians and artists excepted—think and communicate their thoughts, the brain still functions faster, more fluently, and with less effort when processing images.

My own laboratory has conducted numerous studies that clearly demonstrate the superiority of images over words, both in retail environments and on the web. In one such study,[28] Mindlab compared the speed and ease with which people could make sense of complex data when it was presented to them in the form of either words or images. The differences were startling. Data provided in the form of images reduced the mental effort required to make sense of them by around 20 percent. Not only did our subjects perform the task more efficiently, they had better subsequent recall of the information. Neuroscientist Dr. Lynda Shaw explains why this occurs:

> The visual brain is this incredibly flexible and adaptable design to help us see and remember and make sense of everything around us. If we can stop feeling overwhelmed... we can actually start enjoying this information, and by enjoying it we might be able to increase our brain capacity because we're using it better.[29]

A finding like this comes as less of a surprise when we realize that humans have been thinking in images for millions of years, but using writing for just a few thousand. While *Homo Erectus*, one of our earliest ancestors, was walking the earth some two million years ago, there is general agreement that the writing of language, rather than only numbers, was not invented until about 3200 BCE. The power of the image was recognized by advertisers almost as soon as it became possible to print illustrations, first by means of drawings and later through the use of photographs. During the late nineteenth century, for instance, women buying a packet of Quaker Oats were being persuaded that they were purchasing more than a breakfast cereal. They were buying, as well, into the noble virtues of rectitude, honesty, and family values; then, as now, potent emotional triggers for the American psyche. And it was all down to the company's inspired choice of logo: the image of a bewigged and black-coated Quaker.

What does a member of the Religious Society of Friends have to do with breakfast cereals? The answer is, of course, absolutely nothing. But what this does do is create a subconscious association in the consumer's mind between the brand and positive attributes such as wholesomeness and tradition. These are all linked to "feel good" emotions, and in this role the Quaker became an early example of a hidden persuader. He allowed mothers to look on providing food for their family not simply in terms of nutrition but, says Gary Cross, a Professor of History at Penn State University, as "something to inspire confidence, an indication that you were doing a good job as a mother."[30]

Engineering emotions through color

As we saw when considering the retailing environment, color plays an enormously important role in generating emotions, acting directly on the emotional regions of the brain in profound ways. Red, for example, increases physical arousal, which is one reason it is so often used as a warning.

Color can even affect the way in which experienced referees judge the outcome of matches. Sports psychologists at the University of Münster, Germany, showed 42 referees video clips of martial arts bouts in which one combatant was wearing red and the other blue. They then replayed the clips after digitally manipulating the clothing so that the colors were swapped around. In close matches this resulted in the scores being exchanged, with competitors now dressed in red being awarded an average of 13 more points than when they had been dressed in blue.[31]

We used this finding in a study comparing three sets of advertisements for take-away meals. These were identical except in one respect, the color scheme. In the first the predominant color was red, in the second blue, and in the third green. Brain activity showed that the most emotional engagement occurred with the red scheme, followed by blue and then green.

Another example is Cadbury's brand identification with the colour purple. Bailey Dougherty, Account Director at Boom! Marketing, a leading Canadian experiential marketing agency, believes that the net worth of the color to Cadbury's is "almost priceless," since

it is associated with a series of feel good emotions. Cadbury Purple is regal yet accessible—and you may have noticed, that seeing the colour does make you think of chocolate.[32]

If brands, or cued representations of brands such as Cadbury purple, are embedded in an entertaining context, they can be influential without being consciously recognized or recalled. Cues that predict rewards are potent hidden persuaders that result in impulsive eating.

What makes a baby face?

A company making a baby product intended to illustrate its print campaign with an illustration of an attractive, smiling baby. But what sort of baby face would the intended customers, young mums, identify with most readily? This was one of the earliest studies I conducted, back in the 1990s, a good decade before the term neuro-marketing was even invented. After attaching sensors to the heads and bodies of the young mothers who volunteered to take part in my research, I showed them a series of baby faces that an artist had skillfully retouched to alter minor aspects of their features.

In some, the nose had been made more snubbed; in others the smile broadened or a dimple added, subtracted, or expanded, the pupils made slightly wider or more narrow; the whole shape of the face was also subtly changed. What I was looking for here were the facial characteristics that would act most effectively as what is called a "biological releaser."[33] This relates to the fact that the young of many species—lion cubs, lambs, puppies, and human babies—share several characteristics: disproportionately large heads and big eyes. These infantile characteristics trigger a powerful protective emotion in adults and so help ensure that the young will be cared for and safeguarded during their vulnerable early years.

In addition to measuring the way the mothers' brain was responding, their heart rate and excitement level rising or falling, we also used eye trackers to see what parts of the face were studied most closely and which were ignored. Finally, I recorded the extent to which their pupils widened or narrowed as they examined the images. This provides a good measure of their like or dislike for the baby, since the more we are attracted to something the wider our pupils become. After testing 60 subjects, I was able to identify the baby face producing the strongest emotion in the mothers, and this became the focus of an extensive and successful advertising campaign.

Engineering emotions through music

"Extraordinary how potent cheap music is!" exclaimed Noël Coward in *Private Lives*. That is a message that advertisers as well as musicians have long known and now neuroscientists have started to explore it. Music has equal emotional engineering power to pictures, and in some circumstances is far superior to them in triggering emotions, from joy to fear and depression to spine-tingling excitement. For instance, what are called "sonic signatures"—those short bursts of notes that introduce many news programs or announce that Windows is loading—are triggers that alert your brain almost instantly to what is happening.

In the previous chapter, I explained how music is used to manipulate everything from shoppers' moods to the speed with which they move through a store. Here, I want to describe a study that Mindlab conducted for a drinks company to investigate the most evocative background music for a beer commercial. We were asked to compare responses to a track from a recording by a world-famous (i.e., expensive) singer–songwriter with different versions of a tune created by a less well-known (i.e., cheaper) composer. The scores were added to a number of different versions of the commercial and, once again, our volunteers were wired up and their mental and physical responses recorded as they watched. Our conclusions saved the client a considerable sum of money in performing rights, as we were able to demonstrate that the less famous version worked slightly better across most of the commercials than that by the headline artist.

Music is vital to brand managers because, when used successfully, it enables them to trigger an involuntary memory for their product almost instantly. It takes only a few bars of a tune to bring the brand to the forefront of the consumer's mind, due to a process known as "involuntary musical imagery" or INMI. Dr. Lassi Liikkanen, a researcher at Aalto University, Finland, comments:

INMI is defined as a conscious experience of reliving a musical memory without deliberately attempting to do so. It is also known by other colloquial terms such as earworms, sticky tunes, or tune in the head phenomenon.[34]

Although the causes of INMI remain unknown at the time of writing, researchers hypothesize that it activates memory mainly through recall and recognition. The more often one hears a simple piece of music, the more likely it is to stick in one's head and be almost impossible to banish from the forefront of one's mind, at least for a while. That may be irritating for the consumer, but it is music to the ears of marketers, advertisers, and retailers.

It is worth mentioning a new method of delivering attention-grabbing sounds via mobile devices. Known as earcons, these are audible icons that appear to come from a specific area of the device's screen. You might, for instance, hear the sound of a steak sizzling when you click on the icon for a restaurant, or the noise of gently breaking surf when you look at the image of a sunny tropical beach. Earcons serve as barely registered persuaders to check out the eatery or go to the travel agent.[35]

Engineering emotions with word power

The power of words to trigger powerful emotions is well known to direct marketing copywriters, who pen heart-wrenching begging letters on behalf of good causes. However, words can have a powerful effect even when they are not so overtly seeking to pluck the consumer's heart strings.

Dan Jones, a leading hypnotist and expert on the hypnotic power of words, explains:

Many brands manipulate your decision making with emotive words and other linguistic tricks. Emotional states are trance states and memories are state dependent, so if advertisers can trigger an emotion linked with their brand and with some real world event, that will subconsciously remind you of the brand each time you experience the same emotion. It's a form of autosuggestion. The effectiveness of autosuggestion when used repeatedly and frequently has been known since Emile Coue promoted the use of autosuggestion for self-help with phrases like "Each day in every way I am getting better and better."[36]

Take the McDonald's slogan, "I'm lovin' it." The phrase was coined by Paul Tilley for the DDB advertising agency in 2003 and has been translated into more than 20 languages. But why "*I'm* lovin' it," why not "*You're* lovin' it"?

Instructing people to behave in a particular way risks a backlash. It creates a psychological resistance, although not necessarily at a conscious level, that leads them to do the exact opposite. Because television viewers will relate the words "I'm lovin' it" to the actors speaking those lines in an advertisement, the message slides easily into their heads and becomes a brain worm. Then, because they hear the same phrase repeatedly, just like a catchy tune, they start silently to repeat the line themselves. By linking the emotion of love with the McDonald's brand and saying "I'm" instead of "You're," through autosuggestion consumers are giving themselves a command to "love" McDonald's.

Another way in which brands use emotive words to influence our buying is by focusing on emotions associated with our basic needs. We all have needs to feel safe, to feel secure, to feel a close connection with others, and to feel that we belong. So if a brand is marketed as helping you to get one of these needs met, then that increases the chances of people feeling more drawn to that brand. In Britain, the AA (Automobile Association) has used the slogan "To our members we're the fourth emergency service," which triggers emotions associated with our need to feel safe and secure. Cadbury's Milk Tray had the slogan "And all because the lady loves Milk Tray," playing on the emotional need to feel a close connection and bond with a significant other person, and encouraging our decision making when trying to choose a small yet romantic gift that "the lady" will love.

Many brands use vague language so that what they are presenting could apply to almost anyone. This linguistic trick, known as the Forer or Barnum effect, is widely used by psychics to tell people something that sounds specific and very personal, while actually applying to a large number of them. The psychic might, for example, say something like: "You want to appear confident and happy to others and put on a smile, yet deep down you know you have times when you doubt yourself and times when you feel low and would rather be anywhere else than there." Their clients will relate to this experience, thinking that it sounds insightful and accurate. In terms of brands, neither the Co-op's "You can always get it at the Co-op" nor ASDA's "Saving you money every day" states anything specific, but they both convey a sense of action and certainty.

Some brands use *implications* in their language as a way of exerting a subtle influence on people. Implications generate action without arousing resistance, because consumers often fail to realize that they are being manipulated. For instance, Alka-Seltzer's message "Plop, plop, fizz, fizz, oh what a relief it is" was a subtle way of playing on consumers' emotions. Everybody wants to feel well and find relief from discomfort. What many failed to notice was that the slogan also gave an implicit command about how to use the product, by "telling" the customer that they needed to take two tablets—"plop, plop, fizz, fizz"—not only one. By encouraging greater use of its tablets, Alka-Seltzer, of course, also greatly increased its sales.

In the previous chapter I described the "feel—felt—found" device that Apple sales agents are taught to use in order to overcome customer objections. Another widely used technique, which can be employed with both the written and the spoken word, is a way of transforming products into benefits. This follows the simple formula "x has y, which means z."

For instance, a shopkeeper trying to sell you a camera might say: "This has an f1.4 lens and a top shutter speed of 1/10,000th of a second." However, these product details will only appeal to System R thinking, as I described in Chapter 5. The shopper will have to expend mental energy in order to understand what relevance, if any, such information has for them.

By transforming those features into benefits, the appeal is made directly to the emotionally driven System I. For example, the salesperson might say to a young mother interested in buying a camera: "Imagine you are taking a picture of your child's birthday party and want to capture the atmosphere perfectly. Well, the wide-aperture, f1.4 lens will enable you to snap great shots without having to use flash."

A father might be told: "Imagine your son playing football in his school's top team. A big match is taking place and you want to make sure you capture all the action. By using this camera with its top shutter speed of 1/10,000th of a second, you can get pin-sharp memories of even the fastest shot at goal. By adding this telephoto lens you will be able to be almost part of that action."

We are narrative people who love to be told a story. By transporting the customer from the store to the birthday party and sports field, the salesperson not only engages their automatic thought processes, but also engineers positive emotions.

To test the emotional power of benefits, I wired up subjects to measure activity in both brain and body while they read different versions of a sales pitch. On every occasion, those listing benefits rather than providing product details produced a more positive response and a greater readiness to make a purchase.

The importance of appropriate emotions

As I mentioned earlier, the emotions that brands seek to engineer need to be both powerful and appropriate. By this I mean that the feelings generated must be congruent with the product and with the specific emotional needs of the consumer at that moment in their life. In the drama of our existence, each of us, as Shakespeare put it, "plays many parts." Some of these we create for ourselves; most are imposed on us by others: by our parents, teachers, partners, family, employers, social, political and religious leaders, and, more generally but no less powerfully, by our culture. We feel that an emotion is appropriate when it matches the ways in which we believe each of our different roles should be played.

For most of history, a majority of women have been raised and socialized to play a role akin to those of the Stepford Wives. In this 1970s science fiction classic, all the men in the fictional town of

Stepford, Connecticut, were married to submissive, fawning, mindless, docile, and impossibly beautiful women—women who had, in fact, been brainwashed into that subservient role by the men. However absurd this may seem today, for extensive periods of recent history this was precisely the role many women believed themselves destined to perform. And it was one on which some advertisers were only too eager to capitalize.

In 1921, the Washburn Crosby flour-milling company of Minneapolis created the perfect housewife, home maker, and mother in the form of Betty Crocker. Betty was the woman who never was, an advertising fiction created in response to letters from customers asking for information about baking. Rather than answer these impersonally, the company decided to invent a woman to reply on their behalf.

The name Betty was chosen because it sounded cheery, wholesome, and folksy; the surname was a tribute to Washburn Crosby's director William Crocker. Her portrait was a composite of the faces of all the women in the company's Home Service Department. From the first, Betty's mission was to engineer two powerful emotions in her readers and listeners: pride and guilt. The pride was in her accomplishments as a home maker, aided by purchases of the company's Gold Medal–brand flour that would produce feelings of happiness, contentment, and fulfillment; the guilt that if she did not turn herself into the perfect baking machine, she might lead her family down the road to ruin. In one of Betty's radio shows she warned the women of America: "If you load a man's stomach with boiled cabbage and greasy fried potatoes, can you wonder that he wants to start a fight, or go out and commit a crime?"[37]

Betty's weekly cookery program, which when it started in 1924 was the first ever such show in the US, soon had a huge audience of intensely loyal listeners. Between lessons on baking, which naturally featured Washburn Crosby's products prominently, Betty emphasized the importance of women being good housewives, a role that, she assured them, "satisfied aspirations as great as women could have in any occupation." For her millions of fans, Betty Crocker was no advertising fiction but a real person to be admired, respected, trusted, and emulated, all of which could be done through the simple expedient of buying the brand of flour she recommended.

The range of emotions that can be manipulated in this way is extensive. We have already considered some of the most widely used: anxiety, guilt, and our need for security. Here I want to turn the spotlight on the one emotion that has proved massively successful in differentiating brands: pride.

Engineering pride

Of all the emotions that brand managers seek to engineer, pride literally takes pride of place. And it's all down to our biology. Geoffrey Miller, professor of evolutionary psychology at the University of Mexico, explains:

> *Humans evolved in small social groups in which image and status were all–important, not only for survival, but for attracting mates, impressing friends, and rearing children. Today we ornament ourselves with goods and services more to make an impression on other people's minds than to enjoy owning a chunk of matter—a fact that renders "materialism" a profoundly misleading term for much of consumption.*[38]

The power of the brand to evoke feelings of pride, status, and superiority is revealed by what happens in the brain of fashion-savvy shoppers, such as those bargain hunters on 6th Avenue in New York that I described in Chapter 1, when confronted by fake designer-label products, or even those that, while genuine, they have been incorrectly told are counterfeit. Even when the quality, look, and feel of a fashion item without a famous brand name attached to it are identical to the genuine article, if they believe it to be fake the brain- and body-monitoring equipment shows not even a slight frisson of excitement. There is no speeding up of electrical patterns in the brain; no increase in heart rate; no rise in excitement-related skin conductance. Equally, if fashion shoppers are shown an excellent copy of a designer-label item, such as a fake Louis Vuitton bag or a replica of a Patek Philippe watch, the same mental and physical buzz occurs as if they had been handed the real thing—but only so long as they remain ignorant of the fact that it is merely a copy. As soon as the truth is told, their excitement vanishes.

The techniques of emotional engineering discussed so far have all operated in the open. Although there are sometimes embedded commands within the text or subtle alternative meanings conveyed by an image, no attempts are made at concealment. All of the techniques are easily spotted, as long as you know what to look for. The same cannot be said about the forms of engineering described in the next chapter, in which we enter the disturbing and highly controversial world of subliminal priming and persuasion.

8

The Power of Subliminal Priming
and Persuasion

We have lots of choices. Or do we? What and how much we
consume stems more from unconscious choices than from
mindful deliberation. Advertising capitalises on this automa-
ticity to exploit the insatiable need for fulfilment that burdens
many modern humans in industrialised countries.
　—*Erika Rosenberg, "Mindfulness and Consumerism"*[1]

Over a six-week period in the summer of 1957, some 50,000 people
supposedly became the unknowing victims of a remarkable experiment in mind control. When the news broke, the American public
was outraged, a short-lived, multimillion-dollar business was created, and a perfect storm of media hysteria was provoked. Yet the
experiment that created the controversy never in fact happened.

Five years later, James McDonald Vicary, the man who had perpe-
trated the deception, confessed that it had all been a publicity stunt
intended to drum up business for his struggling market research
firm. As a result of his actions, "subliminal advertising," the revolutionary new technique that he claimed to have invented, disappeared
into the dustbin of history, where it stayed for the next 40 years. Even
today there are some psychologists, and even more advertising professionals, who continue to reject the idea that subliminal advertising exists. One advertising executive has described this presentation
of stimuli below the conscious awareness as an urban myth.[2]

In his 1981 book *The Trouble with Advertising*, John O'Toole,
Chairman of one of the world's largest advertising agencies, Foote,

Cone & Belding Communications, stated unequivocally that there was no such thing as subliminal advertising. He insisted:

> *I have never seen an example of it, nor have I ever heard it seriously discussed as a technique by advertising people... it is demeaning to assume that the human mind is so easily controlled that any-one can be made to act against his will or better judgement by peremptory commands he doesn't realise are present.*[3]

Recent brain research has demonstrated, however, that the critics were wrong. While some studies have failed to find any statistically significant effect, could not be replicated, or had methodological flaws, others have clearly shown that subliminal advertising is indeed able to exert a profound effect on consumer preferences, not in the crude way suggested by James Vicary, but through a far more subtle and effective influence known as *priming*.

In this chapter, I will recount the strange background to subliminal advertising, explain where early users went wrong, and describe how it is currently being widely used to influence our buying decisions.

Vicary's "experiment"

During the summer of 1957, a movie theater in Fort Lee, New Jersey was showing *Picnic*. The film, a romance starring William Holden and Kim Novak, was billed as a love story between two people "Electrically attracted to each other... Overwhelmingly engulfed by it... Guiltily in love!" With six Academy Award nominations, *Picnic* proved a box office hit. But what the audiences who packed the theater's 2,500-seat auditorium did not know was that James Vicary, a 42-year-old market researcher, proposed using them as unwitting lab rats. Vicary, founder of the Subliminal Projection Co., had—or so he subsequently claimed—installed a device of his own invention in the projection booth. This, he later told journalists, was able to project advertising messages onto the screen so rapidly that they were invisible to the naked eye. Despite not being consciously perceived, he claimed, they still influenced audiences by affecting their subconscious.

He explained that as the film was being shown he had projected "THIRSTY? DRINK COCA-COLA" and "HUNGRY? EAT POPCORN" at five-second intervals throughout the movie, but because they were flashed up for only three milliseconds the audience was never consciously aware of them.

Vicary called a press conference in New York to unveil his new invention. A writer from *New Yorker* magazine described how "some fifty journalists turned up and all sat obediently and receptively, if a bit sadly, in our little mortuary chairs, allowing our brains to be softly broken and entered."[4]

Vicary began by enthusiastically describing his new "subliminal projection" technology, which, he claimed, was set to "revolutionize advertising by promoting products directly to the needs and desires of the unconscious mind."[5] His purpose, he insisted, was a benign one: He wanted to spare people the need to watch endless advertisements on television, read them in newspapers and magazines, or listen to them on the radio. Instead, commercial messages could, in the words of one journalist, be "beamed" directly into their brains without them ever knowing it. He then outlined the results of his Fort Lee cinema experiment, claiming that it had led to an increase in Coca-Cola sales of 18.1 percent and in popcorn sales of a whopping 58 percent. He offered no explanation for the differences in these two percentages and gave no further details about the conditions under which he had conducted the tests. He also declined to provide any information about his invention, since patents were still being applied for and so details must remain secret.

The lights were then dimmed and journalists watched a short color film, *Secrets of the Reef*, containing subliminal images of the Coca-Cola trademark. Despite the logo being flashed up 169 times over the colorful shoals of fish, it was consciously seen only three times, when he deliberately slowed down the film and allowed it to become visible. Vicary ended his press conference by asking for questions. These, he later admitted, revealed "hostility, resistance and unease." It was a foretaste of the outrage soon to come.

When asked whether manipulating people without their knowledge or agreement was ethical, he replied that the reason he had called the press conference was to raise public awareness of the power of subliminal advertising and to enable the implications of the techniques to be discussed openly and rationally. He disputed the use of the word "manipulation," which, he protested, was pejorative and inaccurate. Subliminal advertising, Vicary insisted, "reminded" people to buy, it did not *oblige* them to do so. Members of the cinema audience who had bought Coca-Cola or popcorn had only done so because those briefly flashed-up messages had reminded them that they were hungry or thirsty. There had, he emphasized, been no effect on those who were neither.

Following up on the massive publicity generated by his press conference, Vicary rapidly began offering his services as a "motivational research consultant," while continuing to perfect subliminal advertising. "This innocent little technique," he assured advertising agency bosses and the CEOs of major manufacturers, "is going to sell a hell of a lot of goods."

Perhaps through a fear of missing out on the next big thing in advertising, Vicary's approaches were greeted with contracts and retainers that are reported to have amounted to $4.5 million, or around $22.5 million at today's value. How much, if anything, of these vast sums was even paid out is open to question, with many commentators describing such claims as further evidence of Vicary's ability to spin a story.

The man who fell to earth

Who was James Vicary? What was his background and how did he attain such a lasting and controversial reputation?

He was born in Detroit, Michigan, on April 30, 1915. The death of his father when James was 6 years old, which Vicary would later describe as the "most devastating event of his life," left the family in serious financial difficulties.

At the age of 15 James began working as a copy boy for the Detroit Free Press Forum, a local Gallup Poll group. Six years later he was studying sociology at the University of Michigan, where he organized the university's Bureau of Student Opinion. After the Second World War he set up the James M. Vicary Company, which specialized in the analysis of brand and product names. Among his prominent clients were TIME Magazine, the Ford Motor Company, General Mills, and Colgate-Palmolive.

Vicary wrote widely on public opinion research and different forms of testing and his trenchant, often controversial views soon attracted media attention. On one occasion, for example, he suggested that women baked cakes as a "surrogate for childbirth"; on another, he theorized that when shopping in supermarkets women entered a state of "hypnoidal trance."[6]

In *The Hidden Persuaders*, Vance Packard described Vicary as "perhaps the most genial and ingratiating of all the major figures operating independent depth-probing firms." He was a man whose work "exemplified the power advertisers sought over consumers by probing and exploiting unconscious psychological rationales in order to stimulate consumption."

By the time Vicary called the press conference to announce the results of his subliminal advertising experiment, therefore, he had attained both renown as a researcher and infamy as a manipulator of men's minds. Within weeks of that somewhat hostile press conference, however, he was to suffer a spectacular fall to earth.

The backlash

One journalist described subliminal advertising as "the most alarming and outrageous discovery since Mr. Gatling invented his gun,"[7] while *Newsday* proclaimed it "the most alarming invention since the atomic bomb." The *Los Angeles Times* denounced him for being "as evil as a Nazi war criminal" and said that he ought to be shot. *Saturday Review* editor Norman Cousins began a leading article, entitled "Smudging the Subconscious," with the words "Welcome to 1984." He went on to warn: "If the device is successful for putting over popcorn, why not politicians or anything else? If it is possible to prompt the subconscious into making certain judgements of human character, why wouldn't it be possible to use invisible messages for the purpose of annihilating a reputation or promoting it?" Cousins concluded his polemic by urging the authorities "to take this invention and everything connected to it and attach it to the center of the next nuclear explosive scheduled for testing."[8]

So if Vicary had hoped to be seen as a hero for, as he put it, "sparing Americans the annoyance of being bombarded by countless advertisements," he was swiftly and brutally disillusioned. To understand why subliminal advertising generated so much ill-informed hysteria, one has to consider the political mood of the nation. The Korean War, which had ended four years earlier, had led to thousands of American soldiers being held captive by North Korea. Some were persuaded by the enemy to broadcast statements denouncing the US as a war-monger and extolling the virtues of Communism. Medical and military experts attributed this to systematic psychological manipulation on the part of the captors. Terms like "mind control" and "thought reform" entered the language and the popular imagination.

In this frenetic atmosphere, Vicary's research rapidly came to be perceived, by press and public alike, as a form of brainwashing, a potential weapon of tyranny and subversion, a technology capable of transforming American society into the dystopian nightmare prophesied by Aldous Huxley in his 1931 science fiction novel *Brave New World*.

A year later, in a book entitled *Brave New World Revisited*,[9] Huxley described "subliminal projection machines" that would disperse propaganda and advertising messages. He suggested that such subliminal techniques could all too easily become a "powerful instrument for the manipulation of unsuspecting minds." He claimed:

The scientific dictator of tomorrow will set up his whispering machines and subliminal projectors in schools and hospitals... and in all public places where audiences can be given a preliminary softening up by suggestibility increasing oratory or rituals.

In less than 12 months, subliminal persuasion had, in the public's mind, been transformed from an advertising technique to a technology capable of undermining democracies, controlling and manipulating individual minds, and destroying freedoms while preserving an illusion of freedom. A few weeks later, all three of the major US networks, CBS, NBC, and ABC, announced a ban on all forms of subliminal advertising in their television and radio programs.

In June 1958, Vicary abruptly disappeared from New York. He left behind no bank account and no indication as to where he had gone. Five years later, he resurfaced to give an interview to *Advertising Age*, in which he confessed that the whole affair had been a fabrication whose purpose was to try to save his near-bankrupt marketing business. He remarked sadly:

All I accomplished, I guess... was to put a new word into common usage, and for a man who makes a career out of picking the right names for products and companies, I should have my head examined for using a word like subliminal. [10]

The following month, the British Institute of Practitioners in Advertising ordered members not to use subliminal messages in any form of advertising or self-promotion. The Subliminal Projection Co. went out of business and advertising executives, perhaps ashamed of having been taken in by such an obvious hoax, queued up to deny that they would ever have used it.

Subliminal messages were nothing new

Although Vicary may have honestly believed that he was breaking new ground, the idea that people can be influenced through stimuli, visual or auditory, below ("sub") their threshold ("limen") of conscious awareness, dates back to ancient Greece. In the fifth century

BCE, Greek philosopher Democritus wrote that "much is perceptible which is not perceived by us" to describe the idea that we can be affected by sights and sounds of which we remain unconscious.[11]

The most direct early forerunner of Vicary was research undertaken by Austrian neurologist Otto Poetzl in 1917. He showed his subjects pictures of landscapes for one hundredth of a second and asked them what they had seen. Not surprisingly given the very short exposure time, the answer was not very much. He then asked them to return the next morning and describe their dreams. He found that some of these contained fragments of the pictures that had been briefly seen the day before. In other words, the subliminal information had been unconsciously registered by the brain and incorporated into their dreams.

During the 1930s, James G. Miller, a Harvard psychiatrist, demonstrated that very faint images can be perceived on a subliminal level. In what he claimed to be a study of extra-sensory perception (ESP), Miller asked his subjects to sit facing what appeared to be a large mirror. They were told to stare intently into the mirror while he went into another room and attempted to project images of cards to them by telepathy. From time to time he would use a telephone to ask what card he was mentally "sending" them. He was, in fact, projecting very faint images of the cards on the back of the mirror, and the real purpose of his experiment was to see whether these would be perceived subliminally.

The results supported his hypothesis. With the projector switched on, Miller's subjects guessed the card correctly far more often than they could have done by chance alone. When the projector was turned off, however, their performance dropped to chance levels. All of the subjects attributed their responses to ESP or intuition, with not one saying that they had consciously perceived the projected images.

In a second phase of the experiment, Miller gradually increased the illumination of the images so that they would be readily apparent to any new person entering the room. In spite of this, many of the subjects continued to believe that the cards were products of their imagination, and expressed surprise and shock when the existence of the projector was made known to them. Clearly, something is going on in people's brains when they are exposed to subliminal stimuli, although it was to be many years before brain imaging technology arrived to help explain what that something may be or what it implies.

What subliminal advertising is and is not

So what exactly is subliminal advertising and what evidence is there that it actually changes opinions, influences attitudes, and increases sales?

Technically, a stimulus is perceived subliminally only if people are consciously unaware of having seen or heard it. Only briefly presented words and images that are not intended to be consciously perceived and are not consciously recognized may be described as subliminal. The distinction is important, since the term is frequently, and inaccurately, applied to other advertising techniques.

There are four ways of presenting information in such a way that it either always or usually bypasses the conscious brain and communicates its message directly to the subconscious:

- Subliminal messages, which are delivered too rapidly ever to be consciously seen or heard.
- Supraliminal messages, which can be, and sometimes are, seen or heard.
- Embeds, a form of supraliminal message, often of an emotionally arousing or disturbing form, buried inside another image or sound.
- Messages hidden in clear sight but not usually spotted due to a psychological effect known as inattentional blindness.

Subliminal messages
In a study conducted in my own laboratory, participants were shown pictures of people performing everyday activities. These were

preceded by a subliminal image, which was shown for just 10 milliseconds, depicting either a positive or a negative event, for example a cuddly puppy or a blood-stained corpse. Our subjects were then asked to evaluate the personalities of the people in the pictures. Did they, for example, look friendly or standoffish, welcoming or unwelcoming, outgoing or introverted, sociable or unsociable, and so on?

We found that the pictures seen following the subliminally projected positive image were evaluated far more positively than those following the negative image. In addition, our subjects were wired up to record activity in their brain and body, as described in previous chapters. These sensors indicated greater mental and physical arousal in response to the negative than the positive image.

Physical prowess can also be subliminally influenced, as a study by Henk Aarts and his colleagues at Utrecht University clearly demonstrated. In this research, 42 undergraduates of Utrecht University were briefly exposed to three groups of five words. One group described aspects of physical exertion (e.g., effort, vigorous), the second were positive adjectives (e.g., good, pleasant), and the third were neutral adverbs (e.g., furthermore, around). The students were then informed that they were taking part in a study designed to test the suitability of a new research instrument, a device that measured handgrip force. They were instructed to squeeze the handgrip with their dominant hand as soon as the word "squeeze" appeared on the computer screen and to stop the instant the word disappeared.

The researchers found that those who had been primed with both exertion-related and positive words had faster reaction times, squeezed the handgrip more quickly when the command appeared, and produced greater force. Aarts commented:

These results confirm that subliminally priming exertion prepares people to display forceful action, but when these subliminal primes are accompanied with a positive stimulus it motivates people to spend extra effort.[12]

What works with images and words also works when using symbols. Robert Zajonc, from Stanford University, reports on an experiment in which participants were shown 10 polygons for just 1 millisecond each. Afterwards, they were presented with a pair of polygons consisting of one already seen and one not previously viewed. They were then asked to say which of the two they thought they might have seen before and which they liked best. Researchers found that the previously seen shape was preferred, even though none of the participants knew which they had seen earlier.[13]

As I will explain in a moment, while evaluating personality, increasing physical strength, and looking at polygons may seem to have little to say about shopping behavior, subliminal studies like these reveal a great deal about the subconscious influences on our purchases. However, let's first consider the other three forms of influence without conscious awareness: supraliminal messages, embeds, and triggers hidden in plain sight.

Supraliminal messages

During the 2000 US presidential campaign, George W. Bush ran a $2.5 million advertisement condemning Al Gore's prescription drug plan, which was derided as "excessively bureaucratic." The ad ended with the phrase "bureaucrats decide" appearing, breaking into fragments, and dancing around the screen. Many Democrats reported that during this sequence, the word "RATS" appeared in large letters for one thirtieth of a second. Alex Castellanos, a veteran advertising strategist who was responsible for the commercial, dismissed accusations of an attempt to subliminally influence voters. He claimed that the use of the word was "purely accidental" and insisted: "We don't play ball that way. I'm not that clever."

Whether or not it was deliberate, this is *not* an example of subliminal advertising. Although often incorrectly described as subliminal, the use of a "single-frame cut," which involves inserting just one frame or a video image into a sequence of images, is more accurately termed *supraliminal*. Such insertions can be seen and, as in the case of the RATS controversy, frequently are. The outcry that typically follows would seem to make their use counter-productive; indeed, they are banned in many countries.

Embedded messages

Take a look at the picture below and study it carefully before reading on.

Figure 8.1

From The Secret Sales Pitch, *by permission of August Bullock*

What do you see? Provided that the picture is new to you and that you respond like most people, you will see an illustration of four somewhat strange-looking flowers.

If that's what it currently looks like to you, then cherish that image! I am now going to reveal something that will change the way you see those flowers for ever. Embedded in this image is the word SEX. If you still can't see it, look more closely at the space between the first and second flower from the left, where the letter *S* will appear. The *E* is located between flowers two and three, and the *X* between flowers three and four.

In 1969, while presenting a course on media studies, psychologist Wilson Bryan Key, a former journalist, market researcher, and military photo analyst, noticed something odd about an illustration accompanying an article in *Esquire* magazine. In an interview with Dominic Streatfeild, he explained what he had noticed and to what this discovery led:

> *I was lecturing... on one of the beatnik poets of the day. And I looked at the picture, I think it was of him, a painting of him, upside down. And there on the bookshelf behind him was an erect penis as a bookend. I walked around the table: "Jesus Christ! That shouldn't be there!" Then I started poking around and within three months I had a two foot pile of the stuff in my office... I knew that they were putting something into this printing. And then I discovered the S E X business.* [14]

Over the next few years, Key "revealed" words describing sexual activity embedded in advertising images ranging from ice cubes in a glass of gin to the folds of Boy Scout uniforms. He highlighted what he claimed were phallic and other emotionally charged images, such as skulls and devils, not only in advertising photographs, paintings, drawings, and designs, but also in movies and film posters. Their purpose, he confidently asserted, was to make people buy things that they do not want or need.

When in 1974 he published *Subliminal Seduction*, the first of four books he wrote on the subject, Key found a ready audience for his conspiracy theories. Within a few months nearly 9 million copies had been sold, elevating him to celebrity status, although, as Vicary had found almost 20 years earlier, much of the attention he attracted was hostile. Key recalled in 2005:

> *Oh, yeah. I was threatened! Phone calls at 3 in the morning and a voice says "We know where you live, we know what your*

child looks like. We're gonna get you and you'll never know where it's coming from!" It's a little unsettling. So finally I... left town.[15]

Evidence in support of Key's assertions can be found in a 1984 study by William E. Kilbourne, Scott Painton, and D. Ridley.[16] After reading *Subliminal Seduction*, they located two advertisements in national magazines that they suspected contained sexual subliminal embeds. One, for Marlboro Lights, appeared to them to depict two cowboys riding through rocky terrain with the image of a penis concealed among the boulders. The second, for Chivas Regal, seemed to show the back of a nude woman embedded below the neck of the whisky bottle.

A retouch artist was instructed to airbrush out these apparent embeds. The researchers then displayed the original advertisement, with the embeds, for half a minute to one group of subjects. A second group saw the airbrushed versions. In both cases, arousal was measured by means of sensors attached to the fingers. The researchers reported that those who were shown the original advertisements produced an arousal as much as 20 percent higher than for the cleaned-up version.

It should be noted that other similar studies have failed to find any results, while some that did have been severely criticized on methodological grounds. As a result, the question of whether supraliminal embedded images and words, sexual or not, can affect purchasing decisions remains unresolved.

Hidden in plain sight

Choose any one of the six cards shown in Figure 8.2. Study it carefully, and note the suit, the face value, and its position in the sequence.

Figure 8.2 The playing card test – first sequence

Now turn to page 272 and study the sequence again. You may be amazed to discover that I was able to read your mind and know precisely which of the six cards you would select, and then remove it from the line-up.

In fact, of course, I did nothing of the sort. I am a neuro-psychologist, not a mind reader. Your chosen card is missing because *all of* the cards have been changed. By asking you to focus intently on just one of them, I hoped that you would pay little or no attention to the others. Maybe it worked—it does nine times out of ten when presented in my lectures—or perhaps you weren't taken in for a moment.

What this does illustrate is the fact that we tend to be consciously aware only of what we attend to. In a famous demonstration of what we might call the "failing to see the trees for the wood" effect, Daniel Simons and Christopher Chabris of Harvard University videotaped two teams of three players, one team wearing white tops and the other black, passing an orange ball to one another.[17] People watching the video were asked to count the number of passes made by either the black- or the white-shirted team. While the play is progressing, a girl dressed in a gorilla costume stalks across the screen, pauses for a few seconds in the center of the group, beats her chest, and strides off. Amazingly, almost half (46 percent) of those watching the video failed to notice the gorilla at all. When I have shown this video during my own presentations, a similar proportion of the audience also miss seeing the beast. They are so intently focused on counting the passes that its presence is never recognized.

The original researchers found that people tracking passes between the black-topped players were more likely to notice the gorilla than those attending to the white-shirted team. This was because the gorilla was perceptually similar to the players they were actively tracking and, as a result, became more "visible." What is noteworthy about missing one thing by focusing on another is that once the item hidden in plain sight—or the embed, for that matter—is pointed out, it becomes impossible not to see it. You will always now spot the gorilla, see through the playing-card trick, and notice the word SEX in the illustration in Figure 8.1.

However, can things that were present yet unseen due to inattentional blindness affect our behavior? The evidence strongly suggests that they can. Travis Carter and his colleagues at the University of Chicago decided to see whether a brief exposure to the American flag would have any effect on voting attitudes and intentions, even if no attention was drawn to that potent national symbol. In 2008, before the presidential election, they conducted an online survey about political orientation, feelings of patriotism and nationalism, exposure to news stories, and attitudes toward specific issues. Participants were also asked to rate their warmth toward the presidential candidates (Barack Obama and John McCain) and the vice-presidential candidates (Joseph Biden and Sarah Palin).

The survey came in two versions, with a single small difference between them. On one there was a very tiny American flag (72 × 45 pixels) located in the top left corner of the form. When the US flag was included in the design, voters were more likely to favor the Republicans than those whose form did not display the Stars and Stripes. As the researchers reported:

> A single exposure to an unobtrusive American flag shifted participants' voting intentions, voting behavior, attitudes, and beliefs toward the Republican end of the branch of the government.[18]

A year after Obama's election and with the Democrats still holding power in both houses of Congress, a further variant of this study was conducted. On this occasion, participants visiting the laboratory were shown photographs of buildings and asked to estimate the time of day when they were taken. Two of the photos showed the American flag, hanging from a flag pole or on the front of the building. In the other two the flags had been digitally removed. Participants' attention was not drawn to the flags in any way. Next, they completed a shortened form of the survey used in the previous experiment. Once again, the unattended image produced a swing to the political right. And when these researchers retested the participants almost a year later, the influence of the flag remained unchanged. As they note:

This finding suggests that the American flag introduced a shift toward the Republican worldview, even during a Democratic administration. Again, the effect was not moderated by political ideology or any other measured variable, which suggests that the flag produced the same conservative shift for both liberal and conservative participants.

Brand preferences and unconscious priming

Imagine you have volunteered to take part in what you are told is a study to measure how accurately you are able to detect minor changes in a string of letters. Seated in a small cubicle, you watch intently as a string of capital letters appears, briefly, on the computer screen before you. Every now and then there is a lower-case letter, for example a *b* among a string of *BBBBBB*s. Your task is to report the number of occasions on which lower-case letters appear.

That test completed, you are asked to suck a salty sweet called a *dropje*, common in the Netherlands, which has a letter embossed on one side. The researcher asks you to try to identify this letter using only your tongue; in fact, the real purpose is to make you feel thirstier due to the salt. Another group of participants are not given the sweet and are simply asked to say how thirsty they feel.

Finally, you are asked to say whether you would sooner quench your thirst with Lipton Ice or Spa Rood (a local brand of mineral water). You choose the Lipton Ice. Although this choice seems to have been made from your own free will, it slightly puzzles you. Normally you prefer mineral water when thirsty, but for some reason today the tea strikes you as preferable.

What you did not know was that what appeared to have been a free choice was actually the product of subliminal manipulation. While you were studying those strings of letters, the word Lipton Ice (or a neutral control word) was flashed onto the screen for 23 milliseconds. As a result, you were subconsciously persuaded to ask for tea rather than water. This study, by Johan C. Karremans and his colleagues at the Department of Social Psychology at Radboud University, Nijmegen,[19] is an example of what is termed priming, a way of conditioning the consumer's brain to favor one brand over another that is both effective, powerful, and very widely employed.

At first glance this may seem to vindicate Vicary's claims all those years ago. Nevertheless, two points need to be borne in mind. First, Lipton Ice, the product that was subliminally primed, is a refreshing beverage, so it makes sense for someone to choose it as a thirst quencher. Second, and even more important, the priming only influenced those who were already thirsty. Among participants with little or no thirst, the priming had little or no effect.

Measuring what can never be consciously known

The development of brain scanning and EEG has enabled direct studies of how priming affects the way we think. In 2007, researchers at University College, London reported the first physiological evidence that invisible subliminal images can indeed affect mental processes below the level of conscious awareness.[20] A team from the Institute of Cognitive Neuroscience, led by Bahador Bahrami, discovered that the brain is able to register such briefly flashed images, even when the individuals themselves are adamant that they have not seen anything. Using fMRI, the researchers investigated the impact of subliminal images on the primary visual cortex, located in the occipital lobe at the back of the brain. Lying in the scanner, subjects were asked to perform one of two tasks while pictures of everyday objects, such as pliers and an iron, were presented in a way that prevented them entering conscious awareness.

In one task, participants were asked to spot the letter *T* in a stream of other letters; in the other, to pick out a white letter *N* or a blue letter *Z* from the same stream. During the first task, the brain scans showed that the primary visual cortex had indeed detected the subliminal images. In the second challenge, however, no such neural activity was observed. Because this task demanded greater concentration, the brain blocked out the subliminal images.

While my own laboratory has been exploring the effects of subliminal advertising on shoppers' behavior using the type of technologies described elsewhere, we have also been at the forefront of developing new ways of using a very different technique. This approach, Implicit Association Testing, does not depend on measuring electrical changes in the brain or physical arousal, but focuses instead on a less complicated effect of priming: its influence over reaction time.

Exploring the consumer's subconscious mind over the internet

In the mid-nineteenth century, Franciscus Donders made a discovery that greatly assisted the study and understanding of cognitive processes. In a fairly basic experiment, he measured the different reaction times of left- or right-handed responses to stimuli presented on the participants' left or right side. He found that people took fractionally longer to respond to a stimulus if it appeared on the opposite side of their body to the hand with which they were required to respond. In other words, they took slightly longer to respond to a signal from the left with their right hand than to one from their left, and similarly with a right-sided signal to which they had to respond with their left hand.

With this discovery, Donders sowed the seed for one of the most robust measures used in neuromarketing today, the Implicit Association Test (IAT). This can be employed quickly and easily to explore unconscious thought processes, what I have termed in this book System I thinking. Whether we are aware of responding or not—and whether it is contrary to our beliefs or not—this implicit system is always in play.

On page 94, I gave a simple example of automatic thinking, the four questions that lead most people to the answer "yolk." Capturing such responses is precisely what IAT is all about. Phil Barden, Managing Director of Decode Marketing UK, explains:

> *You're testing for automaticity of association and because it's under time pressure, people don't have the chance for the—as we call it—"pilot system" in the brain, to kick in and post-rationalize. So it's [about] capturing that pure, intuitive response.*[21]

For example, if I asked people whether they were racially prejudiced, most would immediately deny that they were. While some could be speaking the truth, others will be knowingly lying in order to conceal a socially unacceptable opinion. For a surprisingly large number, however, that denial will be inaccurate, but on a level of which they are not consciously aware. This was the finding of Harvard University's Project Implicit, which since 1998 has been gathering data via a publicly accessible, internet-based IAT (go to https://implicit.harvard.edu/implicit). In one of these tests they measure the speed with which people categorize simple pairings such as "White" + "Gun" and "Black" + "Gun," or "White" + "Wealth" and "Black" + "Wealth."

The stronger the unconscious association, the more rapidly that person will react when asked to pair two items together; the weaker the association, the slower the reaction time. The results of this test led the researchers to conclude that, sadly, a majority of those responding via the internet held unconscious racial biases.

Nevertheless, it is very important to make a distinction here between prejudice associations and prejudice behavior. A prejudice association could be as innocuous as feeling more threatened by a group of young males as compared to a group of young females. While this may not always be a rational response, it is one often founded in some level of emotional sense.

IAT has been used to explore a wide range of concepts, including gender stereotyping,[22] self-concept,[23] and self-esteem,[24] the use of contraception,[25] and female authority,[26] as well as a multitude of brand and product associations among consumers. It is also widely employed to measure how effectively an advertisement changes a person's implicit beliefs in a product or service.

In an IAT study conducted by Mindlab, the effectiveness of advertising for the Samsung Galaxy smartphone was compared with that for the Apple iPhone. Participants were asked to sort each phone into pairs of categories such as "Innovative/Conventional," "Smart/Stupid," "Efficient/Inefficient," and the speed with which they made these associations was measured.

They were then shown different advertisements, some for the Galaxy smartphone and others for unrelated products. After watching these, they completed a second comparison task. The results clearly demonstrated that the Galaxy advertising weakened the association between Apple and innovation, while the association between Samsung and innovation remained the same. This turned out to be highly relevant, as it predated the controversy and ensuing legal battle between Apple and Samsung, in which Apple was ultimately knocked off the top spot in the smartphone market.

Because IAT can explore subconscious thought processes without the need to attach electrodes to the head or put people in brain scanners, it can be used just as easily over the internet as in the laboratory. My own company has developed a suite of tools for doing just that. By utilizing the power of the World Wide Web, we are able to recruit and evaluate people fitting almost any required demographic profile. The tests are conducted in the familiar surroundings of participants' own home or office, and produce results that are just as insightful and accurate as those obtained under more controlled conditions.

Brand priming in the world of shoppers

In the previous chapter I described the power of brands to influence shopping behavior. This chapter has explored the role of subliminal and supraliminal advertising in priming consumers to respond in a particular way. Brands are symbols of aspirations, representing desired self-qualities, such as sophistication or status. As a result, brand priming can activate goals linked with these desired outcomes and so elicit goal-directed behavior.

We can be primed, for example, to prefer Coke to Pepsi, or to select a "Happy Meal" in preference to a bowl of salad. Studies have shown that fast-food symbols such as the McDonald's Golden Arches prime diners to eat more quickly and become more impatient. The presence of a credit card symbol, discreetly located in the laboratory, primed subjects to spend more money. We are surrounded by priming cues that, through advertising and marketing, come to influence our attitudes, emotions, and behaviors as consumers.

As Johan C. Karremans from the University of Nijmegen points out, despite the fact that "Vicary's advertising techniques appear to have existed only in Vicary's fantasies... if certain conditions are taken into account, his fantasies may indeed become reality."[27]

For many this is the most deeply troubling aspect of our consumer society. When it comes to shopping, there could be no such thing as free choice or random behavior. However much we may like to believe that we are acting independently and spontaneously, we are really driven by unconscious brand priming. Although we are blissfully unaware of this, it ultimately determines our purchasing decisions and consumption choices. Nowhere are these cues to be found in greater abundance or more cleverly concealed than on television, the topic I investigate in the next chapter.

9

When Your Television
Watches You

Advertising... is both the creator and perpetuator of the dom-
inant attitudes, values, and ideology of the culture, as well as
the social norms and myths by which most people live... [it]
helps to create a climate in which certain attitudes and values
flourish and others are not reflected at all.
  —*Jean Kilbourne, "The more you subtract the more you add"*

As people watch television, in many homes their television will be
watching them back. These sets belong to viewers who are paid
to allow cameras to be installed either inside or beside their television, to record not only what but *how* they view: how often they
change channels, whether they continue watching or change channels when commercials are shown, what other activities they are
involved in when programs are on. These activities have been found
to include talking, yelling and gesticulating, snacking, eating, reading, leaving the room, cuddling, playing computer games, dancing,
struggling over the remote control, and having sex! All of these data
are analyzed to provide program makers and advertisers with an
in-depth understanding of viewers' responses to what was shown.

My own laboratory has conducted similar research that uses
cameras linked to cell phones, which transmit images back to us in
real time. This enables us to provide broadcasters with immediate
feedback about how well, or how badly, their new show or commercial is being received. In some studies we have also recorded brain
activity, heart rate, and skin conductance, physical movements,

eye-blinks, and postural changes during television programs, to gain an insight into subconscious responses to what is seen and heard. I will be describing some of the findings from our research later in this chapter.

With millions of pounds worth of production costs and advertising spend at stake, advertising agencies and their clients can no longer afford to take any chances. What they want is reliable, scientific proof that their campaign is working and their money being well spent—that their advertising has created the perfect sales pitch.

The power of the box in the corner

The 90-year-old brainchild of Scottish inventor John Logie Baird, television has transformed social habits, revolutionized retailing, and even changed the way we think. In the twenty-first century, television's ability to influence our lives, determine our purchasing choices, and dictate our patterns of consumption is partly a result of advances in neuroscience and brain imaging. Analysis of the ways in which viewers respond, second by second, to what they are seeing and hearing can be used to change small aspects of a commercial in order to enhance its persuasive power. These modifications are often extremely slight and subtle, possibly a change of a single color, an adjustment to voice tone, a few words added or subtracted from the text, a different type of background music.

My own interest in researching the power of television is both professional and personal. As an 18-year-old in the late 1920s, my mother, a dancer, performed on the world's first television programs, broadcast from studios at 2 Savoy Hill in London. She recalled the informality of early production, with Baird himself wandering around in carpet slippers and making mugs of tea for cast and crew. She also described the strangely colored makeup that performers were obliged to put on, to enhance contrast on the tiny screens of the day, and the difficulties of keeping one's balance performing pirouettes against a black-and-white-striped background while being "scanned" by a moving dot of light. This dot, produced by a rapidly rotating disc, generated the fairly crude images characteristic of television's early days.

The medium has grown to become a technology whose reach and influence are unparalleled. By means of commercials, it has the power to elevate some brands to superstar status while relegating others, which may be equal or superior to the chosen few, to virtual obscurity. No less importantly, it fundamentally shapes the social landscape, transforming attitudes, molding opinions, and manipulating choices. It provides the backdrop against which people live out their lives, so commonplace as to be almost invisible yet so powerful as to be virtually invincible. And I am not only referring to the ubiquitous box in the corner. Today's viewers want their entertainment and information any time and anywhere: on computers, tablets, and smartphones, time shifting to watch when convenient to them rather than the network. Since television influences our response to all of the persuasive techniques so far discussed in this book, we should start by examining just how it achieves its dominance as the ultimate hidden persuader.

Shaping viewers' worldview

In the US, 92 million homes (98 percent of households) own at least one television, with 80 percent owning two or more. A similar level of penetration is found throughout the developed and, increasingly, much of the developing world. The introduction of television into the largest cities in the People's Republic of China during the 1980s, for instance, has been hailed as the most important cultural event apart from the Cultural Revolution, and almost every urban Chinese family now has a set.[2]

A survey commissioned by Ericsson's ConsumerLab found that people now spend up to a third of their leisure time on this activity. In the US, where people watch for around seven hours each day, the average viewer will spend 20 years of their life in front of the box. In the UK, some 4.5 hours each day are spent watching, amounting to around 13 years of continuous viewing. Today alone, the human population will devote around 3.5 *billion* hours to watching television on an estimated 0.5 billion sets worldwide.

Small wonder, then, that television programs and advertisements now play a greater role and exert far more influence on the socializing of many children than their school, their religion, and even their parents. Jean Kilbourne, Visiting Research Scholar at Wellesley Centers for Women, Massachusetts comments:

> *Advertising is an increasingly ubiquitous force in our lives, and it sells much more than products. We delude ourselves when we say that we are not influenced by advertising, and we trivialize and ignore its growing significance at our peril.*[3]

It is only within the last 20 years, however, that the true power of television to change society has begun to be appreciated and researched. Because its output appeared so simple, some would say simple-minded, researching its influence was for a long while something many academics avoided. As Robert Allen from the Department of History at the University of North Carolina admits:

> *For many people (myself included) television has the same status in their lives as the food they eat for breakfast or the way their faces look in the morning; it is something so much a part of day to day existence, that it remains invisible as something analyzed or consciously considered.*[4]

In addition, recent technological advances, such as the introduction of television on smartphones and over the internet, have changed this pattern of use. A survey for Accenture revealed that the number of consumers watching broadcast or cable television in a typical week declined from 71 percent in 2009 to 48 percent in 2011. The survey, which questioned 1,000 consumers in Brazil, China, France, Germany, India, Japan, Russia, South Africa, Sweden, and the US, also reported that the number of consumers intending to purchase a television set over the next 12 months had fallen from 35 percent in 2010 to 32 percent in 2011. This does not mean, of course, that people have suddenly stopped watching television or videos and are returning to books or deserting to radio. Rather, it reflects the fact that consumers are watching in different places and on different devices, including smartphones, laptops, and tablets.

In the battle for eyeballs, cloud computing is also having a significant effect on viewer behavior. More than half of those canvassed in the Accenture survey reported switching to online services and the cloud. Nearly a third had stopped or almost stopped renting or buying DVDs, nearly four out of ten play games online, while almost three in ten stream online content. This melding of traditional television with online services and the decreasing distinction between computers and television form the topic of the next chapter.

The world as reality television

In the movie *Being There*, from the novella by Jerzy Kosinski, Peter Sellers plays Chance, an illiterate gardener who has spent his entire life behind the walls of an estate owned by an eccentric millionaire. His only knowledge of the real world is through television. After his benefactor dies, the estate's lawyers evict him from his home and he wanders aimlessly and helplessly through the streets of Washington, DC, where he regards everything as though it was happening on television. Confronted by an urban street gang, he threatens to "turn them off" with his television remote. Riding in a police car, he remarks that the world as seen through the windscreen is "just like TV only you can see much further!"

While a satire, this film reflects the way many heavy television viewers are increasingly starting to perceive the world. And their world, according to George Gerbner's *Cultivation Theory*, is heavily biased by the medium's formulaic and stylized narrative content. "Its drama, commercials, news and other programs bring a relatively coherent world of common images and messages into every home," he explained. As a result it cultivates, during the child viewer's earliest years, the "predispositions and preferences that used to be acquired from other sources."[5] The effect of spending hours every day engaged with a "reality" that is in fact not a reality, together with the surroundings under which television is typically watched (that is, in the comfort and security of one's own home), produces a state of mind characterized by impulsive rather than rational thinking. As a result, consumers are encouraged to passively accept as reality representations that are often significantly skewed by the narrative structure of television programs. Despite never having had any direct contact with those they watch on television, many viewers still believe they really "know" about them: how they live, what they possess, and the consumption choices they make. This pseudo-knowledge shapes their own expectations, satisfactions, motivations, and desires. As Professor Walter Ong of St. Louis University comments:

> *It is hard for us to realize how little of our information comes from direct experience with the physical environment, and how much of it comes only indirectly, from other people and the mass media... they leave us with a greater dependence on others for shaping our ideas about how things are in the world. While becoming aware of places and events far from the direct experience of our daily lives, we have given up much of our capacity to confirm what we think we know.*[6]

How television viewers view the world

In their book *Age of Propaganda*, Anthony Pratkanis and Elliot Aronson of the University of California at Santa Cruz pose the following important question:

> *Why are the pictures of the world painted by the mass media so persuasive?... we rarely question the picture that is shown. We seldom ask ourselves, for example, "Why are they showing me this story on the evening news rather than some other one?"*
>
> *The pictures that television beams into our homes are almost always simply taken for granted as representing reality.*

*Once accepted... [they] guide our thoughts and actions...
determining which issues are most pressing, and decreeing the
terms in which we think about our social world.*[7]

Research bears out this assertion. Viewers who spend four or more
hours watching television each day hold significantly different opinions from those who spend far less time obtaining their information
from the television. They believe, for example, that there is a far higher
prevalence of crime, violence, alcoholism, drug abuse, and prostitu-
tion in society than is actually the case. They are also more likely to be
racially prejudiced; to overestimate the number of people working as
doctors, lawyers, or athletes; to regard women as more limited in their
abilities and interests than men; and to think that older people are
fewer in number and less healthy than they were 20 years ago, even
though the exact opposite is true. Finally they are more likely to view
the world as a dangerous, sinister, and selfish place.[8] Jack McLeod
and Steven Chaffee from the University of Wisconsin comment:

*Given that television is a medium in which viewers regularly
suspend their disbelief, often in what some believe to be a passive cognitive state, cultivation theory posits that heavier viewers of television will have beliefs about the social world that
are more consistent with televised social representations. To
the heavy television viewer, the real world becomes more like
the TV world.*[9]

Shanto Iyengar of Stanford University and Donald Kinder of the
University of Michigan conducted a series of ingenious experiments
in which the content of evening news programs was manipulated
over a seven-day period. Some of these newscasts focused on
weaknesses in US defense, a second group on pollution, while the
third concerned itself with the economy. The participants, who saw
only one of the three sets of specially edited programs, had their
views, opinions, and attitudes on these topics assessed before and
after their week of viewing.

In line with the researchers' predictions, the saturation news coverage caused each group to consider the extensively covered topic they were shown as the most urgent and important challenge their country faced:

When primed by television news stories that focus on national defense, people judge the president largely by how well he has provided, as they see it, for the nation's defense; when primed by stories about inflation, people evaluate the president by how he has managed, in their view, to keep prices down; and so on.[10]

As Harvard political scientist Bernard Cohen noted:

The mass media may not be successful much of the time in telling people what to think [but] it is hugely effective in telling people what to think about.[11]

The ultimate selling machine

Until the arrival of the internet and online shopping, television was influential in the movement of product more rapidly and successfully than at any time in retail history. In 1981, Lowell Paxson created the Home Shopping Network (later rebranded HSN) as the world's first cable television retailer. Within nine years this was being received, around the clock, by 64 million US households.

It offered what the producers termed "advertainment," a store in the viewer's front room in which they could buy anything from tacky knick-knacks such as cubic zirconium jewelry to fashion, kitchenware, toys, and computers. No longer were shoppers obliged to spend time flicking through the pages of a catalog, filling in and posting order forms, and waiting a week to ten days for the goods to arrive. All they had to do was pick up the phone and dial; a minor inconvenience now further simplified to a button press on the remote control or a few clicks on the computer mouse. Today the two most successful television retailers, HSN and QVC, produce a revenue in excess of $10 billion annually.

As well as being a means of helping to sell specific products through advertising or product placement, or simply by the fact that a celebrity is seen wearing, driving, or using a particular brand, television also creates the climate in which consumerism flourishes. Since programs frequently portray affluent consumers, heavy viewers come to see society not only as richer than it actually is, but as a place where everyone has an innate entitlement to such wealth. As I shall explain in a moment, this skewed worldview is drummed into their brain from the moment they are old enough, around the age of 2, to operate the television remote. Many advertisements, and not a few programs, are constructed in such a way as to create comparisons that make viewers either feel inferior themselves to the people appearing on television, or rate other products or people as in some way inferior.

Women who view advertisements for perfumes that use extremely attractive models, for example, report lower levels of satisfaction with their own appearance. And in one study, men rated a potential blind date as far less attractive after watching an episode of *Charlie's Angels*, a show featuring extremely attractive women, than they had done prior to seeing the program.

These television-induced feelings of insecurity and self-doubt form part of a widely used sales technique known as "hurt and heal," in which consumers experience pain before being offered a cure through the simple expedient of buying the product. The next time you are watching commercials, whether for a product, a service, or even a political party, note how frequently advertisers resort to this tactic.

So far from being a passive mirror reflecting society as it is, television is an all-pervasive and powerful medium of persuasion—one that consistently and persistently promotes the notion that the road to true happiness, social acceptance, and romantic commitment is by means of continual acquisition and consumption. This influence applies from the very beginning of our viewing.

"Alas, regardless of their doom, the little victims play"

These lines, from "Ode on a Distant Prospect of Eton College" by nineteenth-century poet Thomas Gray, could fairly if somewhat cynically be applied to the tele-generation, those whose formative years were spent in the presence of television.

Psychologist John Broadus Watson boasted in his 1924 book *Behaviourism*:

> *Give me a dozen healthy infants, well-formed, and my own specific world to bring them up in and I'll guarantee to take any one at random and train him to become any type of specialist I might select, regardless of his talents, penchants, tendencies, abilities, vocation, and race of his ancestors.*

That pretty much sums up the aims of those whose business is to target youth; only in this case, they are less concerned about these youngsters' careers than in making sure that they grow into enthusiastic consumers. Nowhere is the persuasive power of television greater than when directed at children and adolescents. Between the ages of 8 and 13, for example, American children spend some 3.5 hours daily in front of the television and watch around 40,000 commercials annually. Even a decade ago, Professor James McNeal of Texas A&M University, once described as the "godfather of kids marketing," estimated the total advertising and marketing spend aimed specifically at children to be $15 billion.[12]

According to Juliet Schor, the typical American infant can recognize logos at the age of 18 months and ask for products by brand name when aged 3. By their third or fourth birthday, "children start to believe that brands communicate their personal qualities, for example that they are cool, or strong, or smart."[13]

By the time they start school, children have committed hundreds of brand names to memory. By the age of 6, girls will often demand the latest fashions, use nail polish, and be familiar with the words of pop songs. By age 8, boys will start enjoying beer commercials (a firm favorite among this age group) and begin playing violent video games. What causes them to adopt these prematurely adult habits and appetites is, mostly, the persuasive power of television advertising.

Branded for life

Advertising aimed at children is generally based on extensive psychological and, increasingly, neuroscientific research. As a result, commercials are directed, lit, photographed, scored, and edited for maximum appeal to the sensory and cognitive capacities of their preteen audience. In *The Real Toy Story*, investigative journalist Eric Clark explains:

> *For girls and for boys, there are different approaches. Girls prefer light, airy music, female voices, pastel colours, and soft images... Boys go for adventurous music, loud voices, strong images and colours.*[14]

Toys are filmed and photographed in such a way as to ensure maximum psychological engagement. Doll commercials, for example, nearly always open with the doll looking directly into the camera, and hence into the eyes of the child. The purpose is to trigger a direct emotional attachment between child and doll. Typically, the doll will have been given the physical features of a disproportionately large head, wide eyes, and pudgy limbs that act as the "care-engendering" biological releasers that I described in Chapter 6. The embedded message here is: "I want to be your friend. I want to play with you."

Ads aimed at boys contain combat and violence, because advertisers know that aggression appeals to young males and so shifts products. "Boys' spots are usually aggressive, battle-orientated," admits commercial director Leo Zahn. "There is a constant attack and destruction."[15] These displays of aggression are enhanced by the way the commercial is edited, with rapid cutting creating a fast pace that emphasizes action-oriented, stereotypical masculinity.

Because bright colors are especially attractive to children, they are far more likely to feature in commercials aimed at this age group than are more subtle and muted tones. These add to the cartoon-like hyper-reality locations often used. Stop motion, computer graphics, and other film techniques are also frequently employed to give the toys an appearance of movement, the suggestion that they have a life of their own.

The importance of being "cool"

Once they reach the teenage years, adolescents are, in the words of Juliet Schor, "subjected to unremitting pressure to conform to the market's definition of cool."[16] For most young people, girls especially, adolescence is a period of self-doubt and insecurity. The brain does not become fully mature until the early 20s and the teenage brain is struggling to master the social rules, values, and aspirations that form the sense of self. As a result, teenagers are insecure, open to peer pressure, and inexperienced in the ways of the commercial world. They are also more vulnerable to the seductive power of television advertising than at any other time in their lives.

Many ads focus in on these insecurities and the teenager's need for social acceptance by their peers. Media executive Nancy Shalek explains:

> *Advertising at its best is making people feel that without the product you're a loser. Kids are very sensitive to that. If you tell them to buy something, they are resistant but if you tell them that they'll be a dork if they don't, you've got their attention. You open up emotional vulnerabilities, and it's very easy to do with kids.*[17]

Does it work? Absolutely. Is it ethical? You decide

In a paper entitled "Priming effects of television food advertising on eating behavior," Jennifer Harris and her colleagues at Yale University divided 118 children aged between 7 and 11 into two groups. One group watched a cartoon that included four 30-second food commercials, the second one without any advertisements for food. The foods selected were, in the words of the researchers, "Of poor nutritional quality using a fun and happiness message (a high-sugar cereal, waffle sticks with syrup, fruit roll-ups, and potato chips) and were chosen to represent the types of food commercials that are most commonly shown on children's TV."

While watching the cartoons, both groups of children were provided with a large bowl (150g) of cheese crackers and told that they could snack on these if they wanted. After the cartoon was over and the children had left, the crackers remaining were weighed. As the researchers had predicted, children who saw the cartoon with food advertising ate almost half as many (45 percent) crackers as those who saw the nonfood version. A similar effect was found in a second experiment along the same lines, this time using adult participants. Harris reports:

> *Food advertising that promoted snacking, fun, happiness, and excitement, i.e., the majority of children's food advertisements, directly contributed to increased food intake. These effects occurred regardless of participants' initial hunger, and the amount consumed after viewing snack advertising was completely dissociated with adult participants' reported hunger.*[18]

In recent years, and under pressure from regulators, television advertising of high-fat, high-sugar foods to children has undergone a decline. That is the good news for parents and health professionals. The less good news, as I will explain in the next chapter, is that this advertising is moving to mobile devices, where it is not only far more effective, but also much harder for parents and healthy eating advocates to control.

Now that we have examined some of the ways in which television is able to exert such a transformational influence over individual attitudes and the social milieu, we should turn our attention to the way in which commercials are tailored, tweaked, and fine-tuned to make them as persuasive as possible. For it is here that the insights offered by neuromarketing are making their greatest impact.

Learning without awareness

For decades, the traditional way to measure advertising awareness, and therefore advertising effectiveness, was simply to ask people if they remember seeing the commercial for a particular brand. For both advertising professionals and their clients, this remains one of the core metrics, or measures, used in tracking advertisements.

This strongly suggests that viewers must pay attention to commercials in order to transfer knowledge of the brand to long-term memory. As Philip Kotler, co-author of the world's most popular marketing textbook, observes: "The advertiser has to turn the 'big idea' into an actual ad execution that will capture the target market's attention and their interest."[19]

However, is this really the case? Do viewers actually need to attend consciously to television advertising in order to recall the brand or be motivated to buy it? The answer, as I shall explain in a moment, is that they do not. The second point that arises is whether viewers actually watch television in a way that would result in continued, conscious awareness of what is being broadcast. Once again, the research evidence strongly indicates that in many cases they do not.

As I explained in Chapter 2, Herbert Krugman's pioneering study of a young woman while she watched television suggested that brain activity while watching was different to that while reading. In front of the television more slower alpha waves were recorded, suggesting a relaxed frame of mind. When reading a magazine, by contrast, the brain waves were dominated by faster, attention-related beta waves. These findings were confirmed in later studies.

In his 1978 book *Four Arguments for the Elimination of Television*, Jerry Mander noted how the mere act of watching television itself, aside from what is being viewed, sets up a state of mind akin to hypnosis. This is enhanced by the semi-darkness in which television is usually watched and the fact that the eyes remain fixed, for lengthy periods, at a single distance. The muscles are often relaxed and there is a slowing of both heart rate and breathing, conditions typically present with some forms of hypnotic induction, all occurring not in the real world but in a parallel yet different one created by the broadcasts themselves. As Mander comments, "It is simpler to hypnotise someone in a confined space where external reality is removed."[20]

Today, with television often being viewed on the move, on smartphones, tablets, and computers, the viewer's actual state of mind remains unknown. To the best of my knowledge, at the time of writing no EEG research has been conducted under these conditions. However, given the busy, bustling, attention-demanding surroundings in which advertising is now being watched, it seems very unlikely that viewers are paying anything but the most cursory of attention to the majority of commercials. The challenge facing advertisers and their clients is therefore to construct ads in such a way that they can sneak past the barriers of viewers' distraction and indifference to lodge in their brain and influence their shopping choices.

It is here that neuromarketers play an increasingly important role. Before we look at how their insights are being used, let us consider the extent to which conscious attention and awareness really are essential to a commercial's success.

Attention, memory, and advertising awareness

As I explained in Chapter 1, the surprising discovery that consumers remember advertisements to which they have paid no conscious attention was first reported more than a century ago by the American psychologist Walter Dill Scott. He described a woman who, although she claimed never to have looked at any of the advertisements in the tramcars on which she traveled to and from work each day, still "knew them all by heart and... held the products they advertised in her highest esteem."[21]

That she could do so, and that present-day viewers are equally aware of and influenced by commercials to which they have never paid attention, is rendered possible through a process known as "implicit learning." Implicit learning is possible because we also possess an "implicit memory," of whose contents we are not consciously aware.[22] When it comes to measuring advertising effectiveness, implicit (that is, subconscious) memory is superior to explicit (that is, conscious) memory in three key ways:

- It is significantly more durable.
- Its capacity is greater.
- It does not depend on our paying attention.[23]

The problem for researchers has been how to discover whether someone has learned something explicitly or implicitly if they cannot remember having learned it at all. Unlike dogs, which prick up their ears when paying attention, humans provide no reliable nonverbal clues to indicate that they are doing so. Even if you use eye tracking, as most neuromarketing companies do, to investigate where and for how long someone was looking at an advertisement, this does not necessarily mean that they were attending to it. As I demonstrated in the previous chapter, it is perfectly possible to look at things without really attending to what we are seeing.

Brain-imaging studies have now partly answered this problem by enabling researchers to monitor mental activity as it is happening. One of the key measures employed by all neuromarketing companies is the level of attention revealed not by what the person says, but by what changes in their brain activity indicate. The same technology is also now being used to evaluate the third component of effective television advertising: emotional engagement.

The emotional power of television advertising

To be effective, advertising must satisfy three requirements: It must be personally meaningful to the viewer, be culturally relevant, and, perhaps most importantly, create feelings of warmth and positive affect. Triggering a meaningful emotional response is essential to the persuasive power of the brand, since all purchasing decisions have a strong emotion-based dimension to them.[24] Emotion can also be strongly manipulated outside conscious awareness. Indeed, as neuroscientist Joseph LeDoux has observed: "Our emotions are more easily influenced when we are not aware that the influence is occurring."[25]

One common method for generating warm and positive emotions among many viewers is via an appealing image: a cute child, say, or a cuddly animal. These images have been shown to work even when they have no connection with the brand being promoted. In a study by John Kim of Oakland University and his colleagues,[26] a close-up of a kitten was paired with the logo of a fictitious pizza house. Even though there was no logical connection between the two, their mere association caused those who viewed the commercial to express a more positive attitude toward and a greater liking for that pizza house.

The choice of image obviously varies according to the emotion that the advertiser wants to induce: attractive and scantily clad models for sexual desire, sweeping landscapes for awe, rugged cowboys for virile masculinity, or soft drapes for a sophisticated fragrance.

The persuasive power of repetition

Another way to impress your brand name on the viewer is through constant repetition. If you have ever sat wearily through the umpteenth repetition of an all too familiar television commercial for a soap powder, shampoo, or detergent, you may have wondered why it was being shown. Surely advertisers must see that they are wasting their money by showing the same advertisement three times during a 30-minute show, since this does nothing to persuade viewers to buy their product. Indeed, one of the most consistent and common complaints of viewers is the annoyance they feel at having to watch the same old stuff over and over again.

From the manufacturer's perspective, repetition offers a way to ensure that their message is viewed by multiple, and sometimes overlapping, target audiences. Advertising agencies also like it because, since a proportion of their fee often comes from media costs, the more exposure their ad gets, the more money they receive. Furthermore, the very high cost of making commercials today—their budgets are often greater than the programs during which they are shown—makes repetition a more cost-effective way of using them.

Nevertheless, there is an even more compelling reason for advertisers either showing the same commercial, or a slightly modified version of it, beyond the point at which it irritates their potential customers. While hardly the most creative form of persuasion, repetition is one of the most effective.

The recognition of the power of constant exposure to a brand or an idea to influence and manipulate people has a long history. Edward Bernays, the pioneering PR spin doctor whose work I described in Chapter 1, made full use of it to drum up American support during the First World War. In the 1930s, Nazi propaganda head Joseph Goebbels based his entire campaign on the simple premise that people will regard as true information with which they are most familiar. He commented:

> *Propaganda must... always be essentially simple and repetitious. In the long run only he will achieve basic results in influencing public opinion who is able to reduce problems to their simplest terms and who has the courage to keep forever repeating them in this simplified form despite the objections of intellectuals.*[27]

While working at the University of Michigan in the 1960s, social psychologist Robert Zajonc demonstrated that exposure to a familiar stimulus caused people to rate it more positively than they did those that, while similar, were unfamiliar. What sparked his interest in the subject was the fact that overall, positive words are used more frequently than negative ones in everyday speech. In a random sample of one million English words, "good" occurs 5,122 times and "bad" only 1,001. "Pretty" (1,195) is used more often than "ugly" (178); "on" (30,224) more frequently than "off" (3,644); and "first" (5,154) is more commonly used than "last" (3,517).

In one study, Zajonc presented two groups of subjects with meaningless Chinese characters, explained that they represented adjectives, and asked them to state whether the connotations were positive or negative. One group had been repeatedly exposed to these symbols in advance, while the second was unfamiliar with them. As he had hypothesized, the group who had seen the symbols many times previously rated them more positively than did the second group. They also experienced what two nineteenth-century researchers, Gustav Fechner and Edward B. Tichener, described as the "glow of warmth" that is felt in the presence of anything familiar. When asked by Zajonc to rate their own mood, those looking at the previously seen characters described themselves as feeling more hopeful and positive about life than did subjects unfamiliar with the symbols. He observed:

> *Consumer research shows that we prefer products or styles that we have seen more often, regardless of whether we have prior practical experience with the product.*[28]

Interestingly, in the light of the previous chapter, Zajonc also demonstrated that subliminal exposure produced the same effect.[29] In other words, exposure can exert its effect without conscious thought being required; or, as he put it, "preferences need no inferences."[30]

How many times should an advertiser repeat a commercial in order to ensure what is referred to in the industry as "wear-in," while avoiding boring viewers to the point of distraction, a condition dubbed "wear-out"?

Psychologist Herbert Krugman suggested that at least three repetitions were needed to make any impact on the viewer. More recent research suggests that it all depends on the *type* of advertisement involved. Studies by Professor Connie Pechmann of the University of California and David Stewart of Loyola Marymount University showed that advertisements appealing to the emotions required fewer repetitions than those making greater intellectual demands.[31] That is to say, those involving subconscious thought processes were absorbed more easily and effectively than those requiring conscious reflection and deliberation. From this it is clear that the three measures of greatest importance to the effectiveness or otherwise of a television advertisement are attention, memory, and emotion.

Unfortunately, for the reasons given earlier, *asking* viewers how much attention they were paying, what emotions they were experiencing, and how accurately they are able to recall what they have seen does not work. It is not that viewers are unwilling to provide such information, but rather that they are unable to do so. In the words of cognitive psychologists George Lakoff and Rafael Nunez:

> *Most of our thought is unconscious—that is, fundamentally inaccessible to our direct, conscious introspection. Most everyday thinking occurs too fast and at too low a level in the mind to be accessible. Most cognitions happen backstage.*[32]

That is, in the subconscious mind.

Jolts and viewer attention

When analyzing graphs depicting the rise and fall of viewer attention during a typical television advertisement, one typically sees a sharp increase at frequent intervals. In some 30-second commercials this occurs 24 times. Called "jolts,"[33] these spikes are triggered by such things as changes of scene or camera angle, sudden sounds, and so on; anything, in fact, that interrupts the flow of viewers' thoughts. Every jolt compels them to pay attention as they strive to make sense of what they are seeing and hearing. To neuroscientists, these jolts correspond to the "orientation response" (OR), an inborn and automatic reaction to anything new and different in our surroundings.

First identified in 1927 by Russian physiologist Ivan Pavlov as the "what-is-it?" reflex, the OR sharpens our attention and focuses it on specific aspects of our surroundings. Part of the primitive "fight, flight, or freeze" survival mechanism, it takes place in the mid-brain, just above the spinal cord. As a result, it operates subconsciously while drawing the conscious mind's attention to anything different, unexpected, novel, and therefore potentially dangerous.

Viewers don't need to *learn* to regard cuts as significant because, even though these only exist in the artificial world of film and television, they are still sufficiently close to important aspects of the real world to have significant psychological consequences. Just as unexpected sights in the world around us trigger the orienting response, so too do these mechanically imposed visual novelties. By constantly jolting the brain into generating an OR, commercials increase implicit attention and enhance implicit recall.

The use of cuts, especially rapid cuts that impose ever faster motion and novelty, has increased significantly in recent years. Over the past decade, the average shot length (ASL) has been reduced by half, allowing twice as many shots in every commercial. As a consequence, viewers who have grown up with television are more visually literate than those who, like myself, were born before television became a mass media. The downside of this ease with which rapidly changing images are interpreted has been an ever-decreasing attention span among younger viewers. This inability to attend to a single topic for any length of time has been noted by teachers on both sides of the Atlantic.

During the 1980s, I conducted an experiment among 9- to 12-year-olds during which I wired them up to equipment that would switch a video recorder off if they became inattentive. The youngsters, who had sensors attached to their fingers, sat in comfortable armchairs watching a cartoon that they really enjoyed and wanted to see. Despite this, the longest period for which they were able to stay attentive was, on average, 15 minutes. After that, they started to lose concentration and the machine was automatically switched off. When I repeated the experiment in 2011, the longest period of sustained attention achieved was just 7 minutes.

This chapter has considered some of the ways in which television exerts its powerful influence over society and consumers. In the next chapter, I will investigate how mobile marketing is transforming both sales and selling.

10

The Marketing Power of Mobile Media

Business as usual is a death sentence for any brand that wants to communicate via social and mobile channels. Consumers... have endless channels of communications that they know better than you do to check up on the truth of any claim. And they probably never trusted you much in the first place anyway.
—*Steve Smith,* Mobile Insider *columnist*[1]

At a press conference on January 27, 2010, Steve Jobs spoke of his hunch that Apple just *might* be on to something with its newly launched iPad. That turned out to be the understatement of the decade. Within three years, more than 200 million units had been sold worldwide and the company was predicting a billion more sales over the next five years. The effect of the iPad and other tablets on the way products and services are marketed has been profound.

ABI Research reports that around a quarter of owners currently use their tablets to make purchases of £30 or more each month, with one in ten spending nearly £60 over the same period. Mobile devices also encourage impulse-driven sales. An in-depth study from Google and Nielsen of mobile search habits found that two-thirds of mobile searches triggered further action within an hour. In over a quarter (28 percent) of cases this took the form of a purchase, while in more than half (55 percent) it involved a call or visit to a store.[2] Mobile commerce as a whole is predicted to increase from $12 billion a year at present to more than $31 billion by 2017.[3]

At conference after conference I have heard speaker after speaker delivering the same warning to advertisers and brand managers: Mobile devices have created a "connected generation," whose informed and hyper-cynical outlook has changed all aspects of advertising and marketing—for ever.

Man's best friend is the mobile

Research and anecdotal evidence have revealed the intimate relationships that owners have with mobile devices, especially their smartphone. "They say they will never leave home without it," comments Steve Smith, editor of *Mobile Marketing Daily* at Media Post. "They even report feelings of withdrawal from leaving their phones at home."[4]

Accepting that mobile devices can become an owner's trusted friend and adviser, what other advantages do they have over flesh-and-blood sales professionals? Here are ten standout benefits that our research has identified. When it comes to marketing, mobile devices:

Possess more knowledge
Because they are able to store, access, and manipulate huge volumes of data, digital devices have access to almost limitless "knowledge," not merely about the products themselves but also about their user. In the next chapter I will explain how such insights are obtained.

Provide trusted recommendations
Mathematical techniques, such as Bayesian networks or collaborative filtering, enable digital devices to predict what an individual customer is likely to buy and offer appropriate recommendations. Companies such as Amazon have been in the forefront of pioneering the use of data in this way, offering customers suggestions for books, music, or gadgets based on previous purchases.

Are more responsive
By making shopping faster, easier, and simpler, digital technologies encourage people to shop more frequently. By reducing complex

activities to one or two simple steps, or preferably only one step, the consumer is able to make purchases far more easily and, of course, far more impulsively. Dr. B.J. Fogg, Director of the Persuasive Technology Lab at Stanford University, points out:

> *If you purchase products on Amazon.com, you can sign up for "one-click" shopping. With one click of a mouse, the items you purchase are billed automatically to your credit card, packed up, and shipped off. The reduction strategy behind "one-click" shopping is effective in motivating users to buy things.*[5]

In a rapidly moving, highly competitive global marketplace, automating transactions in this way will often mean the difference between a sale and a fail.

Get their timing right

Because mobile technology travels with the user, it can offer a marketing message at the most opportune moment. Getting the timing right is, however, far from simple. It means taking into account many factors, including the physical setting, the social context, and the transient physical and mental state of the consumer. Devices capable of detecting and responding to their owner's emotional and physical state are currently under development. These will adjust their sales messages according to the user's goals, routines, location, and even the social context, offering suggestions only if these would not prove distracting to others nearby. If the device detected tiredness, for example, it might suggest a cup of coffee and indicate the closest branch of a Starbucks or Costa Coffee. If the owner seemed depressed, it could propose a visit to a health club or beauty parlor.

In his book *Persuasive Technology: Using Computers to Change What We Think and Do*, Fogg describes how two of his students created a prototype of a toy bear fitted with global positioning system (GPS) technology that enabled it to "know" its precise location at any given moment. Their idea was that the toy would either be given away or sold cheaply by McDonald's. Whenever the bear was close to one of the fast-food restaurants, it would start singing a jingle about how delicious its food tasted and how much he would like to have some. Although the toy never went into production, one can imagine how persuasive such a timely message might be when a family drove or walked past a McDonald's.[6] One can also easily imagine the extent to which parents might quickly come to resent the constant sales message and wonder just how long such a toy could survive.

That, of course, brings us to the second point about getting the timing right. Context is no less important than the availability of a particular product. In the case of the McDonald's bear, for example, a simple tweak to the software could have ensured that it only sang the jingle at an appropriate time of day, say close to lunch or supper.

Can personalize offers

A recent trend in advertising and marketing has been the drive for personalization, the development of sales messages that satisfy the specific needs of the individual concerned. Mobile devices, for the reasons I give in the next chapter, can "know" more about their owner than even someone's most intimate companion. As a result, they can offer products and services that are tailor-made to that individual's needs.

As I will explain in Chapter 11, this kind of information is increasingly being harvested from a wide variety of social media. If, for example, a shopper has expressed a dislike for McDonald's but a preference for Burger King, the message could take this into account when providing directions. By utilizing knowledge of an individual's likes and dislikes, the cell phone is able to transform itself from useful gadget to trusted friend. Given the commercial potential of marketing, it is hardly surprising that major multinationals such as Coca-Cola, PepsiCo, McDonald's, Kellogg's, and Burger King are leading the way in developing mobile and location-marketing technologies.

Prove endlessly persistent

As any salesperson knows, when it comes to selling, persistence pays. And when it comes to being persistent, digital marketers win hands down. Mobile devices never feel snubbed or rejected and, unless programmed to do so, never take "no" for an answer.

Offer anonymity

While, as I explained in Chapter 5, many shoppers respond positively to the attention of a human sales assistant, on other occasions they much prefer the anonymity of digital transactions. Such confidentiality is especially important when people are purchasing items of a very personal nature.[7]

Are ubiquitous

Mobile devices are rapidly becoming an ever-present component of everyday life. You can find some form of digital capability embedded in cars and trucks, television sets and wristwatches, washing machines, refrigerators, and toothbrushes. This means that, in the ways I describe below, almost any appliance could be transformed into a mobile marketing platform. In this way, sales messages can be taken into places such as the bathroom and bedroom, where no human salesperson would be welcome.

Are connected

Radio-frequency identification (RFID) chips are low-cost transmitters widely used to track consumer purchases. Similar technology can also be used to introduce "ambient intelligence" into a wide range of household devices. Your refrigerator, for example, could be fitted with a radio receiver that used RFID data from chips embedded in consumables such as milk to alert the owner when certain key staples were running low. A message to this effect would be flashed up on the user's computer, tablet, or cell phone.

The device could also, of course, send the same message over the internet to a supplier. This would enable a supermarket to send a timely alert to the owner. The store could also tempt them to make further purchases by offering discounts or flagging up special offers. All the consumer would have to do is press a button on their smartphone to complete the purchase.

For many busy, time-pressed consumers, such an automatic service would be a welcome boon. Their refrigerator and store cupboards could continuously monitor consumables, from bread and eggs to lavatory paper and wine, sending in an order to the supermarket whenever stocks became low, without reference to the owner. The first they would know was when a delivery vehicle arrived with the required products.

The same mobile devices could be fitted inside a car to alert the owner, and perhaps a nearby garage, when an oil change was needed or tire pressures were low. A business suit might warn the wearer that it required pressing or an electric toothbrush indicate that its brushes needed changing or to use more toothpaste. David Wright, an expert in this kind of "ambient intelligence," says:

> In the near future, every manufactured product—our clothes, money, appliances, the paint on our walls, the carpet on our floors, our cars, everything—will be embedded with intelligence, networks of tiny sensors and actuators, which some have termed "smart dust."[8]

All of this information, if also sent to retailers or manufacturers, would enable prompt and relevant marketing messages to be sent to the users.

Are scalable

Digital technology can scale up quickly and easily when demand grows, and scale back or change tactics just as rapidly should consumer interest wane or needs change. While it takes time to recruit and train human sales agents, computer programs can be modified and improved over a far shorter period.

With these ten key benefits of digital technology in mind, let us now look at some of the ways in which they are being utilized to market products and build customer loyalty.

Digital marketing via game playing

Games have come a long way in the four decades since Pong arrived in amusement arcades in the early 1970s. Not only have graphics become far more detailed and sophisticated, but, most recently, the introduction of virtual reality has blurred the distinction between what is real and what is digitally generated by enhancing what the player sees, hears, feels, and smells.

Virtual reality creates a computer-generated environment in which players immerse themselves in a make-believe world that offers not only lifelike graphics and stereo sounds, but smells and haptics, a virtual sense of touch and resistance. A player might, for example, extend her hand to "catch" a virtual tennis ball. As it "landed," she would seem to "feel" the weight, the "roughness" of the ball's texture, and the "shape" of the sphere as her fingers closed around it.

Digital marketing by means of games uses state-of-the-art animation, high-definition video, and augmented reality to transport players into a new and emotionally arousing environment. Such total immersion in what is often a bizarre and terrifying virtual world reduces their control by depleting the mental resources needed to inhibit impulsive behavior.

Requiring players to focus intently on the game and indulge in effortless action results in a loss of the sense of self, together with a distorted impression of the passage of time. Interactive and immersive video games enable digital marketers to integrate advertising and product placement so smoothly into the action that, for the average player, these become virtually indistinguishable from the game itself.

Hotel 626: A study in terror, engagement, and memory

Hotel 626 was a highly sophisticated and ingenious online marketing campaign launched by Frito Lay in 2008. Its purpose was to restore the popularity of two flavors of potato chips, Doritos Black Pepper Jack and Smoking Cheddar, which had fallen out of favor with younger consumers. The company decided to "stop talking to Moms" and talk instead to the people who actually ate their products: teenagers. Its marketing department developed a Halloween-based promotion designed to appeal specifically to tweens and teens that would bring these two flavors "back from the dead."

The blurb announcing Hotel 626, which was only available during the hours of darkness, explained that visitors would find themselves "trapped in a haunted hotel, from which they had to do anything to escape." To register for this multimedia, augmented reality computer game, players entered their names and email addresses on the website. Having done so, they found themselves trapped in a nightmarish building from which they had to escape by undertaking a series of unpleasant and scary challenges. These involved using webcams, cell phones, and microphones. Live Twitter feeds were set up to engage users to share the experience, while a Facebook app encouraged players to "send a scare" to friends via their social networks. This marketing strategy not only mixed real and virtual realities, but encouraged the consumption of a rewarding food to be blended with the highly intense emotional experience of escaping from the terrors of the hotel. Such arousal is likely to leave a permanent mark on the player's implicit memory, contributing to brand loyalty and establishing a powerful emotional connection with Dorito's.

At less than $1 million, small change for a major marketing campaign, Hotel 626 proved a runaway success. More than 4 million young people from over 136 countries checked in and played the game for an average of 13 minutes—almost an eternity for food marketers, who are typically delighted if they can hold the attention of consumers for 30 seconds. In just three weeks, 2 million bags of the relaunched flavors had been sold. In 2009, Hotel 626 won the most prestigious award in marketing, the Cyber Lion, at the Cannes Advertising Awards. It also spawned an even more terrifying game, Asylum 626, the following year. This featured a blood-chilling chase through an insane asylum by nurses wielding chainsaws and incorporated even greater player involvement.

By purposely integrating virtual and real worlds, the game designers were able to provide a deeply emotional and immersive experience for young players. Faced with danger, for example when having to fend off an attack by a chainsaw-wielding maniac while trapped in a closet, players can send out a message asking friends to help save them. Those who agree will be asked to scream into their microphones or hit as many keys on their keyboards as possible to distract the assailant. In another scenario, players are presented with two photos of Facebook friends and forced to choose who will live and who... probably won't.

"We leave it to the imagination what happens," says Hunter Hindman, the campaign's Creative Director. "There's some fairly gruesome sound design and some leading things to indicate that the friend you do not save is not doing so well."[9]

Hindman went on to explain how, in the second game:

We employed head tracking in one scene, so the player literally must move to avoid an attack. We used the webcam in new and innovative ways to actually place the player into the game play itself. We asked people to give us more access and information this year, telling them upfront that the more they gave us, the scarier the experience. We used social networking in ways that hadn't been done before.

Specifically, we bring their friends into the experience and the game play itself. All of these changes began to add up to us to a more immersive, more frightening experience.[10]

In the final scene of the video game, players had to use a special code or marker, imprinted into bags of the two flavors, which when presented to a webcam triggered a 3D key that allowed them to escape.

Critically, both of these games were targeted at adolescents, those in a period of life marked by mood swings and feelings of social awkwardness. The brain's prefrontal cortex, which has a critical role in decision making, does not reach full maturation until early adulthood. As a result, the hormones associated with maturity and the still developing frontal cortical area make tweens and teens especially vulnerable to fear-related stimuli, and so far more receptive to the rewarding properties of junk food.

Researchers at the University of California Irvine[11] report that digital marketing "purposefully evokes high emotional arousal and urges adolescents to make consumption decisions under high arousal," exacerbating their tendency for poor decision making when emotionally aroused, so that they self-medicate using foods high in sugar and fat. These findings confirm an earlier study by Microsoft, which reported that such campaigns "evoke stronger emotional connections with consumers and more positive emotional association from the brands."[12]

Mobile marketing

More and more companies are optimizing their websites to run on cell phones and encouraging users to download location-based apps. These tell networks where the person is and what they are doing in order to present them with the most relevant information. This new form of digital marketing is known as SOLOMO, standing for the three components driving traffic to a website: Social, Local, and Mobile.

"So-Lo-Mo isn't a fad that's going away," says writer Lindsay Scarpello. "It's here, it's real, and it's important for brands and retailers, as well as marketers, to get hip to this trend."[13]

Paradoxically, the almost universal use of cell phones has proved damaging to at least one area of marketing: the impulsive purchase of magazines, chocolates, sweets, and chewing gum while shoppers are queuing at the checkout. Instead of browsing such items, an increasing number of shoppers are now taking out their phones for some digital distraction as they wait to pay. This is a habit that US magazine executives have dubbed, with reference to the vision-restricting headgear worn by race horses, the "mobile blinder."

David Carey, president of Hearst Magazines, which publishes *Cosmopolitan* and 19 other magazine titles in the US, acknowledges that "A number of people, if stalled for a minute, will steal a look at their email or news feed... Everyone that has products at checkouts has to battle for consumer attention."[14]

According to the Alliance for Audited Media, single-copy sales of magazines have fallen by almost 10 percent over a 12-month period, with the trend being even more pronounced for celebrity gossip, women's, sex, and fashion titles. *Cosmopolitan*, with the highest single-copy sales of any US magazine, suffered a decline of 18.5 percent, and *People*, *In Touch Weekly*, *US Weekly*, *Glamour*, and *Star Magazine* all reported double-digit declines in single-copy sales over the same period. Such sales are of great importance to the magazine industry and its advertisers because they most accurately reflect consumer demand.

There are many reasons for this decline, but undoubtedly a key part of the publisher's difficulties lies in the multiplicity of competing attractions now available to consumers, which can frequently be accessed more easily, often more cheaply, and sometimes freely. Buying a magazine or newspaper involves a trip to the newsagent or store and the expenditure of hard-earned cash. Downloading a magazine or just an article from the web, by contrast, can be done with a couple of button pushes almost anywhere and at any time. Such transactions have the additional benefit of offering the "processing fluency" discussed in Chapter 2. As I have explained, the speed and ease with which items can be obtained are a powerful incentive to make impulse purchases.

Some publishers and marketers are now fighting back against "mobile blinders" by positioning their magazines in different parts of the store and having attention-grabbing digital features, such as a QR code, on their covers. *Cosmopolitan*, for example, used such a code that enabled readers who scanned it with their smartphone to enjoy a surprise deal. Marketing people are developing ads specifically for cell phones that offer special deals and promotions. It is all part of a furious battle for shoppers' attention, which has become one of the most valuable and hard-to-capture territories ever fought over.

Interactive mobile advertising

Brainient, a UK-based company, has developed a unique way of increasing engagement and the amount of time spent watching commercials by enabling people to interact with them. In his offices, Brainient's founder and CEO, Romanian Emi Gal, told me how his system works. "Watching videos used to be a lean-back experience," he says. "Now it's lean forward."[15]

In 2009, to capitalize on the growing trend for watching video on handheld devices, Gal pitched to media agencies the idea of creating interactive advertisements. Now he has more than 100 global clients, including Coca-Cola, Volvo, and the *Pirates of the Caribbean* franchise, which run some 50 Brainient-powered campaigns each month.

What is an interactive ad? It could be as simple as a button on an online video clip that shows you behind-the-scenes footage or arranges a test drive while you watch a car commercial. But it could also be a Kinect-enabled, gesture-activated movie trailer, such as the one Gal created in 2012 for the launch of *The Hobbit*. "All you have to do is raise your hand and wave it around to find out more," he explains.

If viewers are persuaded to interact with a video in this way, Gal claims that they are more likely to watch it: 10 percent click on interactive advertisements compared to just 1 percent for non-interactive commercials, engagement increases by 480 percent, and people spend 120 percent longer watching.

Mobile marketing and augmented reality

In augmented reality, digitally generated elements are overlaid on the real world when viewed through a pair of special glasses. While wearing these, a shopper will see relevant information superimposed on their surroundings. When sightseeing in an unfamiliar city, for example, the augmented reality glasses flash up information about nearby historical landmarks. If the wearer is shopping, they overlay special offers, with arrows directing the customer to the store concerned. At meal times, the glasses could direct the person to the nearest McDonald's, Wendy's, or Burger King.

One such device is Google Glass, a wearable computer in the form of a pair of smart-looking glasses that have an integrated heads-up display and a battery concealed inside the frame. The tiny prism display is positioned just above the eye-line, enabling the wearer to view the display merely by looking up. Embedded in the glasses are a camera, microphone, GPS, and, according to reports, a method of transferring sounds through the bones of the skull. The device is voice controlled, allowing the user to command such functions as taking still pictures or videos, or sending messages via speech to text arranging a meeting with friends, or to ask for directions. The glasses will also enable video-conferencing technology, with the ability to stream what is being viewed.

Apps are being developed for such glasses that will allow users to identify their friends in a crowd and send emails. These augmented reality devices will provide companies with one of the most powerful forms of hidden persuasion ever devised: a helpful, trusted guide who knows all there is to know about your surroundings, even if you are a stranger in town, and who can take you by the hand and lead you wherever you want to go; or, at least, wherever the program's commercial sponsors want you to go.

Effective mobile marketing, the ability to sell products across all digital platforms, crucially depends on possessing a detailed and intimate knowledge of individual consumers: their likes and dislikes, foibles and follies, desires and dislikes, strengths and weaknesses.

In the next chapter I will describe how by harvesting Big Data and combining the insights this provides with the curious human tendency to invest digital devices with human feelings, it becomes possible to develop marketing messages so personally persuasive that they are almost impossible to resist.

11

The Ultimate Brain Sell

*Today computer technology is being designed to apply tradi-
tional human techniques of interactive persuasion, to extend
the reach of humans as interactive persuaders. This is new ter-
ritory, both for computer technology and for human beings.*
                            —B.J. Fogg, Persuasive Technology

Over the next few years, advertising and marketing will increasingly
be generated by computers and disseminated to consumers without
the need for any human intervention. This is not to say, of course,
that humans will have no part to play in the process. The development of an overall advertising and marketing strategy will still be in
the hands of flesh-and-blood specialists. It is they and not computers who will decide where and how brand messages and product
features are to be communicated. However, the precise moment at
which that message is sent and much of the content will be left to
digital machines—or, more precisely, to the algorithms run on those
machines.

The success of such an approach does, nevertheless, depend on
two crucial assumptions: that people are really capable of forming a close psychological bond with a computer, tablet, or smartphone; and that these systems will continue to be able to access
vast amounts of detailed personal information about consumers.

In this chapter, I want to examine the extent to which both of
these assumptions hold true. We start by considering the relationship between humans and intelligent machines.

"My Tamagotchi just died!"

The intensity of the emotions that can be aroused by digital life forms was first brought home to me in the late 1990s. Among my students was a bright and seemingly well-adjusted man in his early 20s whom I will call Mark. One afternoon, I found him sitting alone in the somewhat gloomy Student Union bar. He was hunched over a glass of beer and looking extremely sad. Fearing he had suffered some terrible bereavement, I sat down beside him to offer what comfort I could.

Fighting back his tears, Mark explained that he had, indeed, suffered a loss, one that caused him great sadness laden with feelings of deep guilt. As a result of his inattention and neglect, his Tamagotchi had died. For those unfamiliar with this product, a Tamagotchi is a handheld digital pet created in 1996 by two Japanese inventors. The egg-shaped device has a small screen, on which creatures such as animals, objects, or people appear, together with three buttons. The owner's task is to nurture the creature, by pressing the appropriate buttons, until it "grows" into an adult. As with a human child, how it develops depends on the amount of care and attention it receives. If neglected, it "dies." Distracted by exams and a new girlfriend, Mark had failed to provide his Tamagotchi with the "nourishment" needed for "survival." Before dismissing Mark as a neurotic, it is important to realize that many of the more than 76 million Tamagotchi owners worldwide have reported similar feelings of sadness over such a loss. For them, the death of this digital creature generates feelings of unhappiness similar to those of an actual bereavement. They are not alone.

In a recent study, a group of consumers were allowed to play for a while with a feline-like robot called iCat. They were then instructed to switch iCat off and informed that in doing so they would erase the robot's memory. "It was," explains Joline McGoldrick, Director of Research at Dynamic Logic, "akin to killing the robot." Researchers found that participants who had enjoyed a "positive emotional experience" with the "animal" hesitated three times longer before pressing the "off" switch than those who felt the experience had been less than helpful.[1]

The extraordinarily deep emotional relationship that even highly intelligent and well-educated people can form with computers was first revealed as long ago as 1966. At a conference organized by the Association for Computing Machinery, Dr. Joseph Weizenbaum introduced delegates to Eliza.[2] Named after Eliza Doolittle in Shaw's play *Pygmalion*, his computer program performed the role of a therapist. It was a simple piece of code, lacking in any intelligence and working through simple pattern recognition and the substitution of keywords. Despite these significant limitations, the effect on those who interacted with "her" was remarkable. Weizenbaum recalls:

Eliza created the most remarkable illusion of having understood in the minds of many people who conversed with it. They would demand to be permitted to converse with the system in private, and would, after conversing with it for a time, insist, in spite of my explanations, that the machine really understood them.[3]

He recounts how on one occasion he came into his office to find his secretary busily engaged with the "therapist." "Excuse me Professor," she exclaimed in embarrassment, "but do you mind waiting outside until the session is finished?"

Byron Reeves and Clifford Nass of Stanford University observe:

Computers, in the way that they communicate, instruct, and take turns interacting, are close enough to human that they encourage social responses. The encouragement necessary for such a reaction need not be much. As long as there are some behaviors suggesting a social presence, people will respond accordingly... consequently, any medium that is close enough will get human treatment, even though people know it's foolish and even though they likely will deny it afterward.[4]

In one study, these researchers told participants that they were to be tested on a series of facts presented on a computer screen. Having shown them the information, the computer then asked how much they knew about the subject. It was explained that if they had limited knowledge on the topic, further information would be provided. In reality, no matter what response they made, everyone was given exactly the same additional facts. The participants then sat the test and were provided with their score. Next, the computer rated its own performance as a teacher. No matter what score the participant had obtained, the computer commented on how great a job it had done.

Participants were next divided into two groups and asked to report on how well or badly *they* felt the computer had performed. The only difference between the two groups was that one carried out the evaluation on the same computer they had used previously, while the second group completed an identical evaluation on a different computer. Reeves and Nass report:

> *Participants who answered questions on the same computer gave significantly more positive responses than did participants who answered on a different computer. The computers got the same treatment that people would get. The respondents who interacted with the same computer throughout the experiment related more positively on 20 of the 22 adjectives presented.*[5]

It was as if the students felt a closer bond to the original computer than to the new machine and were somehow concerned about hurting its feelings.

"When working with a computer perceived to be similar in personality, users judge the computer to be more competent and the interaction to be more satisfying and beneficial," explains Fogg.[6] In one of his studies, two groups of participants solved problems using one of two computers. The first was labeled "teammate" while the second was unlabeled. Researchers found that when the computer was identified and subsequently perceived as "part of their team," participants described it as "more similar to them, in terms of approach to the task, suggestions offered, interaction style, and similarity of rankings of items needed for survival."[7] They also regarded it as smarter and friendlier, as providing higher-quality information, and as performing better.

As a result of extensive research into the relationship between humans and intelligent-seeming machines, we can say with confidence that a close, even emotionally intense psychological bond can develop. The more intelligent and responsive the digital device appears to be, the more people will come to trust its "judgments" and follow its "recommendations"—both of which put it leagues ahead of most sales professionals when they try to close a deal.

By harnessing the power of supercomputers that have been constructed to "think" in much the same way as the human brain, it becomes possible to construct and disseminate new advertising and marketing messages virtually instantaneously. However, in order for this to be done effectively, the device must have access to significant amounts of data about each individual consumer's likes and dislikes, what they might be interested in buying, and what, through clever marketing, they might be persuaded to buy.

In other words, they need knowledge of what it will take to transform a need into a want-need. That brings us to the second condition necessary for automated advertising and marketing success: an intimate and up-to-date knowledge of consumers as individuals.

Harvesting Big Data

In his dystopian novel *1984*, George Orwell warned: "Big Brother is watching you." More than 50 years later, Big Brother is still watching—but with an important difference.

Today, billions of internet users have become the enthusiastic accomplices of their own surveillance. Freely and willingly, they are prepared to disclose the most intimate details of their personal lives to complete strangers. As a result, the information that major companies such as Google, Amazon, Facebook, and Twitter possess about consumers has never been more detailed nor more extensive. In the trade this is known as Big Data.

While data harvested from social networking sites, such as Facebook, MySpace, and LinkedIn, yields details about an individual's personal profile, valuable commercial information is also collected from a wide range of digital sources, including online shopping, patterns of web browsing, cell-phone activity, and the use of credit, debit, and loyalty cards. The personal information gathered in this way includes:

- Names of family members together with their ages
- Present and past addresses
- Financial status and credit rating
- Marital status
- Phone numbers, landline and mobile
- Computer IP addresses
- Social class and ethnicity
- Religious beliefs
- Educational attainments
- Current and past employment records and whether they have a criminal record
- Details of their current location plus all the places they have been over the past several weeks
- Their tastes in music, films, books, magazine articles, snacks, gadgets, paintings, jokes, fragrances, fashions, food, and drink
- Political leanings
- Sexual orientation together with information about any sexual fantasies they have sought to satisfy via the web

All of these, plus many other personal details, are used to develop marketing strategies designed to bypass the conscious brain and deliver commercial messages directly to the nonconscious regions. Information gathering begins at birth and continues until the consumer draws their last breath.

And legitimate companies are not the only ones to take an interest in the details of people's private lives. Criminals, ranging from teenage hackers to organized criminal gangs and state-sponsored cyber spies, prowl the World Wide Web. According to Peter Warren, chair of the Cyber Security Institute, two million criminal websites are set up each month and 60,000 new viruses are released every day. He warns:

> There are around five super gangs whose internet based activities mean that we are now in the era of the super-criminal, crime gangs whose power is so great that they too now pose a threat to our lives and livelihoods.[8]

The Facebook wars

"Ask a kid what Facebook is for and they'll answer 'it's there to help me make friends,'" comments media theorist Douglas Rushkoff, author of *Program or Be Programmed*. He adds:

> Facebook's boardroom isn't talking about how to make Johnny more friends. It's talking about how to monetise Johnny's social graph... Ask yourself who is paying for Facebook. Usually the people who are paying are the customers. Advertisers are the ones who are paying... We are not the customers of Facebook, we are the product. Facebook is selling us to advertisers.[9]

One man who would agree wholeheartedly is 25-year-old Austrian law student Max Schrems. While completing a university assignment, he asked Facebook to provide him with all the information it held on him. To his astonishment, he was sent a 1,200-page document containing personal data grouped into 57 categories. Schrems, who compared this amount of personal information to the voluminous files of the Stasi, East Germany's much feared secret police, was outraged. Instead of handing in his class project, he set up an advocacy organization called Europe vs. Facebook and encouraged tens of thousands of users to demand copies of whatever data was held on each of them. The young law student's readiness to stand up to the social networking giant struck a chord with users. Within weeks of its establishment, his site had received 40,000 inquiries.[10]

Ginger McCall, an attorney at the Washington-based Electronic Privacy Information Center, comments:

Social networking sites are often not transparent about what information is shared and how it is shared. Users may be posting information that they believe will be viewed only by their friends, but instead, it is being viewed by government officials or pulled in by data collection services.

As we shall see, Facebook is by no means unique in gathering personal data, and to the company's credit it offers users myriad ways to control their privacy. The privacy settings page has dozens of different options that can be toggled on or off. Furthermore, when they make a mistake, the team behind Facebook seem to learn from it. Recent updates have significantly simplified that page to help ensure that users are not overwhelmed by the initial dashboard of options.

What causes critics to regard it as a threat to individual freedom, social values, and even to the web itself is the company's sheer size. The internet took 30 years to gain 750 million users; Facebook achieved it in just 8. If Facebook were a continent, it would be the fourth most populated one in the world. This astonishing growth rate is transforming the way the web works. Many businesses, for instance, now ignore traditional web marketing and confine their online presence solely to Facebook.

The company has given birth to the billion-dollar social gaming giant Zynga and devoured the photo network Instagram. The photographs posted on Facebook now number in excess of 3 billion. Whereas in the recent past the internet was organized around data, it is now, as a result of Facebook, organized around people.

Technical writer Steven Johnson observes:

*It should come as no surprise that we now find ourselves grav-
itating toward a new platform grounded in those social maps.
And the bigger we make the platform, the stronger its gravita-
tional pull.*

In an article for *Wired* magazine entitled "Can anything take down
the Facebook juggernaut?" he pointed out that the internet, which
included everything from emails and file trading to voice-over-IP
phone calls, was always technically larger than the World Wide Web.
Only through its widespread adoption was the web able to become
the more powerful. Johnson adds:

*The web became the main attraction. Facebook now threatens
to perform that same jujitsu against the web itself. The difference, of course, is that no one owns the web—or in some
strange way we all own it. But with Facebook we are ultimately
just tenant farmers on the land; we make it more productive
with our labour, but the ground belongs to someone else.*[11]

Facebook "Likes" reveal more than most users realize

For marketers, one of the most fruitful pieces of information provided by Facebook could well be its users' "Likes." Research by
Michal Kosinski and David Stillwell, from Cambridge University's
Psychometric Centre, and Thore Graepel from Microsoft Research
has shown that Likes can be used to create remarkably insightful
personal profiles. These include accurate predictions of a user's
age, IQ, race, personality, sexual orientation, religious beliefs, and
political leanings, and whether or not they smoke cigarettes, take
drugs, or drink alcohol. Since this information is, at the time of
writing, publicly available, it offers considerable scope for the creation of highly personalized marketing messages.

To conduct their study,[12] the researchers first created a Facebook
app called myPersonality. Volunteers undertook this complete psychological test that assessed their intelligence, competitiveness,
and general satisfaction with life. It also measured personality traits

such as levels of extraversion and introversion. The responses of 58,000 US Facebook users, together with data from their profile and friends network, were then analyzed using a statistical model that predicted personal attributes based on Likes alone. The results proved remarkably accurate in predicting a wide range of demographic variables with considerable commercial potential.

Homosexuality, for example, was determined with 88 percent accuracy for men and 75 percent for women. African-Americans were distinguished from Caucasian Americans with 95 percent accuracy; and Republicans from Democrats with 85 percent accuracy. Religious beliefs had an accuracy of 82 percent; whether the user smoked cigarettes (73 percent), drank alcohol (70 percent), or took drugs (65 percent) were equally predictable. Even seemingly irrelevant personal details, such as whether users' parents separated before the user reached the age of 21, were determined with an accuracy of 60 percent.

Their statistical model also accurately predicted far harder to gauge traits such as IQ, emotional stability, openness, and extraversion. The openness trait, which distinguishes those who welcome change from those who dislike it, was identified from Likes with the same accuracy as a personality test score. Other Likes produced a strong, although sometimes apparently incongruous or random, association with a personal attribute. For example, a preference for Curly Fries was linked with a high IQ, while the belief that "spiders are more afraid of us than we are of them" was more prevalent among nonsmokers than smokers.

The researchers point out that only a small minority of Facebook users actually clicked Likes that explicitly revealed any of these attributes. For example, fewer than 5 percent of gay users clicked obvious Likes such as gay marriage. The accuracy of the model's predictions thus depended on aggregating huge amounts of the more popular, if less informative, Likes such as music and television shows.

The resulting detailed and dependable personal profiles would, the researchers suggest, prove of great commercial value to marketers and advertisers. Nevertheless, they also recognize the potential for exploitation. Michal Kosinski says:

> *I am a great fan and active user of new amazing technologies, including Facebook. I appreciate automated book recommendations, or Facebook selecting the most relevant stories for my newsfeed. However, I can imagine situations in which the same data and technology is used to predict political views or sexual orientation, posing threats to freedom or even life.*

His colleague David Stillwell agrees, adding:

> *I have used Facebook since 2005, and I will continue to do so. But I might be more careful to use the privacy settings that Facebook provides.*

If you regard the commercial use of personal information gathered by Facebook as an invasion of privacy, you may be even more concerned to learn that, compared with what other market research companies know about you, this organization is barely scratching the surface of knowledge about people's identity.

As with all online retailers, Amazon's appetite for gathering information on its customers' habits is insatiable. If you read a book on your Kindle, for example, not only will the company have a record of its title, but also any phrases you may have highlighted, the pages you turned, whether you read from first to last page or dipped into and out of different sections, and, if so, which they were. By analyzing these data, the company is able to customize its marketing to match your personal interests and tastes. If, for example, you read John Schofield's *Cromwell to Cromwell: Reformation to Civil War* from beginning to end at a single sitting, but dipped in and out of Zen Martinoli's *5 Minute Fitness*, the next time you logged in Amazon would be likely to recommend more historical novels than keep-fit manuals.

However, while some of the companies likely to harvest your personal data, such as Google, Amazon, Apple, and Microsoft, will certainly be known to you, others have little or no public profile and operate well below the radar.

With headquarters in Little Rock, Arkansas, and annual revenues of $1.15 billion, Acxiom has been described as "one of the biggest companies you've never heard of."[13] A global corporation, with offices in the UK, France, Germany, the Netherlands, Poland, Australia, China, and Brazil, as well as all across the US, Acxiom holds details on almost every American household and over half a billion consumers worldwide, in total some 1,500 items of information on each man, woman, and child. "Think of Acxiom as an automated factory," commented one of its employees. "The product we make is data."[14]

Despite its size and the zetabytes (that's 10 followed by 21 zeros) of data held in its servers, Acxiom represents only 12 percent of the personal information market. That leaves 88 percent of the information on consumers being harvested and marketed by other companies, some of which are far more secretive about their business. In "Big Data, Big Deal," a white paper produced by Acxiom, Jed Mole, David McKee, and Ian Fremaux observe:

> *Somewhere within the avalanche of data are buried significant patterns and behaviours which signpost buying, churn, brand support or aversion... there is a great challenge in taking raw data from the huge variety of possible sources, integrating these into systems and producing actionable insights which feed operational systems.*

Google for spies?

The extent of the technical expertise and financial investment now being poured into Big Data analysis is demonstrated by a program called RIOT. Developed by Raytheon, the world's fifth largest defense contractor with annual sales in excess of $24 billion, RIOT has the capability not only to track people anywhere in the world, but also to predict their future behavior, and has been dubbed a "Google for spies" by some commentators.[15] The acronym stands for Rapid Information Overlay Technology. RIOT not only harvests personal information, from such websites as Twitter and Facebook, but also uses GPS data to identify an individual's location.

One source of such information lies in the location tags automatically embedded into photographs taken on a smartphone. Another is from data provided by Foursquare, a mobile phone app used by over 25 million people to notify friends and colleagues of their whereabouts. Data from Foursquare enables RIOT to identify the ten places most frequently visited by that individual over a seven-day period, together with the times at which they made those visits.

In a dramatic demonstration of how this information can be used to follow an individual around the country, the company tracked— with his knowledge and consent—one of its own employees for a week. Among the information it gleaned about his movements, the company showed that Nick, the target, visited a gym regularly at 6 am. "We know where Nick's going, we know what Nick looks like," says Brian Urch, Raytheon's principal investigator. "Now we want to try to predict where he may be in the future."[16]

Not surprisingly, security services around the world have expressed considerable interest in RIOT after Raytheon showcased it to US government and security leaders at a conference for "secretive, classified innovations." No less interest is likely to be shown by marketing and retailing companies, which could use RIOT and the innovative algorithms for analyzing the Big Data it will undoubtedly inspire, to create the ultimate selling tool. By knowing where potential customers are likely to be and what they are likely to be doing at any given time, advertising messages could be fine-tuned to anticipate and meet their precise needs.

According to Michael Bevans, Head of Advertising and Publisher Solutions at Yahoo!, this will enable online marketing to:

- Provide the *right* message (or comment) about the *right* product to the *right* person at the *right* time.

- Engage the user with information meaningful to them.
- Allow a brand to cultivate awareness and affinity based on a shared set of interests.
- Engage with an audience based on *purchase intent* for a product or service.[17]

Called behavioral targeting, this increased accuracy enables advertisements to be directed solely at consumers whose recent online behavior indicates that the product category is relevant to them. It offers marketers the ability not only to take account of the recency and intensity of the consumer's online activity, but also to make accurate predictions about their future interests and purchases. Behavioral targeting takes account of the fact that websites searched for, checked, and viewed provide a strong indicator of future interests.

Social media and mobile marketing

Recognizing that young people would be the primary consumers of social media, Coca-Cola quickly developed a strategy to target a teen or young-adult audience. It knew that people in this age group are major users of cell phones and the internet and that it would be possible to develop a deep emotional connection with them by personalizing the offers made and the way information is presented on the web. It realized, in the words of Coca-Cola social media marketing executive Adam Brown, the "importance of fishing where the fish are."

This fishing has produced massive catches. According to Brown:

Everyday there are about 1,000 blogger posts that talk about us, 3,000 tweets, although this has been doubling now about every six weeks, about 15 YouTube videos that talk about us go live everyday, about 100,000 videos on YouTube now that talk about us and about 50 pictures go up on Flickr every day. There are about 50,000 pictures on Flickr that feature Coke.[18]

The fact that Coca-Cola currently has some 22 million Facebook fans, with 25,000 new "friends" added every day, demonstrates the extraordinary power of arguably the most persuasive and far-reaching integrative marketing campaign so far developed. The My Coke program involved digital advertising techniques, ranging from behavioral targeting with user-generated content, to social media surveillance, search engine optimization, and mobile location marketing. In order to register for My Coke rewards—the program initially offered 4 billion unique redemption codes worth a cumulative $50 million in prizes—the consumer had to provide personal details and a cell-phone number.

Coca-Cola linked with advertising partners Tacoda, Mediavest, and FICO to map out behavioral targeting plans to reach the maximum number of people who would have an interest in My Coke rewards. As a result, the program offered up to 1,500 versions of the site, based on customer preferences. A consumer who prefers Sprite and likes to cook, for example, might receive Sprite coupons and advertisements for cooking programs. A consumer who drinks Diet Coke and enjoys movies would be targeted for movie promotions and Diet Coke discounts.

An indication of the campaign's success can be seen from the fact that "one third of all members told an average of 3.7 people about the company's brands and the My Coke Rewards program."[19]

According to Carol Kruse, Coca-Cola Vice President for Global Interactive Marketing, by 2008 the rewards program had become the largest "ever launched for the Coca-Cola Trademark... a multi-year, online driven, mega-rewards program that allows consumers to choose from a pool of experiences and rewards."[20]

By embedding brands, or cues that prime people for a particular brand (such as Cadbury's use of the color purple, which I described in Chapter 6), within an entertainment context, an influence can be exerted that engenders the need to be consciously recognized or recalled. By personalizing a commercial message in a way that has direct appeal to the consumer's known interests, desires, attitudes, and motivations, a company is able to develop deep emotional connections between consumers and brands. This connection operates at such a deep level within the brain that it is no longer recognized as an implanted commercial message and seems, instead, to be the way the consumer always makes sense of the world.

Creating mobile empathy

How would you respond if the next time you switched it on, your smartphone or computer remarked in concerned tones, "You seem a bit down today. Would you like me to play your favorite movie to cheer you up?" or "You seem tired. Why don't you stop for a coffee?"

The idea that a digital device could empathise with you, let alone express an emotion of its own, may seem bizarre and even freaky. But within a few years, empathic computers could have become widespread. Peter Robinson, Professor of Computer Technology at the University of Cambridge, explains:

> *We're building emotionally intelligent computers, ones that can read my mind and know how I feel. Computers are really good at understanding what someone is typing or even saying. But they need to understand not just what I'm saying, but how I'm saying it.*[21]

Because our facial expressions provide such vital clues to the way we are feeling, much of the effort is going into developing software that will read the user's emotions via a built-in camera. Robinson and his team have developed a program that uses a camera to locate and track more than 20 "feature points," including the edge of the nose and the corners of the mouth, as well as key movements, such as nodding or shaking the head, or raising the eyebrows. Combinations of movements are then used to identify underlying emotions.

Researchers are also working on a system that combines an analysis of expressions with gestures to infer emotions. With an accuracy of around 65 percent, this program can correctly identify an emotion almost as often as another human. Other systems under development predict emotions by analyzing intonations in speech. Somebody who is depressed, for example, will speak in a particular way, just as someone who is happy and excited will have a specific frequency and speed to their speech.

However, merely understanding emotions is not enough. Robinson wants computers to express emotions as well, whether they are cartoon animations or physical robots. In Japan, engineers have already made significant advances in constructing robots with feelings. One of these is called Nao. When unhappy "he" hunches and looks downcast; if scared "he" cowers and remains motionless until "calmed" by being gently stroked on the head. Robinson points out:

> *An emotionally aware computer has many commercial applications. Imagine a computer that could pick the right emotional moment to try to sell you something, a future where mobile phones, cars and websites could read our mind and react to our moods.*[22]

Social media and personalized billboards

Imagine a fashion-conscious 22-year-old female executive who passes an advertising billboard on her way to work each day. Sometimes she glances at the poster, but mostly she just hurries past. Now consider how she would react if, as she came close, that billboard flashed up a message addressing her by name: "Hi Michele. I know how much you love Jimmy Choo shoes. Just to let you know they are on sale at the Jane Doe fashion boutique just across the street from here. Say I sent you and there'll be another 20% off just for you!"

If the next passer-by was a young man, the poster would present another personalized message, perhaps suggesting trainers or the latest video game, depending on his interests. Again, by using facial recognition and information harvested from that individual's online activities, the poster would be able to address him by name and make him an offer that he might find it very hard to refuse.

This type of personalized advertisement was first imagined by Steven Spielberg in his 2002 movie *Minority Report*. Today, fact has overtaken fiction, with very similar devices being field-tested in a number of major cities. These interactive billboards are able to identify the age and sex of people—although not as yet their names and other personal details—as they are either walking past or standing waiting for a bus or train.

Immersive Labs, a New York–based company, has developed a system using facial-recognition software to create displays that react to people in real time. "The real focus is artificial intelligence, so that ads can learn and improve over time," says Immersive Labs CEO Jason Sosa. "The software may learn that it's better to play a Coca-Cola ad at this time of day, or when the weather's like this."[23]

The same system can also be used to learn more about the way customers behave while shopping: how long they spend looking at an advertisement, their progress around the store, dwell time, peak shopping periods, or how customers respond to vending machines and "end caps," the displays at the end of aisles. Other companies are exploring ways of using pictures posted on social media sites to identify individuals, then drawing on the likes and dislikes they have posted, to make them offers with the greatest persuasive appeal.

David Jones, global CEO of ad agency Havas and Euro RSCG Worldwide, told CNN:

> *What we're going to see is the boring world of retail and the sexy world of digital will come together, and it'll be an unbelievable change. The biggest single revolution that we'll see in digital is all around location-based [advertising].*[24]

The possibilities are indeed intriguing, especially if you start thinking about potential interactions with other systems. For example, billboard facial-recognition systems could be linked to payment facial-recognition systems so that discounts advertised would be automatically granted when a customer pays.

Social media and embedded television messages

In our laboratory we have conducted studies into ways in which information derived through data mining social media might be used in a new form of television advertising. If this took off, it might even eliminate the commercial breaks that viewers find intrusive and frequently take steps to avoid. This would involve what is known as "permission marketing," in which consumers sign up to receive advertising of specific interest and relevance to their life. The technique, which is being developed by a number of companies, involves marketing messages appearing for a few seconds within a television program. The messages would relate to products being shown at that moment as part of the show. What my laboratory was asked to investigate was how viewers would respond to such messages. Would they find the information provided useful and interesting, or merely aggravating and intrusive?

To conduct the study, the results of which were later presented to the Astra satellite company, we obtained permission to use the popular television show *Come Dine with Me* as a template. The program is based around the idea of having strangers invite one another to their homes for dinner on consecutive nights. The guests then award their host points for the quality of the food and hosting skills, with the winner taking home £1,000.

We arranged that while the preparation of the meal was being shown, details of the equipment used, such as price, availability, and manufacturer, would briefly appear in a pop-up box on the screen (Figure 11.1). Which pop-up box appeared could be adjusted according to the interests of any particular viewer, based on information derived from social media. Each box includes a photograph and the name of the product, together with the best price. By using the remote control, viewers could elect to view further details, purchase the item right away, or move the box to a "dock" for review

Figure 11.1 A scene from *Come Dine with Me*. Three pop-up boxes appear providing details of the kitchen equipment being used.

Come Dine With Me image courtesy of ITV Studios/Channel 4/Screenocean.

once the program had finished. Our research showed that not only did viewers welcome these brief product messages—which only appeared because they had given permission for them to do so— but attended to them, frequently made on-the-spot purchases, and found the information useful.

Necessary evil or needless invasion of privacy?

It is not only commercial organizations that are collecting Big Data. In June 2013, a former US intelligence worker, Edward Snowden, revealed details of a top secret electronic surveillance program run, since 2007, by the US National Security Agency. Known officially as US-984XN and code-named PRISM, it targeted computer users living outside the US. Set up by President George Bush in 2007, PRISM involved the downloading of terabytes of information gleaned from emails, videos and voice communications, photos, file transfers, login notifications, and social networking. According to leaked documents the information was collected "directly from the servers of these U.S. Service Providers: Microsoft, Yahoo, Google, Facebook, PalTalk, AOL, Skype, YouTube, Apple." It was also reported that Britain's equivalent of the NSA, Cheltenham-based GCHQ, has also been secretly gathering intelligence from the same internet companies through an operation set up by the NSA.

While the extent of the operation and the alleged participation of major internet players, something those companies strenuously deny, may come as a shock to many, the fact that such data is of interest to counter-intelligence agencies should surprise no one. Every major player, especially China and Russia, is engaged in exactly the same practices and for precisely the same reasons.

Unless you want to disconnect yourself totally from modern society—that is, never use the internet, carry a credit or debit card, use a cell phone, or engage in any form of electronic transaction—then this is the price to be paid. In the final chapter I will suggest some simple, basic ways to minimize your exposure to what will, without a doubt, become an increasingly inquisitive and deceptive World Wide Web.

But how worried should consumers be about having their personal details used in this way? Professor Chris Hankin, Director of the Institute for Security Science and Technology at Imperial College London, comments:

> *The real power of social media mining is establishing a "pattern of life" from which anomalies might stand out, whether an emerging disease outbreak, discontent with local policing methods, or broad approval for the latest design of a smartphone. The hyper-connectivity of a large proportion of the world's population is almost regarded as a right and, whether they like it or not, it gives widespread public access to their thoughts and actions.* [25]

Other commentators have expressed concern. While all the companies involved emphasize that online data is gathered "without any personally identifiable information being disclosed," some argue that such anonymity is simply impossible to ensure.

John Taysom, Senior Advanced Leadership Initiative Fellow at Harvard University, asks:

> *But what data constitutes personally identifiable information? PII is a predetermined list of attributes that could identify an individual. But... it is not clear what information alone or in combination is not personally identifying. As citizens we need therefore to lobby... in favor of a more dynamic notion of identifying data. Identifiably personal information (IPI, if you must) is any set of data which by inspection could lead to the identification of an individual from a group, with a given level of confidence in a given time. This is likely to be a much broader set of data than that which is currently referred to as PII.*[26]

He warns that without this revision, "the application of analytics to 'big data' (for which read 'your data'), whether to benefit society or to boost profits, could turn data science into data surveillance."

Digital tribes

Whether you feel that personal data collection is a monstrous invasion of privacy or a practical and efficient means of ensuring that shopping is made faster, easier, and more relevant depends, at least to some extent, on your age. This, in turn, dictates the "digital tribe" to which you are most likely to belong:

- *Digital Natives* include anyone born from the late 1980s onward. Because the World Wide Web started in 1991, they have never known life without the internet. As a result, say John Palfrey and Urs Gasser in their book *Born Digital*, they "live much of their lives online, without distinguishing between the online and the offline. Instead of thinking of their digital identity and their real-space identity as separate things they just have an identity."[27]

- *Digital Settlers*, while not born into the internet era, helped to shape it. Often highly sophisticated users of the internet, they are equally at home in an analog world.
- *Digital Immigrants* were middle-aged at the start of the digital age and so came late to a world of instant communication and multiple connectivity. While by no means all of them are Luddites—so-called silver surfers, men and women in their late 50s and older, are among the internet's most active and enthusiastic users—they are also comfortable when using more traditional ways of socializing and communicating. They find it just as easy to talk face to face as in cyberspace. They continue to write and post letters, favoring snailmail over email, and they are often suspicious of and cynical about the digital age.

Digital Natives are the least likely to regard data gathering as an invasion of their privacy; indeed, most welcome the ease and speed with which it enables them to use the internet—where, for example, they can shop online thanks to "cookies" that companies implant on their computing devices. They enjoy making friends online, sharing personal information, exchanging opinions, swapping photographs, and being sent recommendations for movies, music, books, and holidays that perfectly match their interests.

What they frequently fail to appreciate as they enjoy the apparently "free" services offered by search engines, the "free" information provided by many commercial websites, and the "free" opportunities for socializing available on social networking sites is that nothing is ever really free. As blogger Andrew Lewis succinctly put it: "If you are not paying for it, you're not the customer; you're the product being sold."

It is by combining a deep knowledge of an individual consumer's subconscious wants and needs with a greater understanding of psychology and neuroscience that it will become possible for advertisers, marketers, and retailers to devise sales strategies that read consumers' thoughts, influence their emotions, and stimulate them to shop—and this is creating the ultimate brain sell.

12

Let the Buyer Be Aware

It's caveat emptor on aisle three. Consumers must realize that, as a group, they are easily manipulated, and companies are counting on that.

—*Donald MacGregor*[1]

When in lectures and talks I describe the power and technology behind the brain sell, audience reactions fall into one of two main categories. Some people express fascination with and great excitement about the future direction of advertising, marketing, and retailing. They emphasize ways in which our growing knowledge of the buying brain will open the way to ever richer, more personally specific, and enjoyable consumer experiences—and, of course, to ever more effective, and profitable, ways in which advertisers, marketers, and retailers will be able to influence consumers.

The second reaction is shock and outrage. Some people feel themselves almost physically violated by the extent of the personal knowledge that many major companies possess and alarmed at the prospect that they may, by some means or another, be "brainwashed" into buying products that they do not need and cannot afford.

Such concerns have led consumer rights and advocacy groups to press for ever-tighter regulation of advertising and marketing, urging governments to ban some types of market research and data-collection techniques outright and to significantly restrict others. In my view, however, rules and regulations imposed in a few jurisdictions are unlikely to have any effect. Unscrupulous companies will easily flout the law, while ethical ones, facing severe commercial pressures, may strive to discover legal loopholes or face being driven out of business. Besides that, with the exception of advertising and marketing to children and teenagers, especially of high-fat, high-sugar foods, it is surely up to consumers to safeguard their own interests by becoming better informed of the commercial forces ranged against them.

As I explained in the Introduction, one of my purposes in writing this book has been, with an insider's knowledge and experience, to enhance such awareness on the part of consumers. I aim to help you better appreciate the multiplicity of ways in which major corporations, with unlimited intellectual talent and very deep pockets, are able to influence your buying decisions.

If you gain such knowledge, you will be able to enjoy the many very real benefits that neuroscience and modern advertising, marketing, and retailing have to offer, while avoiding the traps lying in wait for the unwary.

The good news for consumers, and indeed for the many honest advertisers, marketers, and retailers, is that the world of commerce is becoming ever more transparent. We live in an age in which every company is under growing pressure to deliver a return on the time and money it has invested that exceeds those of its rivals. At the same time, consumer pressures are requiring ever greater transparency. If such openness is denied, or perceived as being denied, it can rapidly erode the foundations of trust and credibility on which long-term commercial success crucially depends.

Heightened visibility does, of course, also bring about greater scrutiny and criticism when companies fail to follow through on their promises or are seen as operating in a devious or underhand way. Today, as never before, it is mandatory for companies to deliver their messages and their products directly and sincerely to customers. The alternative is to face the wrath and negative publicity generated by tweeters, bloggers, radio show callers, and both social and traditional media. All of these often highly emotionally charged and not infrequently inaccurate, subjective judgments will command consumers' mindspace and resist attempts to explain or clarify the situation. Once lost, reputation may never be regained.

Yet the vast amounts of information about consumers now available and the greater insights into what motivates, excites, and delights them offer advertisers, marketers, and retailers an opportunity to win the loyalty and trust of customers in a way never before possible. It is true that companies can fail horribly at this, but they can also excel magnificently.

The Japanese distinguish between *atarimae hinshitsu* and *miryokuteki hinshitsu*. The former describes what the customer expects a product or service to do. When you buy a watch, for example, you expect that it will keep accurate time. When you see your hairdresser, you expect that he or she will style your hair well. This is the functional requirement, the quality that satisfies by meeting customer expectations.

Miryokuteki hinshitsu describes the quality that fascinates by exceeding customers' expectations: the watch that looks stylish as well as telling the time accurately, the hair styling that boosts your confidence by making you look and feel more attractive.

The brain sell techniques discussed in this book offer companies the chance to excel by providing a quality that fascinates with every product they sell and every service they provide. And it is knowledge of such techniques and how they are used that offers the key to both customer satisfaction and customer protection.

Protecting yourself against the persuaders

So what practical steps can you take to safeguard yourself against the new hidden persuaders that now abound in the retailing landscape?

Five tips on the internet

Some simple precautions may be sufficient to foil potentially costly criminal attacks and identity thefts. While these may sound all too obvious to the computer literate, it is amazing how often they are neglected even by experienced users.

1. Beware internet cafés. Free wi-fi may seem tempting, but it's about as safe and sensible as drinking from a half-empty beer bottle that you find lying in the street.
2. Avoid easily hacked passwords. Some people still leave their mobile devices on the factory default setting of 0000 or use the word "password" as their password. Remember that personal details, such as your mother's maiden name, that of the family pet, or your favorite pop star, can be all too easily discovered on the net, so don't use them as a password.
3. Despite the inconvenience, change your passwords regularly and never use the same one on all your sites.
4. Beware "phishing" expeditions in which strangers send you apparently enticing files to be opened, claim that you or your company has a parcel awaiting delivery, or attempt to disguise themselves as a message from your bank or building society. When in doubt, chuck it out.
5. Finally, if you have children, educate them to appreciate just how hazardous the World Wide Web can be. While this is a task probably more easily handled by adults who are themselves Digital Natives, it is essential that every parent understands the extent to which the internet teems with hidden persuaders. The current media emphasis is on the risks of exposure to hard-core, and sometimes extremely violent, pornography or of being groomed by predatory pedophiles posing as children on social networks. Far less has been written about the inculcation of material desires and values. While no parent should deny their child access to computers, cell phones, or other digital devices that have become essential tools for twenty-first-century living, such access should be carefully monitored, especially with younger children. To do otherwise is as irresponsible as allowing a child to play unsupervised beside a fast-flowing river or busy highway.

Five tips on the high street

Impulse purchases, reportedly worth around £24 billion annually to retailers in the US and UK, result from System I not System R thinking. As I explained in Chapter 5, the former operates below the level of conscious awareness and is strongly influenced by our emotions and "gut feelings." This means that you are more likely to fall victim to the hidden persuaders tempting you to buy on impulse in certain mood states.

1. If, for example, you are feeling a bit down or looking for ways to brighten your day, or when bored and killing time, such as while waiting for your flight at an airport, your risk of spending money impulsively significantly increases. So think twice before you splash the cash.
2. Heightened arousal, such as at the cinema, in a theme park, or on holiday, can also lead to consumers indulging in what have been called "splurchases." Money spent on knick-knacks and vacation souvenirs is often regarded as utterly wasted, sometimes within only a few hours of making the purchase, so again, don't act on impulse.
3. Keep in mind, too, the ways in which subtle hidden persuaders, such as aromas, changes in lighting, or colors and music of which you are barely aware, can trigger the desire to spend. When in a major retail environment, such as a supermarket, hypermarket, or shopping mall, be aware that you are inside the belly of a vast and meticulously researched machine specifically designed and engineered to sell to you. There really is no such thing as a free lunch, either online or in store.
4. One technique you could use whenever you are tempted is to spend ten seconds imagining a pink elephant diving into a bowl of blue custard. Such vivid, fantastical images are what psychologists call "thought stoppers." Clinicians use them to help people break obsessive habits by stopping such ideations dead in their tracks. Since the conscious mind can only hold one idea at a time, the pink elephant and blue custard imagery prevents

it from dwelling on anything else. The distraction may only last a few seconds, but this is often sufficient for the would-be purchaser to step back from the brink of buying and reconsider the whole proposition.

5. It has been said that the five words every salesperson dreads to hear from a potential customer are "I will think about it." By deliberately *not* thinking about a possible purchase, you may well also end up not buying.

Indeed, as a consumer, knowledge is perhaps the most effective defense against the hidden persuaders: knowledge about the techniques being used to sell to you; knowledge that enables you to take the ancient legal maxim of caveat emptor—let the buyer beware—back to its roots and rephrase it as "let the buyer *be aware*."

It is only through an awareness of the power and reach of the persuasion industry that consumers will be able to recognize and resist the myriad powerfully effective marketing and sales techniques confronting them in the world of the brain sell.

Notes

Introduction

1. Packard, V. (1957) *The Hidden Persuaders*, New York: IG Publishing, p. 31.
2. Heath, R. (2012) *Seducing the Subconscious*, Chichester: Wiley-Blackwell, p. 47.

Chapter 1: When Science Met Selling

1. Kilbourne, J. (2004) The more you subtract, the more you add: Cutting girls down to size. In Kasser, T. & Kanner, A.D. (eds) *Psychology and Consumer Culture*, Washington, DC: American Psychological Association, p. 252.
2. James Playsted Wood (1958) *The Story of Advertising*, New York: Ronald Press, p. 27.
3. Ryan, D. & Jones, C. (2009) *Understanding Digital Marketing: Marketing Strategies for Engaging the Digital Generation*, London: Kogan Page, p. 2.
4. Scott, W.D. (1904) The psychology of advertising, *Atlantic Magazine*, January.
5. O'Toole, J. (1981) *The Trouble with Advertising*, New York: Chelsea House, p. 16. John O'Toole was Chairman of the Board of Foote, Cone & Belding Communications, Inc., one of the world's largest advertising agencies.
6. These remarks were especially insightful given the fact that advertising was not, at that time, viewed as a marketing tool. It was seen merely as a way of presenting information about a product or service to the public.
7. Dichter, E. (1964) *Handbook of Consumer Motivations: The Psychology of the World of Objects*, New York: McGraw-Hill, p. 419.
8. Crispin Miller, M. (1975 [1957]) Introduction to Packard, V., *The Hidden Persuaders*, New York: IG Publishing.
9. The Rorschach test involves asking people to say what different patterns remind them of. Although still occasionally used, many psychologists now dismiss it as worthless.
10. Packard, *op. cit.*, p. 81.
11. Ewen, S. (1996) *PR! A Social History of Spin*, New York: Basic Books.
12. *Ibid.*

13. Not that the Freudians' approach had always gone unchallenged, even when they were at their height of their influence. The 1930s had seen the establishment of the Psychological Corporation, headed by a Yale-trained psychologist, Henry C. Link, which offered "the techniques of behavioral psychology" to American companies. Contrasting the approach of what he termed the "old psychology" to his "new" approach, Link explained that while the former studied how "the mind thought," the focus of the latter was how the mind "acted." "The new psychology," he wrote, "is concerned with discovering what advertisements are most effective at getting people to buy. Not what people think or think they think, but what they actually do about certain advertisements is the important question." Link, H.C. (1932) *The New Psychology of Selling and Advertising*, New York, Macmillan, pp. 79–80.

14. Watson, J.B. (1913) Psychology as the behaviorist views it, *Psychological Review*, 20, pp. 158–77.

15. Hunt, M. (1993) *The Story of Psychology*, New York: Doubleday.

16. Camerer, C.F., & Loewenstein, G. (2004) *Behavioural Economics: Past, Present, Future*. In Camerer, C.F., Loewenstein, G., and Rabin, M. (eds) *Advances in Behavioral Economics*, Princeton, NJ: Princeton University Press, pp. 3, 40.

17. Kahneman, D. & Tversky, A. (1979) Prospect theory: An analysis of decision making under risk, *Econometrica*, 47(2), pp. 263–92.

18. Thaler, R. (1980) Toward a positive theory of consumer choice, *Journal of Economic Behaviour and Organisations*, 39, pp. 39–60.

19. Frankish, K., & Evans, J.St.B.T. (2010) The duality of mind: A historical perspective, in Evans, J.St.B.T., & Frankish, K. (eds) *In Two Minds: Dual Processes and Beyond*, Oxford: Oxford University Press, p. 8.

20. Many neuroscientists, myself included, prefer the term "consumer neuroscience." In Mindlab we refer to the data as "neurometrics." However, because the term "neuromarketing" has become so widely known, I will continue to use it in this book.

21. The original comment, in Dutch, reads as follow: "Na dit overzicht kom ik nu tot een omschrijving van neuromarketing. Het doel van neuromarketing is het beter begrijpen van de klant en haar reactie op marketing stimuli, door de processen in de hersenen direct te meten en in de theorievorming en stimuli-ontwikkeling te betrekken. Alhoewel de grootste nadruk ligt op het beter begrijpen van de klant door middel van theorievorming, moet het uiteindelijk ook de manager

helpen bij het ontwerpen van effectievere marketing stimuli. Neuromarketing is kort gezegd gericht op het vergroten van de effectiviteit van marketingactiviteiten door het bestuderen van hersenreacties." I am indebted to my colleague Erwin Hartsuiker of Mindmedia for the translation. Since then there has been a proliferation of new terms made to seem original and exciting by the application of the prefix neuro-, for example neurolaw, neuromarketing, neuropolicy, neuroethics, neurophilosophy, neuroeconomics, and even neurotheology.

Chapter 2: Hidden Persuaders That Shape the Way We Shop

1. Pooler, J. (2003) *Why We Shop: Emotional Rewards and Retail Strategies*, Westport, CT: Praeger.

2. Cialdini, R.B. (1974) *Influence, The Psychology of Persuasion*, New York: William Morrow.

3. Meston, C.M., & Frohlich, P.F. (2003) Love at first fright: Partner salience moderates roller-coaster-induced excitation transfer, *Archives of Sexual Behavior*, 32(6), December, pp. 537–44.

4. Festinger, L. (1957) *A Theory of Cognitive Dissonance*, Palo Alto, CA: Stanford University Press.

5. Aronson, E., & Mills, J. (1959) The effect of severity of initiation on liking for a group, *Journal of Abnormal and Social Psychology*, 59, pp. 177–81.

6. Pollock, C.L., Smith, S.D., Knowles, E.S., & Bruce, H.J. (1998) Mindfulness limits compliance with the "that's-not-all" technique, *Personality and Social Psychology Bulletin*, 24, pp. 1153–7.

7. Eco, U. (1986) *Faith in Fakes*, London: Martin Secker and Warburg, p. 43.

8. Sachs, J. (2013) The story of inadequacy marketing is over, *Wired*, March, pp. 73–4.

9. *Ibid*.

10. Wickelgren, W. (1974) *How to Solve Problems: Elements of a Theory of Problems and Problem Solving*, San Francisco: W.H. Freeman.

11. Levitt, T. (1960) Marketing myopia, *Harvard Business Review*, July–August, pp. 45–56.

12. Michael Bevans, personal communication.

13. Martin Cooper – The inventor of the cell phone, http://www.cellular.co.za/cellphone_inventor.htm, retrieved March 12, 2013.

14. This story is told by Colin Walls in his entertaining blog, http://blogs.mentor. com/colinwalls/blog/2009/06/18/how-to-sell-more-toothpaste, retrieved March 12, 2013. While it seems plausible and I have no reason to doubt it, I have not been able to verify it elsewhere.

15. Jaffe, C. (2011) Beware: Same price, less product, MSN Money, http://money. msn.com/shopping-deals/scam-alert-same-price-less-product-marketwatch. aspx?page=0, retrieved March 12, 2013.

16. Clifford, S. & Rampell, C. (2011) Food inflation kept hidden in tinier bags, *New York Times Business Day*, March 28.

17. Jaffe, *op. cit.*

18. Poundstone, W. (2011) *Priceless: The Psychology of Hidden Value*, Oxford: OneWorld.

19. Ashton, L. (2009) Left-digit bias and inattention in retail purchases: Evidence from a field experiment, Unpublished paper, March, pp. 1–31.

20. Ginzberg, E. (1936) Customary prices, *American Economic Review*, 26(2), p. 296.

21. For example, Basu, K. (2006) Consumer cognition and pricing in the nines in oligopolistic markets, *Journal of Economics and Management Strategy*, 15(1), pp. 125–41.

22. Anderson, E.T., & Simester, D.I. (2003) Effects of $9 price endings on retail sales: Evidence from field experiments, *Quantitative Marketing and Economics*, 1, pp. 93–110.

23. Lacetera, N., Pope, D., & Sydnor, J. (2009) Inattention in the used car market, Working paper, October, pp. 1–38.

24. Hossain, T., & Morgan, J. (2006). Plus shipping and handling: Revenue (non) equivalence in field experiments on eBay, *Advances in Economic Analysis and Policy*, 6(3), Article 3.

25. Morales, A.C., & Fitzsimons, G.J. (2007) Product contagion: Changing consumer evaluations through physical contact with "disgusting" products, *Journal of Market Research*, XLIV, pp. 272–83.

26. Wicker, B., Keysers, C., Plailly, J., Royet, J.-P., & Gallese, V. (2003) Both of us disgusted in *my* insula: The common neural basis of seeing and feeling disgust, *Neuron*, 40, pp. 655–64, October 30.

27. Novemsky, N., Dhar, R., Schwarz, N., & Simonson, I. (2007) Preference fluency in choice, *Journal of Marketing Research*, XLIV, pp. 347–56.

28. Newman, E.J., Garry, M., Bernstein, D.M., Kantner, J., & Lindsay, D.S. (2012) Non-probative photographs (or words) inflate truthiness, *Psychonomic Bulletin & Review*, DOI:10.3758/s13423-012-0292-0.

Chapter 3: *"I Know What You're Thinking!"*

1. Gilbert, D.T. & Hixon, J.G. (1991) The trouble of thinking: Activation and application of stereotypic beliefs, *Journal of Personality and Social Psychology*, 60, pp. 509–17.
2. Whalen, S., & Bartholomew, R.E. (2002) The great New England airship hoax of 1909, *New England Quarterly*, 75(3), September, pp. 466–76.
3. Hoeve, A., The mind miners, *Holland Herald*, http://holland-herald.com/2012/03/the-mind-miners, retrieved March 12, 2013.
4. Burne, J. (2003) A probe inside the mind of the shopper, *Financial Times*, November 28th, http://www.commercialalert.org/issues/culture/neuromarketing/a-probe-inside-the-mind-of-the-shopper, retrieved March 12, 2013.
5. Gehring, W.J., & Willoughby, A.R. (2002) The medial frontal cortex and the rapid processing of monetary gains and losses, *Science*, 295, March 22, pp. 2279–82.
6. In a typical training session, the individual will attach sensors to their fingers and then either watch a pointer moving across a dial or listen to the rise and fall of a sound. As they become more and more deeply relaxed, these physical changes are detected by the equipment and "fed back" to the individual. A video of a typical biofeedback training session can be found at www.brainsell.org.uk. For a video of the brain train in action go to www.brainsell.org.uk.
7. Lewis, D. (1986) *The Alpha Plan*, London: Methuen. This book formed the basis of a BBC *Horizon* program, which can be viewed on the Brain Sell website.
8. BBC *Tomorrow's World*. This video can be viewed on the Brain Sell website.
9. Dabkowski, S. (1996) Big Brother takes a closer look, *Business Review Weekly*, September 9, pp. 56–7.
10. Quoted from *Tomorrow's World, op. cit.*
11. Neuroco undertook work for major UK and US companies. In 2009 it was taken over by Neurofocus, which, owned by Nielsen, is now the largest neuromarketing company in the world. The company was founded by the energetic and charismatic Dr. A.K. Pradeep.

12. Krugman, H. (1971) Brain wave measures of media involvement, *Journal of Advertising Research*, 11(1), pp. 3–9.

13. For example, in 1984 Sidney Weinstein, Curt Weinstein, and Ronald Drozdenko published a paper entitled "Brain wave analysis" in the *Journal of Psychology and Marketing*, 1(1), pp. 17–42. They explained that factors such as cultural, social, personality, and psychological influences could bias buyers' answers in market research studies. By reading electrical activity directly from the brain, they believed that they could eliminate the "problem of extraneous factors biasing verbal responses."

14. McClure, S.M., Li, J., Tomlin, D., Cypert, K.S., Montague, L.M., & Montague, R.P. (2004) Neural correlates of behavioral preference for culturally familiar drinks, *Neuron*, 44(2), October 14, pp. 379–87.

15. *Ibid.*

16. John Ward, personal communication. A full transcript of this interview can be found at www.brainsell.org.uk.

17. Nature Neuroscience (2004) Brain Scam?, *Nature Neuroscience*, 7(7), p. 683.

18. My own company's approach uses neural nets to train a computer about the electrical pattern in an individual's brain while they are viewing images known to produce a particular emotion or level of attention. The pattern produced by the stimuli being tested, let us say this is a beer commercial, can then be compared with the first set of results on a person-by-person basis. By making each participant act within their own control, many of the biases listed in the chapter are avoided and many of the difficulties side-stepped.

19. Dooley, R. (2012) *Brainfluence*, Hoboken, NJ: John Wiley. My full interview with Roger, author of the popular blog Neurosciencemarketing, can be found at www.brainsell.org.uk.

20. Tzramsoy, The fuzzy concept of neuromarketing, http://brainethics. org/?p=795, accessed March 12, 2013.

21. Initial findings from the ARF NeuroStandards Collaboration Project and the "NeuroStandards Retreat," January 12–14, 2011. A PDF of this document can be found on the Brain Sell website, www.brainsell.org.uk.

22. *Ibid.*

23. Uttal, W.E. (2001) *The New Phrenology*, Cambridge, MA: MIT Press, pp. 51–2.

Chapter 4: Why Shopping Isn't "All in the Mind"

1. Hung, I.W., & Labroo, A.A. (2011) From firm muscles to firm willpower: Understanding the role of embodied cognition in self-regulation, *Journal of Consumer Research,* 37(6), pp. 1046–63.

2. Hickey, L. (2005) The brain in a vat argument, *Internet Encyclopedia of Philosophy,* http://www.iep.utm.edu/brainvat, retrieved March 12, 2013.

3. Dr. Samuel Thomas von Sömmering (1755–1830) was a noted German anatomist and physiologist who wrote a number of major books, including *On the Structure of the Human Body,* in five volumes (1791). He believed that nerves acted independently of the brain, which he did not consider essential to the continuance of life.

4. Roach, M. (2004) *Stiff: The Curious Lives of Human Cadavers,* London: Penguin, pp. 199–206.

5. White, R., Albin, M.S., & Verdura, J. (1963) Isolation of the monkey brain: In vitro preparation and maintenance, *Science,* 141, pp. 1060–61.

6. Roach, *op. cit.*

7. Shapiro, L. (2011) *Embodied Cognition,* Oxford: Routledge, p. 27.

8. Van den Bergh, B., Schmitt, J., & Warlop, L. (2011) Embodied myopia, *Journal of Marketing Research*, 48(6), pp. 1033–44.

9. Key, W.B. (1993) *The Age of Manipulation*, Lanham, MD: Madison Books, pp. 95–6.

10. Kalat, J.W. (1998) *Biological Psychology*, 6th edn, Pacific Grove, CA: Brooks/Cole, p. 24.

11. Ley, R.E., Turnbaugh, P.J., Klein, S., & Gordon, J.I. (2006) Microbial ecology: Human gut microbes associated with obesity, *Nature*, 444(21), December, pp. 1022–3.

12. Cited in Fleming, D. (1967) Attitude: The History of a Concept. In Fleming, D. & Bailyn, B. (eds), *Perspectives in American History (Vol. 1)*, Cambridge, MA: Charles Warren Center in American History, Harvard University.

13. Hung & Labroo, *op. cit.*

14. Chandler, J., & Schwarz, N. (2009) How extending your middle finger affects your perception of others: Learned movements influence concept accessibility, *Journal of Experimental Social Psychology*, 45, pp. 123–8.

15. Ackerman, J.M., Nocera, C.C., & Bargh, J.A. (2010) Incidental haptic sensations influence social judgments and decisions, *Science*, 328(5986), pp. 1712–15.

16. Lempert, H., & Kinsourne, M. (1982) Effect of laterality of orientation on verbal memory, *Neuropsychologia*, 20, pp 211–14.

17. Carney, D.R., Cuddy, A.J.C., & Yap, A.J. (2010) Power posing: Brief nonverbal displays affect neuroendocrine levels and risk tolerance, *Psychological Science*, 21(1), pp. 1363–8.

18. Förster, J. (2004) How body feedback influences consumers' evaluation of products, *Journal of Consumer Psychology*, 14(4), pp. 416–26.

19. Casasanto, D. (2009) Embodiment of abstract concepts: Good and bad in right and left-handers, *Journal of Experimental Psychology*, 138(3), pp. 351–67.

20. Oppenheimer, D. (2008) The secret life of fluency, *Trends in Cognitive Sciences*, 12(6), pp. 237–41.

21. Alter, A.L., & Oppenheimer, D.M. (2006) Predicting short-term stock fluctuations by using processing fluency, *Proceedings, National Academy of Science*, 103, pp. 9369–72.

22. Novemsky, N., Dhar, R., Clarj, G.R., Schwarz, N., & Simonson, I. (2007) Preference fluency in choice, *Journal of Marketing Research*, 44(3), pp. 347–56.

23. Van den Bergh *et al.*, *op. cit.*

24. Cacioppo, J.T., Priester, J.R., & Berntson, G.G. (1993) Rudimentary determinants of attitudes: II. Arm flexion and extension have differential effects on attitudes, *Journal of Personality and Social Psychology*, 65(1), pp. 5–17.

25. Choi, C.Q. (2010) How Wii and Kinect hack into your emotions, *Wired*, http://www.wired.com/wiredscience/2010/11/wii-emotion, retrieved March 2011.

26. Ariely, D. & Loewenstein, G. (2006) The heat of the moment: The effect of sexual arousal on sexual decision making, *Journal of Behavioral Decision Making*, 19, pp. 87–98.

27. Baumeister, R.F., Catanese, K.R., & Vohs, K.D. (2001). Is there a gender difference in strength of sex drive? Theoretical views, conceptual distinctions, and a review of relevant evidence, *Personality & Social Psychology Review*, 5, pp. 242–73.

28. Kray, L.J., Locke, C.C., & Van Zant, A.B. (2012) Feminine charm: An experimental analysis of its costs and benefits in negotiations, *Personality and Social Psychology Bulletin*, online July, 109, pp. 1–15.

29. Fisher, J.D., Rytting, M., & Heslin, R. (1976) Hands touching hands: Affective and evaluative effects of interpersonal touch, *Sociometry*, 39(4), pp. 416–21.

30. Saunders, E. (1993) Stock Prices and Wall Street Weather, *American Economic Review*, 83(5), pp. 1337–45.

Chapter 5: Inside the Buying Brain

1. Montague, R. (2006) *Why Choose this Book?* New York: Dutton.
2. These include not just the well-known five senses of seeing, hearing, tasting, touching, and smelling, but also thermoception. Our ability to feel heat and cold is also regarded as the work of more than one sense, not only due to the fact that there are two separate detectors, one for hot and one for cold, but because a third, entirely different type of thermoceptor is located in the brain and used to monitor internal body temperature. Proprioception lets us know where parts of our body are located in respect to other body parts; tension sensors monitor muscle tension; nociception communicates the sensation of pain; equilibrioception enable us to keep our balance; stretch receptors are located in our lungs, bladder, stomach, and the gastrointestinal tract; chemoreceptors are involved in detecting hormones and drugs in the bloodstream; and magnetoception, an ability to detect magnetic fields. All of these are in addition to senses that alert us when we feel hungry or thirsty.
3. Montague, P. R. (2007) Neuroeconomics: A view from neuroscience, *Functional Neurology*, 22(4), pp. 219–34.
4. Schopenhauer, A. (1851/1970) *Essays and Aphorisms*, trans. R.J. Hollingdale, London: Penguin.
5. Other psychologists have named them "Associative vs. Rule Based," "Input Modules vs. Higher Cognition," "Explicit and Implicit," "Impulsive and Reflective." The terms System 1 and System 2 have also been widely used as more neutral descriptions.
6. Lewis, D. (2013) *Impulse: Why We Do What We Do without Knowing Why We Do It*, London: Random House.
7. Kahneman, D. (2011) *Thinking, Fast and Slow*, New York: Farrar, Straus & Giroux, p. 23.
8. Maine de Biran, F.P.G. (1803/1929) *The Influence of Habit on the Faculty of Thinking*, trans. M.D. Boehn, London: Baillière.
9. Bargh, J.A. (2002) Losing consciousness: Automatic influences on consumer judgment, behaviour, and motivation, *Journal of Consumer Research*, 29, pp. 280–85.
10. Barrett, L.F. (2009) The future of psychology: Connecting mind to brain, *Perspectives on Psychological Science*, 4(4), pp. 326–39.

11. Inesi, M.E., Bott, S., Dubois, D., Rucker, D.D., & Galinsky, A.D. (2011) Power and choice: Their dynamic interplay in quenching the thirst for personal control, *Psychological Science*, 22(8), pp. 1042–8.

12. Gigerenzer, G., & Todd, P.M. *Simple Heuristics That Make Us Smart*, Oxford: Oxford University Press, p. 95.

13. Alberts, J.R., & Decsy, G.J. (2004) Terms of endearment, *Developmental Psychobiology*, 23(7), pp. 569–84.

14. Rolls, E.T., Grabenhorst, F., & Parris, B.A. (2008) Warm pleasant feelings in the brain, *Neuroimage*, 41(4), pp. 1504–13.

15. Fiske, S.T., Cuddy, A.J.C., & Glick, P. (2007) Universal dimensions of social cognition: Warmth and competence, *Trends in Cognitive Sciences*, 11(2), pp. 77–83.

16. IJzerman, H.I., & Semin, G.R. (2009) The thermometer of social relations, *Psychological Science*, 20(10), pp. 1214–20.

17. Wiltermuth, S., & Heath, C. (2009) Synchrony and co-operation, *Psychological Science*, 20(1), pp. 1–5.

18. Englich, B., & Mussweiler, T. (2001) Sentencing under uncertainty: Anchoring effects in the courtroom, *Journal of Applied Social Psychology*, 31, pp. 1535–51.

19. Birte, E. (2006) Blind or biased? Justitia's susceptibility to anchoring effects in the courtroom based on given numerical representations, *Law and Policy*, 28(4), pp. 497–514.

Chapter 6: The Persuasive Power of Atmospherics

1. Carbone, L.P., & Haeckel, S.H. (1994) Engineering customer experiences, *Marketing Management*, 3, Winter, pp. 8–19.

2. Kotler, P. (1973) Atmospherics as a marketing tool, *Journal of Retailing*, 49(4), Winter, pp. 48–64.

3. Turley, L.W., & Milliman, R.E. (2000) Atmospheric effects on shopping behaviour: A review of the experimental evidence, *Journal of Business Research*, 49, pp. 193–211.

4. Holbrook, M. & Hirschman, E. (1982) The experiential aspects of consumption: Consumer fantasies, feelings, and fun, *Journal of Consumer Research*, 9, pp. 132–40.

5. Nick Thornton, interview, October 2012.

6. Carbone & Haeckel, *op. cit.*

7. Biddle, S. (2012) How to be a genius: This is Apple's secret employee training manual, Gizmodo.com, August 28.

8. Kim, E., & Yoon, D.J. (2012) Why does service with a smile make employees happy? A social interaction model, *Journal of Applied Psychology*, 97(5), September, pp. 1059–67.

9. A full transcript of this interview can be found at www.brainsell.org.uk.

10. In the famous closing sequence of the 1942 film *Casablanca*, for example, Humphrey Bogart and Ingrid Bergman embrace in the rain while, in the distance, technicians prepare a plane for take-off. In fact, audiences were looking at a small-scale cardboard model of the plane that was being serviced by midgets. Rain and fog were used to help conceal the relative crudeness of this forced perspective.

11. Some 15 years before the term was invented, Gruen was well aware of the importance of creating a powerful shopping experience through the use of atmospherics. When, in 1956, he designed America's first indoor mall, the Southdale Mall in the town of Edina, outside Minneapolis, he constructed a "town square" in the heart of the $20 million building. This included a pond with fishes, huge trees, balconies with hanging baskets, a café, and, perhaps most eye-catching of all, a vast cage filled with brightly plumaged tropical birds. It created a sensation among journalists and attracted visitors from all over the US.

12. Markin, R.J., Lillis, C.M., & Narayana, C.L. (1976) Social psychological significance of store space, *Journal of Retailing*, 52(1), pp. 43–54.

13. Birren, F. (1969) *Principles of Colour: A Review of Past Traditions and Modern Theories of Colour Harmony*, New York: Van Nostrand Reinhold, p. 91.

14. Jacobs, K.W., & Suess, J.F. (1975) Effects of four psychological primary colors on anxiety state, *Perceptual and Motor Skills*, 41(1), pp. 207–10.

15. Babin, B.J., Hardesty, D.M., & Suter, T.A. (2003) Color and shopping intentions: The intervening effect of price fairness and perceived affect, *Journal of Business Research*, 56(7), pp. 541–51.

16. Bellizzi, J.A. & Hite R.E. (1992) Environmental color, consumer feelings and purchase likelihood, *Psychology and Marketing*, 9, pp. 347–63.

17. Puccineli, N.M., Chandrashekaran, R., Grewal, D. & Suri, R. (2013) Are men seduced by red? The effect of red versus black prices on price perception, *Journal of Retailing* 88(2), pp. 115–25, June.

18. Babin *et al.*, *op. cit.*; Singh, S. (2006) Impact of color on marketing, *Management Decision*, 44(6), pp. 783–9.

19. Gorn, G.J., Chattopadhyay, A., Sengupta, J., & Tripathi, S. (2004). Waiting for the web: How screen colour affects time perception, *Journal of Marketing Research*, 41(2), pp. 215–25.

20. Gulas, C.S., & Schewe, C.D. (1994) Atmospheric Segmentation: Managing Store Image with Background Music, Enhancing Knowledge Development in Marketing. In Achrol, R. & Mitchell, A. (eds), *AMA Summer Educators' Conference Proceedings*, Chicago IL: American Marketing Association, pp. 325–30.

21. Smith, P.C., & Curnow, R. (1966) Arousal hypothesis and the effects of music on purchasing behavior, *Journal of Applied Psychology*, 50, pp. 255–6.

22. Milliman, R.E. (1982) Using background music to affect the behavior of super-market shoppers, *Journal of Marketing*, 46(3), pp. 86–91.

23. Dublino, J. (2012) Multi-sensory Dunkin' Donut campaign spikes sales, *Scent Marketing Digest*, April 9, http://scentmarketingdigest.com/2012/04/09/multi-sensory-dunkin-donut-campaign-spikessales, retrieved March 12, 2013.

24. Dublino, J. (2012) McCain Foods to launch multi-sensory bus shelter ads in UK, *Scent Marketing Digest*, February 7, http://scentmarketingdigest.com/2012/02/07/mccain-foods-to-launch-multi-sensory-busshelter-ads-in-uk, retrieved March 12, 2013.

25. ScentAir USA, Scent study: Bloomingdale's, http://www.scentair.com/why-scentair-scent-studies/bloomingdale-s, retrieved March 12, 2013.

26. Sanburn, J. (2011) NYC grocery store pipes in artificial food smells, *Time Magazine Moneyland*, July 20, http://moneyland.time.com/2011/07/20/nyc-grocery-store-pipes-in-artificial-food-smells, retrieved March 12, 2013.

27. ScentAir UK, Scent research, http://www.scentairuk.com/scent_research.html, retrieved March 12, 2013.

28. Doucé, L., Poels, K., Janssens, W. & De Backer, C. (2013) Smelling the books: The effect of chocolate scent on purchase-related behavior in a bookstore, *Journal of Environmental Psychology* (July).

29. Ed Burke, interviewed October 2012.

30. Li, W., Moallem, I., Paller, K.A. & Gottfried, J.A. (2007) Subliminal smells can guide social preferences, *Psychological Science*, 18(12), pp. 1044–9.

31. Kosfeld, M., Heinrichs, M., Zak, P.J., Fischbacher, U., & Fehr, E. (2005) Oxytocin increases trust in humans, *Nature*, 435(2), pp. 673–6.

32. Damasio, A. (2005) Brain Trust, *Nature*, 435, pp. 571–2.

33. Carroll, J. (2008) Time pressures, stress common for Americans, http://www. gallup.com/poll/103456/Time-Pressures-Stress-Common-Americans.aspx, retrieved March 12, 2013.

34. Rudd, M., Vohs, K.D., & Aaker, J. (2012) Awe expands people's perception of time, alters decision making, and enhances well-being, *Psychological Science*, August 10.

Chapter 7: Brand Love: The Engineering of Emotions

1. Peters, T. (1997) What great brands do, *Fast Company*, August /September, p. 96.

2. Pichler, E.A., & Hemetsberger, A. (2007) "Hopelessly devoted to you": Towards an extended conceptualization of consumer devotion, *Advances in Consumer Research*, 34, pp. 194–9.

3. Ahuvia, A.C. (2005) Beyond the extended self: Loved objects and consumers' identity narratives, *Journal of Consumer Research*, 32, June, pp. 171–84.

4. Thomson, M., MacInnis, D.J., & Park, C.W. (2005) The ties that bind: Measuring the strength of consumers' emotional attachments to brands, *Journal of Consumer Psychology*, 15(1), pp. 77–91.

5. Wang, G. (2002) Attitudinal correlates of brand commitment, *Journal of Relationship Marketing*, 1(2), pp. 57–75.

6. Reimann, M., Castaño, R., Zaichkowsky, J., & Bechara, A. (2012) How we relate to brands: Psychological and neurophysiological insights into con- sumer–brand relationships, *Journal of Consumer Psychology*, January, pp. 128–42.

7. Trout, J. (2005) Differentiate or die, *Forbes*, December 5, http://www.forbes. com/opinions/2005/12/02/ibm-nordstrom-cocacola-cx_jt_1205trout.html, retrieved October 16, 2011.

8. Schwartz, B. (2004) *The Paradox of Choice*, New York: HarperCollins, pp. 9–10.

9. Trout, *op. cit.*

10. Miller, G. (2009) *Spent: Sex, Evolution, and Consumer Behavior*, New York: Penguin, p. 37.

11. Reeves, R. (1961) *Reality in Advertising*, New York: Knopf. An early pioneer of television advertising, Reeves was the man who came up with the marketing phrase, still widely used today, Unique Selling Proposition (USP).

12. Zajonc, R.B. (1984) On the primacy of affect, *American Psychologist*, 39, pp. 117–23.

13. Bornstein, R.F. (1989) Exposure and affect: Overview and meta-analysis of research, 1968–1987, *Psychological Bulletin*, 106(2), pp. 265–89.

14. Klein, N. (2000) *No Logo*, London: HarperCollins, p. 20.

15. Knight, P., & Willigan, G.E. (1992) High performance marketing: An interview with Nike's Phil Knight, *Harvard Business Review*, July, p. 92.

16. Schor, J.B. (2004) *Born to Buy*, New York: Scribner, p. 13.

17. Schor, J.B. (1999) *The Overspent American*, New York: HarperCollins, p. 36.

18. Klein, *op. cit.*, pp. 7–8.

19. Aaker, D.A. (1991) *Managing Brand Equity*, New York: Free Press.

20. Directed by Ridley Scott and featuring Anya Major as the anonymous heroine, the commercal was conceived by Chiat/Day.

21. Berger, A.A. (2007) *Ads, Fads and Consumer Culture*, Lanham, MD: Rowman & Littlefield, p. 13.

22. Ledoux, J. (1999) *The Emotional Brain*, London: Phoenix.

23. Lowenstein, G.F., Weber, E.U., Hsee, C., & Welch, N. (2201) Risk as feelings, *Psychological Bulletin*, 127, pp. 267–86.

24. Reimann *et al.*, *op. cit.*, p. 131.

25. Simson, A.K. (2010) Neuromarketing, emotions and campaigns, Unpublished Master's thesis.

26. Wells, M. (2003) In search of the buy button, Forbes.com, http://www.forbes.com/forbes/2003/0901/062.html, retrieved March 12, 2013.

27. Born, C. *et al.* (2006) MRI shows brains respond better to name brand, paper presented to annual meeting of the Radiological Society of North America (RSNA).

28. Study conducted on behalf of Mindjet. Can be downloaded from the Mindlab website, www.mindlab.org.

29. Dr. Lynda Shaw, personal communication.

30. Cross, G. (2000) *An All-Consuming Century*, New York: Columbia University Press.

31. Hagemann, N., Strauss, B., & Leissing, J. (2009) When the referee sees red..., *Psychological Science*, 19(8), pp. 761–79.

32. Bailey Dougherty, personal communication, 2012.

33. Lewis, D. (1978) *The Secret Language of Your Child*, London: Souvenir Press.

34. Liikkanen, L.A. (2012) Involuntary music among normal populations and clinical cases, *ACNR*, 12(4), pp. 12–14.

35. Fox, B. (2002) Audible icons, *New Scientist*, 176(2371), p. 18.

36. Dan Jones, personal communication, 2013.

37. Betty Crocker information was sourced from the Roy Rosenzweig Center for History and New Media, Department of History and Art History, George Mason University, http://chnm.gmu.edu/sidelights/who-was-betty-crocker, retrieved March 12, 2013.

38. Miller, *op. cit.*

Chapter 8: The Power of Subliminal Priming and Persuasion

1. Rosenberg, E.L. (2004) Mindfulness and consumerism. In Kasser, T. & Kanner, A.D. (eds), *Psychology and Consumer Culture: The Struggle for a Good Life in a Materialistic World*, Washington, DC: American Psychological Association, pp. 107–25.

2. Garfield, B. (2000) "Subliminal" seduction and other urban myths, *Advertising Age*, September 18.

3. O'Toole, *op. cit.*

4. New Yorker (1957) Talk of the town, *New Yorker*, April 13, p. 33.

5. *Ibid*.

6. Crandall, K.B. (2006) Invisible commercials and hidden persuaders: James M. Vicary and the subliminal advertising controversy of 1957. Undergraduate Honors Thesis, University of Florida, Dept, of History.

7. Nation (1957) Diddling the subconscious, *Nation*, 5 October 1957, pp 206–7.

8. Cousins, N. (1957) Smudging the subconscious, *Saturday Review*, October 5, pp 20–40.

9. Huxley, A. (2004 [1959]) *Brave New World Revisited*, London: Vintage, pp. 80–81.

10. Danzig, F. (1962) Subliminal advertising – Today it's just historic flashback for researcher Vicary, *Advertising Age*, 33, September 17, pp. 72, 74.

11. Aristotle (1908) *Parva Naturalia*, trans. J.I. Beare & G.R.T. Ross, London: Clarendon Press.

12. Aarts, H., Custers, R., & Marien, H. (2008) Preparing and motivating behavior outside of awareness, *Science*, 319(21), March, p. 1639.

13. Zajonc, R.B. (2001) Mere exposure: A gateway to the subliminal, *Current Directions in Psychological Science*, 10(6), December, pp. 224–8.

14. http://www.dominicstreatfeild.com/2011/03/24/interview-with-wilson-bryan-key, retrieved March 12, 2013.

15. *Ibid.*

16. Kilbourne, W.E., Painton, S., & Ridley, D. (1985) The effect of sexual embedding on responses to magazine advertisements, *Journal of Advertising*, 14, pp. 48–56.

17. Simons, D.J., & Chabris, C.F. (1999) Gorillas in our midst: Sustained inattentional blindness for dynamic events, *Perception*, 28, pp. 1059–74.

18. Carter, T.J., Ferguson, M.J., & Hassin, R.R. (2011) A single exposure to the American flag shifts support toward Republicanism up to 8 months later, *Psychological Science*, July 8.

19. Karremans. J.C., Stroebe, W., & Claus, J. (2006) Beyond Vicary's fantasies: The impact of subliminal priming and brand choice, *Journal of Experimental Social Psychology*, 42, pp. 792–8.

20. Bahrami, B., Lavie, N., & Rees, G. (2007) Attentional load modulates responses of human primary visual cortex to invisible stimuli, *Current Biology*, 17(6), pp. 509–13.

21. Phil Barden, personal communication. To read the full interview go to www.brainsell.org.uk.

22. Nosek, B.A., Banaji, M.R., & Greenwald, A.G. (2002) Math = me, me = female, therefore math = me, *Journal of Personality and Social Psychology*, 83, pp. 44–59.

23. Greenwald, A.G. & Farnham, S.D. (2000) Using the Implicit Association Test to measure self-esteem and self-concept, *Journal of Personality and Social Psychology*, 79, pp. 1022–38.

24. Koole, S.L., Dijksterhuis, A., & Knippernberg, A.V. (2001) What's in a name: Implicit self-esteem and the automatic self, *Journal of Personality and Social Psychology*, 80, pp. 669–85.

25. Marsh, K.L., Johnson, B.L., & Scott-Sheldon, L.A. (2001) Heart versus reason in condom use: Implicit versus explicit attitudinal predictors of sexual behaviour, *Zeitschrift fur Experimentelle Psychologie*, 48, pp. 161–75.

26. Rudman, L.A., & Kilianski, L.A. (2000) Implicit and explicit attitudes toward female authority, *Personality and Social Psychology Bulletin*, 26, pp. 1315–28.

27. Karremans *et al.*, *op. cit.*

Chapter 9: When Your Television Watches You

1. Kilbourne, *op. cit.*

2. Allen, R.C. (1992) *Channels of Discourse, Reassembled*, London: Routledge.

3. Kilbourne, *op. cit.*, p. 252.

4. Allen, *op. cit.*, p. 3.

5. Gerbner, G., Gross, L., Morgan, M., & Signorielli, N. (1986) Living with television: The dynamics of the cultivation process. In Bryant, J. & Zillman, D. (eds), *Perspectives on Media Effects*, Hillsdale, NJ: Erlbaum, pp. 17–40.

6. Ong, Walter, J. (1977) *Interfaces of the World: Studies in the Evolution of Consciousness and Culture*, Ithaca, NY: Cornell University Press.

7. Pratkanis, A.R., & Aronson, E. (1992) *Age of Propaganda: The Everyday Use and Abuse of Persuasion*, New York: W.H. Freeman, pp. 55–6.

8. Gerbner *et al.*, *op. cit.*

9. McLeod, J.M., & Chaffee, S.H. (1972) The construction of social reality. In Tedeschi, J.T. (ed.), *The Social Influence Process*, Chicago: Aldine Atherton, pp. 50–99.

10. Iyengar, S., & Kinder, D. (1987) *News That Matters: Television and American Public Opinion*, Chicago: University of Chicago Press, pp. 114–15.

11. Cohen, B., cited in Rogers, E.M. & Dearing, J.W. (1988) Agenda-setting research: Where has it been, where is it going? In J.A. Anderson (ed.), *Communication Year Book II*, Beverly Hills, CA: Sage, pp. 555–94.

12. McNeal, J.U. (1999) *The Kids Market, Myths and Realities,* Ithaca, NY: Paramount Market Publishing, pp. 14–15.

13. Schor, *Born to Buy,* pp. 19–20.

14. Clark, E. (2007) *The Real Toy Story,* London: Transworld, pp. 239–40.

15. Quoted from interview with Leo Zahn by Castewar downloaded from http://protoncharging.com/1999/07/19/interview-leo-zahn, June 2013.

16. Schor, *Born to Buy*, p. 20.

17. Clark, *op. cit.*, pp. 241–2.

18. Harris, J.L., Bargh, J.A., &. Brownell, K.D. (2009) Priming effects of television food advertising on eating behaviour, *Health Psychology*, 28(4), pp. 404–13.

19. Kotler, P., Armstrong, G., Saunders, J., & Wong, V. (2002) *Principles of Marketing: European Edition*, London: Financial Times/Prentice Hall, p. 668.

20. Mander, J. (1978) *Four Arguments for the Elimination of Television*, New York: HarperCollins, p. 198.

21. Scott, W.D. (1903) *The Theory of Advertising*, Boston: Small, Maynard.

22. Berry, D., & Dienes, Z. (1991) The relationship between implicit memory and implicit learning, *British Journal of Psychology*, 82(3).

23. Shapiro, S., & Krishnan, H.S. (2001) Memory-based measures for assessing advertising effects: A comparison of explicit and implicit memory effects, *Journal of Advertising*, 30(3), pp. 1–13.

24. Mehta, A., & Purvis, S.C. (2006) Reconsidering recall and emotion in advertising, *Journal of Advertising Research*, March, pp. 49–56.

25. LeDoux, J. (1998) *The Emotional Brain*, Weidenfeld & Nicolson, London.

26. Kim, J., Lim, J.-S., & Bhargava, M. (1998) The role of affect in attitude formation: A classical conditioning approach, *Journal of the Academy of Marketing Science*, 26(2), pp. 143–52.

27. Herzstein, R.E. (1987) *The War That Hitler Won*, New York: Paragon House, p. 31.

28. Zajonc, R.B. (1968) Attitudinal effects of mere exposures, *Journal of Personality and Social Psychology*, 9(2, Pt. 2), pp. 1–27.

29. Kunst-Wilson, W. & Zajonc, R. (1980) Affective discrimination of stimuli that cannot be recognized, *Science*, 207(4430), pp. 557–8.

30. Zajonc, R.B. (1980) Feeling and thinking: Preferences need no inferences, *American Psychologist*, 35(2), pp. 151–75.

31. Pechmann, C., & Stewart, D.W. (1988) Advertising repetition: A critical review of wearin and wearout, *Current Issues and Research in Advertising*, 11, pp. 285–329.

32. Lakoff, G., & Nunez, R.E. (2000) *Where Mathematics Comes From: How the Embodied Mind Brings Mathematics into Being*, New York: Basic Books, p. 27.

33. Mander, *op. cit.*

Chapter 10: The Marketing Power of Mobile Media

1. Smith, S. (2013) Chasing authenticity at SXSW, *Mobile Insider*, March 12.

2. Smith, S. (2013) Gone in 60 minutes: Most mobile searches convert in first hour, *Mobile Insider*, March.

3. Walsh, M. (2012) Cross-platform will dictate content, ad strategies in 2013, *Online Media Daily*, February 25.

4. Smith, S. (2013) Tablets evolving into our transaction screen, *Mobile Insider*, Jan 29, Mediapost.com.

5. Fogg, B.J. (2003) *Persuasive Technology: Using Computers to Change What We Think and Do*, San Francisco: Morgan Kaufmann.

6. *Ibid.*, p. 43.

7. Postmes, T., Spears, R., Sakhel, K., & De Groot, D. (2001) Social influence in computer-mediated communication: The effects of anonymity on group behaviour, *Personality and Social Psychology Bulletin*, 27, pp. 1243–5.

8. Pariser, E. (2011) *The Filter Bubble: What the Internet Is Hiding from You*, New York: Penguin, p. 198.

9. Diaz, A.-C. (2009) Goodby and B-Reel enter the asylum for the sequel to Doritos Hotel 626, *Creativity On Line*, September 23, http://creativity-online.com/news/goodby-and-breel-step-into-the-asylum-for-the-sequel-to-doritos-hotel-626/139224, retrieved March 20, 2013.

10. Kevin Ritchie, Doritos continues interactive horror franchise with Asylum 626, *Boards*, 22 Sept. 2009, www.boardsmag.com/articles/online/20090922/asylum626.html (viewed February 24, 2011). Doritos also employed the strategy of interactive packaging for its online music site, Doritoslatenight.com, where users had to point their webcams to a special symbol printed on the bags of Tacos at Midnight and Last Call Jalapeño Pepper in order to view a concert in 3D featuring the groups blink-182 and Big Boi. Aden Hepburn, Doritos late night chips: Augmented reality in a bag! *Digital Buzz Blog*, 11 July 2009, www.digitalbuzzblog.com/doritos-late-night-chips-augmented-reality-with-blink-182-in-a-bag/ (viewed April 11, 2010).

11. Montgomery, K., & Chester, J. (2011) Digital food marketing to children and adolescents: Problematic practices and policy interventions, Washington, DC: National Policy and Legal Analysis Network to Prevent Childhood Obesity, pp. 1–65.

12. Microsoft (2009) Games advertising strikes an emotional chord with consumers, 15 June, www.emsense.com/press/game-advertising.php, retrieved April 11, 2010. See also Microsoft Advertising (2011) Doritos Xbox live arcade game smashes records, June 21, http://advertising.microsoft.com/europe/doritos-xbox-live-arcade-game, retrieved March 20, 2013.

13. Scarpello, L. (2012) The retailer's guide to So-Lo-Mo, Monetate.com, http://monetate.com/infographic/the-retailers-guide-to-solomo/#ax-zz2DWH4zQbG, retrieved March 20, 2013.

14. Emily Steel (2013) Magazine sales suffer from the hard cell, *Financial Times*, February 7.

15. Emi Gal, personal communication, November 2012.

Chapter 11: The Ultimate Brain Sell

1. Mandese, J. (2013) I, advertiser, *Media Post*, February 16.

2. Weizenbaum, J. (1966) ELIZA: A computer program for the study of natural language communication between man and machine, *Communications of the ACM*, 9(1), pp. 36–45.

3. Weizenbaum, J. (1976) *Computer Power and Human Reason*, San Francisco: Freeman, p. 189.

4. Reeves, B., & Nass, C. (1998) *The Media Equation: How People Treat Computers, Television and New Media Like Real People and Places*, Stanford, CA: CSLI Publications, pp. 22–4.

5. *Ibid.*

6. Fogg, B.J. (1997) Charismatic computers: Creating more likeable and persuasive interactive technologies by leveraging principles from social psychology, doctoral dissertation, Stanford University.

7. *Ibid.*

8. Warren, P., & Whyatt, J. (2013) Are you ready for a cyber crime wave? *New Statesman*, February 22–28, p. 6.

9. Douglas Rushkoff, addressing the inaugural Hello Etsy conference in Berlin, 2011.

10. Solon, O. (2012) How much data did Facebook have on one man? 1,200 pages of data in 57 categories. *Wired*, 28 December. http://www.wired.co.uk/magazine/archive/2012/12/start/privacy-versus-facebook.

11. Johnson, S. (2012) Can anything take down the Facebook juggernaut? *Wired*, May.

12. Science (2013) You are what you like, *Science*, 339, 15 March, p. 1259; University of Cambridge Press press release; Proceedings of the National Academy of Science, March 2013.

13. Corporation for Public Broadcasting (2004) Frontline's *The Persuaders*, November 9.

14. Pariser, *op. cit.*, p. 43.

15. Gallagher, R. (2013) Software that tracks people on social media created by defence firm, *The Guardian*, 10 February.

16. *Ibid*.

17. Bevans, M. (2013) What consumers want—But don't know yet! Presentation at QSP summit, March 7.

18. Brown, A. (2009) Coca-Cola: The creation of Expedition 206, http://vimeo.com/8124736, retrieved March 20, 2013.

19. Odel, P. (2006) Coca-Cola bows largest reward program in its history, *Promo Magazine*, March 2, http://promomagazine.com/news/coca-cola_reward-prgm_030206, retrieved March 20, 2013.

20. Kruse, C. (2010) Coca-Cola Vice President for Global Interactive Marketing, Speaker profile, eMarketing Association Executive Conference, 2008, www.emarketingassociation.com/2008/SF/speaker_bios.htm, retrieved August 12, 2012.

21. Peter Robinson, quoted from a Cambridge University Press press release, 2006.

22. *Ibid*.

23. Shayon, S. (2011) Interactive advertising: Here's looking at you, kid. Brandchannel, http://www.brandchannel.com/home/post/2011/04/15/Immersive-Labs-Ads-Looking-at-You-Kid.aspx, retrieved March 20, 2013.

24. *Ibid*.

25. Hankin, C. (2013) Letter to *The Guardian*, February 12.

26. Taysom, J. (2013) Letter to *The Guardian*, February 12.

27. Palfrey, J., & Gasser, U. (2008) *Born Digital*, New York: Basic Books, p. 4.

Chapter 12: Let the Buyer Be Aware

1. Jaffe, *op. cit.*

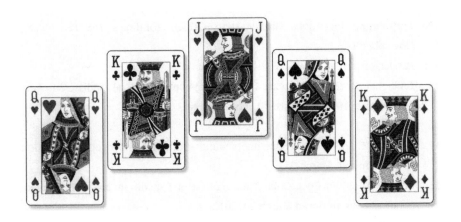

The playing card test—second sequence (see page 177)

Bibliography

Aarts, H., Custers, R., & Marien, H.S. (2008). Preparing and motivating behavior outside of awareness. *Science*, 319(5870), 1639.

Aarts, Henk, Ruys, Kirsten, I., Veling, Harm, Renes, Robert A., de Groot, Jasper H.B., van Nunen, Anna M., & Geertjes, Sarit (2010). The art of anger: Reward context turns avoidance responses to anger-related objects into approach. *Psychological Science*, 21(10), 1406–10.

Adams, Reginald B., & Kleck, Robert E. (2005). Effects of direct and averted gaze on the perception of facially communicated emotion. *Emotion*, 5(1), 3–11.

Aharon, I., Etcoff, N., Ariely, D., Chabris, C.F., O'Connor, E., & Breiter, H.C. (2001). Beautiful faces have variable reward value: fMRI and behavioral evidence. *Neuron*, 32(3), 537–51.

Alexander, M.W., & Judd, B. (1978). Do nudes in ads enhance brand recall? *Journal of Advertising Research*, 18(1), 47–50.

Alpert, M.I., Alpert, J.I., & Maltz, E.N. (2005). Purchase occasion influence on the role of music in advertising. *Journal of Business Research*, 58(3), 369–76.

Ariely, Dan, & Berns, Gregory S. (2010). Neuromarketing: The hope and hype of neuroimaging in business. *Nature Neuroscience*, 11(4), 284–92.

Astolfi, L., Fallani, F.D.V., & Salinari, S. (2008). Brain activity related to the memorization of TV commercials. *International Journal of Bioelectromagnetism*, 10(3), 1–10.

Atkin, Douglas (2004). *The Culting of Brands: When Customers Become True Believers*. New York: Portfolio.

Ayres, Ian (2007). *Super Crunchers: Why Thinking-by-Numbers Is the New Way to Be Smart*. New York: Bantam Books.

Bagozzi, R.P., & Pieters, R. (1998). Goal-directed emotions. *Cognition and Emotion*, 12(1), 1–26.

Ball-Rokeach, Sandra, Rokeach, Milton, & Grube, Joel W. (1984). *The Great American Values Test: Influencing Behavior and Belief through Television*. New York: Free Press.

Barber, Benjamin R. (2007). *Con$Umed: How Markets Corrupt Children, Infantilize Adults, and Swallow Citizens Whole*. New York: W.W. Norton.

Başar, Erol, & Bullock, Theodore Holmes (1992). *Induced Rhythms in the Brain*. Boston: Birkhäuser.

Baum, Eric B. (2004). *What Is Thought?* Cambridge, MA: MIT Press.

Baumeister, R.F., Bechara, A., Damasio, H., & Damasio, A.R. (2000). Emotion, decision making and the orbitofrontal cortex. *Cerebral Cortex*, 10(3), 295–307.

Belliveau, J.W., Kennedy, D.N. Jr., McKinstry, R.C., Buchbinder, B.R., Weisskoff, R.M., Cohen, M.S., & Rosen, B.R. (1991). Functional mapping of the human visual cortex by magnetic resonance imaging. *Science*, 254(5032), 716–19.

Benson, April Lane (2000). *I Shop, Therefore I Am: Compulsive Buying and the Search for Self*. Northvale, NJ: Jason Aronson.

Benson, John (1994). *The Rise of Consumer Society in Britain, 1880–1980*. New York: Longman.

Berger, Arthur Asa (2007). *Ads, Fads, and Consumer Culture: Advertising's Impact on American Character and Society*. Lanham, MD: Rowman & Littlefield.

Bermeitinger, C., Goelz, R., Johr, N., Neumann, M., Ecker, U.K.H., & Doerr, R. (2009). The hidden persuaders break into the tired brain. *Journal of Experimental Social Psychology*, 45(2), 320–26.

Bernays, E.L. (1923). *Crystallizing Public Opinion*. New York: Boni and Liveright.

Berns, G.S., McClure, S.M., Pagnoni, G., & Montague, P.R. (2001). Predictability modulates human brain response to reward. *Journal of Neuroscience*, 21(8), 2793–8.

Bierley, C., McSweeney, F.K., & Vannieuwkerk, R. (1985). Classical conditioning of preferences for stimuli. *Journal of Consumer Research*, 12, 316–23.

Birren, Faber. (1963). *Color: A Survey in Words and Pictures, from Ancient Mysticism to Modern Science*. Secaucus, NJ: Citadel Press.

Bitner, M.J. (1992). Servicescapes: The impact of physical surroundings on customers and employees. *Journal of Marketing*, 56(2), 57–71.

Blythman, Joanna (2004). *Shopped: The Shocking Truth about British Supermarkets*. London: Fourth Estate.

Bor, Daniel (2012). *The Ravenous Brain: How the New Science of Consciousness Explains Our Insatiable Search for Meaning*. New York: Basic Books.

Börjesson, Kristina (2004). *Into the Buzzsaw: Leading Journalists Expose the Myth of a Free Press*. New York: Prometheus Books.

Bradley, M.M., & Lang, P.J. (1999). *Affective Norms for English Words (ANEW): Instruction Manual and Affective Ratings*. University of Florida, Center for Research in Psychophysiology.

Brammer, M. (2004). Brain scam? *Nature Neuroscience*, 7(10), 1015–15.

Broughton, Philip Delves (2012). *Life's a Pitch: What the World's Best Sales People Can Teach Us All*. London: Portfolio.

Budd, Mike, Craig, Steve, & Steinman, Clayton M. (1999). *Consuming Environments: Television and Commercial Culture*. New Brunswick, NJ: Rutgers University Press.

Bullock, August (2004). *The Secret Sales Pitch: An Overview of Subliminal Advertising*. San Jose, CA: Norwich Publishers.

Cacioppo, J.T., Tassinary, L.G., & Berntson, G.G. (2007). *Handbook of Psychophysiology*. Cambridge: Cambridge University Press.

Carbone, L.P., & Haeckel, S.H. (2005). Engineering customer experiences. *Marketing Management Magazine*. IBM Executive Business Institute.

Carr, Nicholas G. (2011). *The Shallows: How the Internet Is Changing the Way We Think, Read and Remember*. London: Atlantic Books.

Chandler, J., & Schwarz, N. (2009). How extending your middle finger affects your perception of others: Learned movements influence concept accessibility. *Journal of Experimental Social Psychology*, 45(1), 123–8.

Chebat, J.-C., & Michon, R. (2003) Impact of ambient odors on mall shoppers' emotions, cognition, and spending: A test of competitive causal theories. *Journal of Business Research*, 56(7), 529–39.

Cheskin, L. (1951). *Color for Profit*. New York: Liveright.

Clark, Eric. (1988). *The Want Makers: Lifting the Lid off the World Advertising Industry: How They Make You Buy*. London: Hodder & Stoughton.

Clark, E. (2011). *The Real Toy Story: Inside the Ruthless Battle for Britain's Youngest Consumers*. New York: Free Press.

Corstjens, Judy, & Corstjens, Marcel (1995). *Store Wars: The Battle for Mindspace and Shelfspace*. Hoboken, NJ: John Wiley.

Coupland, Douglas (2002). *Generation X: Tales for an Accelerated Culture*. London: Abacus.

Coyle, Diane (2011). *The Economics of Enough: How to Run the Economy as if the Future Matters*. Princeton, NJ: Princeton University Press.

Cross, Gary S. (2000). *An All-Consuming Century: Why Commercialism Won in Modern America*. New York: Columbia University Press.

Crossen, Cynthia (1994). *Tainted Truth: The Manipulation of Fact in America*. New York: Simon & Schuster.

Csikszentmihalyi, M., & Rochberg-Halton, E. (1981). *The Meaning of Things: Domestic Symbols and the Self*. Cambridge: Cambridge University Press.

Dagher, Alain (2007). Shopping centers in the brain. *Neuron*, 53(1), 7-8.

Davenport, T.H. (1997). *Information Ecology: Mastering the Information and Knowledge Environment*. New York: Oxford University Press.

De Barnier, V., Maille, V., Valette-Florence, P., & Gallopel, K. (2004). A cross-cultural study of the persuasive effects of sexual and fear appealing messages: A comparison between France, Denmark, Thailand and Mexico. *Marketing Communications*, 14(4), 271–91.

De Chernatony, Leslie, McDonald, Malcolm, & De Chernatony, Leslie (1998). *Creating Powerful Brands in Consumer, Service, and Industrial Markets*. Boston: Butterworth-Heinemann.

De Graaf, John, Naylor, Thomas H., & Wann, David (2005). *Affluenza: The All-Consuming Epidemic*. San Francisco: Berrett-Koehler.

Dichter, E., & Glaisek, R. (1964). *Handbook of Consumer Motivations: The Psychology of the World of Objects*. New York: McGraw-Hill.

Dittmar, Helga (1992). *The Social Psychology of Material Possessions: To Have Is to Be*. New York: St. Martin's Press.

Dittmar, Helga (2007). *Consumer Culture, Identity, and Well-Being: The Search for the "Good Life" and the "Body Perfect."* New York: Psychology Press.

Dixon, N.F. (1971). *Subliminal Perception: The Nature of a Controversy*. London: McGraw-Hill.

Dooley, R. (2011). *Brainfluence: 100 Fast, Easy, and Inexpensive Ways to Persuade and Convince with Neuromarketing*. New York: John Wiley.

Doux, J.L., & Dolan, R.J. (1997). The emotional brain: The mysterious underpinnings of emotional life. *Nature*, 385(6618), 694.

Du Plessis, Erik (2011). *The Branded Mind: What Neuroscience Really Tells Us about the Puzzle of the Brain and the Brand*. Philadelphia: Kogan Page.

Duckworth, K.L., Bargh, J.A., Garcia, M., & Chaiken, S. (2002). The automatic evaluation of novel stimuli. *Psychological Science*, 13(6), 513–19.

Eco, Umberto (1986). *Faith in Fakes: Essays*. London: Secker and Warburg.

Erk, Susanne, Spitzer, Manfred, Wunderlich, Arthur P., Galley, Lars, & Walter, Henrik (2002). Cultural objects modulate reward circuitry. *Neuroreport*, 13(18), 2499–503.

Eroglua, S.A., Machleitb, K.A., & Davis, L.M. (2001) Atmospheric qualities of online retailing: A conceptual model and implications. *Journal of Business Research*, 54, 177–84.

Ewen, Stuart (1996). *PR! A Social History of Spin*. New York: Basic Books.

Falk, Pasi (1994). *The Consuming Body*. Thousand Oaks, CA: Sage.

Falk, Pasi, & Campbell, Colin (1997). *The Shopping Experience*. Thousand Oaks, CA: Sage.

Fiore, A.M., & Kim, J. (2007). An integrative framework capturing experiential and utilitarian shopping experience. *International Journal of Retail and Distribution Management*, 35(6), 421–42.

Firestein, S. (2012). *Ignorance: How It Drives Science*. Oxford: Oxford University Press.

Fletcher, Winston (1992). *A Glittering Haze: Strategic Advertising in the 1990s*. New York: NTC.

Fletcher, W. (2008). Powers of persuasion: The inside story of British advertising. *Journal of Direct, Data and Digital Marketing Practice*, 10, 195–9.

Fogg, B.J. (2003). *Persuasive Technology: Using Computers to Change What We Think and Do*. Boston: Morgan Kaufmann Publishers.

Fogg, B.J., & Eckles, D. (2007). *The Behaviour Chain for Online Participation*. Berlin: Springer-Verlag.

Ford, Brett Q., Tamir, Maya, Brunyé, Tad T., Shirer, William R., Mahoney, Caroline R., & Taylor, Holly A. (2010). Keeping your eyes on the prize: Anger and visual attention to threats and rewards. *Psychological Science*, 21(8), 1098–105.

Förster, J., & Strack, F. (1996). Influence of overt head movements on memory for valenced words: A case of conceptual-motor compatibility. *Journal of Personality and Social Psychology*, 71(3), 421–30.

Franzen, Giep (1994). *Advertising Effectiveness: Findings from Empirical Research*. Henley-on-Thames: Admap.

Franzen, G., & Bouwman, M. (2001). *The Mental World of Brands: Mind, Memory and Brand Success*. London: World Advertising Research Center.

Friese, S. (2000) *Self-Concept and Identity in a Consumer Society: Aspects of Symbolic Product Meaning*. Marburg an der Lahn: Tectum Verlag.

Gabriel, Yiannis, & Lang, Tim (1995). *The Unmanageable Consumer: Contemporary Consumption and Its Fragmentations*. Thousand Oaks, CA: Sage.

Gacioppo, J.T., & Petty, R.E. (1985). Physiological responses and advertising effects: Is the cup half full or half empty? *Psychology and Marketing*, 2(2), 115–26.

Gallagher, Shaun (2005). *How the Body Shapes the Mind*. New York: Clarendon Press.

Gallivan, Jason P., Chapman, Craig S., Wood, Daniel K., Milne, Jennifer L., Ansari, Daniel, Culham, Jody C., & Goodale, Melvyn A. (2011). One to four, and nothing more: Nonconscious parallel individuation of objects during action planning. *Psychological Science*, 226, 803–11.

Gardner, Carl, & Sheppard, Julie (1989). *Consuming Passion: The Rise of Retail Culture*. London: Unwin Hyman.

Garlin, F.V., & Owen, K. (2006). Setting the tone with the tune: A meta-analytic review of the effects of background music in retail settings. *Journal of Business Research*, 59(6), 755–64.

Gatto, J.T. (1991). *The Prussian Connection: The Underground History of American Education: An Intimate Investigation into the Problem of Modern Schooling*. New York: New Society.

Gatto, J.T. (2003). *The Underground History of American Education*, New York: Oxford Village Press.

Gershon, M.D., & Gershon, M. (1999). *The Second Brain: A Groundbreaking New Understanding of Nervous Disorders of the Stomach and Intestine*, New York: Harper Paperbacks.

Gigerenzer, G. (1991). How to make cognitive illusions disappear: Beyond heuristics and biases. *European Review of Social Psychology*, 2(1), 83–115.

Gigerenzer, G. (2004). Mindless statistics. *Journal of Socio-Economics*, 33(5), 587–606.

Gobé, Marc (2001). *Emotional Branding: The New Paradigm for Connecting Brands to People*. New York: Allworth Press.

Goldblum, Naomi (2001). *The Brain-Shaped Mind: What the Brain Can Tell Us about the Mind*. Cambridge: Cambridge University Press.

Gorn, G.J. (1982). The effects of music in advertising on choice behaviour: A classical conditioning approach. *Journal of Marketing*, 45, 94–101.

Gosling, Sam (2008). *Snoop: What Your Stuff Says about You*. London: Profile.

Gosselin, N., Peretz, I., Johnsen, E., & Adolphs, R. (2006). Amygdala damage impairs emotion recognition from music. *Neuropsychologia*, 45(2), 236–44.

Gountas, J. (2008). Marketing metaphoria: What deep metaphors reveal about the minds of consumers. *Journal of Consumer Marketing*, 25(7), 482–3.

Graves, Philip (2010). *Consumer.ology: The Market Research Myth, the Truth about Consumers and the Psychology of Shopping*. London: Nicholas Brealey Publishing.

Grazer, W.F., & Kessling, G. (2011). The effect of print advertising's use of sexual themes on brand recall and purchase intention: A product specific investigation of male responses. *Journal of Applied Business Research*, 11(3), 47–57.

Griskevicius, V., Shiota, M.N., & Nowlis, S.M. (2010). The many shades of rose-colored glasses: An evolutionary approach to the influence of different positive emotions. *Journal of Consumer Research*, 37(2), 238–50.

Guadagno, R.E., & Cialdini, R.B. (2010). Preference for consistency and social influence: A review of current research findings. *Social Influence*, 5(3), 152–63.

Guadagno, R.E., Asher, T., Demaine, L.J., & Cialdini, R.B. (2001). When saying yes leads to saying no: Preference for consistency and the reverse foot-in-the-door effect. *Personality and Social Psychology Bulletin*, 27(7), 859–67.

Gusnard, D.A., Akbudak, E., Shulman, G.L., & Raichle, M.E. (2001). Medial prefrontal cortex and self-referential mental activity: Relation to a default mode of brain function. *Proceedings National Academy of Science USA*, 98(7), 4259–64.

Haberstroh, Jack (1994). *Ice Cube Sex: The Truth about Subliminal Advertising*. Notre Dame, IN: Cross Cultural Publications.

Haig, Matt (2003). *Brand Failures: The Truth about the 100 Biggest Branding Mistakes of All Time*. London: Kogan Page.

Harris, Jennifer L., Bargh, John A., & Brownell, Kelly D. (2009). Priming effects of television food advertising on eating behavior. *Health Psychology*, 28(4), 404–13.

Heath, R. (2012). *Seducing the Subconscious: The Psychology of Emotional Influence in Advertising*. New York: John Wiley.

Heath, R., & Nairn, A. (2005). Measuring affective advertising: Implications of low attention processing on recall. *Journal of Advertising Research*, 45(2), 269.

Heuer, R.J. (1999). *Psychology of Intelligence Analysis*. Washington, DC: US Government Printing Office.

Hine, Thomas (1995). *The Total Package: The Evolution and Secret Meanings of Boxes, Bottles, Cans, and Tubes*. Boston: Little, Brown.

Holdem, C. (2001). Behavioral addictions: Do they exist? *Science*, 294, 980–82.

Hope, Augustine, & Walch, Margaret (1990). *The Color Compendium*. New York: Van Nostrand Reinhold.

Hugdahl, Kenneth (1995). *Psychophysiology: The Mind-Body Perspective*. Cambridge, MA: Harvard University Press.

Hughes, Robert (1994). *Culture of Complaint: The Fraying of America*. London: Harvill.

Hui, M.K., & Bateson, J.E.G. (1991). Perceived control and the effects of crowding and consumer choice on the service experience. *Journal of Consumer Research*, 18(2), 174–84.

Hui, M.K., Dube, L., & Chebat, J.-C. (1997) The impact of music on consumers' reactions to waiting for services. *Journal of Retailing*, 73(1) 87–104.

Humphery, Kim (1998). *Shelf Life: Supermarkets and the Changing Cultures of Consumption*. New York: Cambridge University Press.

Hunt, Morton M. (1993). *The Story of Psychology*. New York: Doubleday.

Ijsselsteijn, W., de Kort, Y., Midden, C., Eggen, B., & van den Hoven, E. (2006). Persuasive technology for human well-being: Setting the scene. *Persuasive Technology*, 3962, 1-5.

Illes, Judy, & Bird, Stephanie J. (2006). Neuroethics: A modern context for ethics in neuroscience. *Trends Neuroscience*, 29(9), 511–17.

Johnson, Steven (2006). *Everything Bad Is Good for You: How Popular Culture Is Making Us Smarter*. London: Penguin.

Johnson-Laird, P.N. (2003). *The Nature and Limits of Human Understanding*. New York: T & T Clark.

Jones, Benedict C., DeBruine, Lisa M., Perrett, David I., Little, Anthony C., Feinberg, David R., & Law Smith, Miriam J. (2008). Effects of menstrual cycle phase on face preferences. *Archives of Sexual Behaviour*, 37(1), 78–84.

Jung, C.G., Franz, Marie-Luise von, & Freeman, John (1964). *Man and His Symbols*. London: Aldus Books.

Kahneman, Daniel (2011) Thinking, Fast and Slow, New York: Farrar, Straus, Giroux.

Kaptein, M., Markopoulos, P., de Ruyter, B., & Aarts, E. (2009). Can you be persuaded? Individual differences in susceptibility to persuasion. *Human-Computer Interaction*, 115–18.

Karremans, J.C., Stroebe, W., & Claus, J. (2006). Beyond Vicary's fantasies: The impact of subliminal priming and brand choice. *Journal of Experimental Social Psychology*, 42(6), 792–8.

Kasser, Tim, & Kanner, Allen D. (2004). *Psychology and Consumer Culture: The Struggle for a Good Life in a Materialistic World*. Washington, DC: American Psychological Association.

Kay, William (1989). *Battle for the High Street*. London: Corgi.

Keil, M.S. (2009). I look in your eyes, honey: Internal face features induce spatial frequency preference for human face processing. *PLoS Computational Biology*, 5(3), e1000329.

Kellaris, J.J., & Cox, A.D. (1989). The effects of background music in advertising: A reassessment. *Journal of Consumer Research*, 16, 113–18.

Key, W.B. (1993). *The Age of Manipulation: The Con in Confidence, the Sin in Sincere*. New York: Madison Books.

Kick, Russell (2001). *You Are Being Lied To: The Disinformation Guide to Media Distortion, Historical Whitewashes and Cultural Myths*. New York: Disinformation.

Kim, J., Lim, J.-S., Bhargava, M. (1998). The role of affect in attitude formation: A classical conditioning approach. *Academy of Marketing Science Journal*, 26(2), 143–52.

Kingdon, M. (2002). The mental world of brands: Mind, memory and brand success. *Journal of Brand Management*, 9(6), 485–6.

Klein, Naomi (2000). *No Logo*. New York: HarperCollins.

Klucharev, Vasily, Smidts, Ale, & Fernández, Guillén (2008). Brain mechanisms of persuasion: How "expert power" modulates memory and attitudes. *Social Cognitive and Affective Neuroscience*, 3(4), 353–66.

Knutson, Brian (2004). Behavior. Sweet revenge? *Science*, 305(5688), 1246–7.

Knutson, B., Fong, G.W., Bennett, S.M., Adams, C.M., & Hommer, D. (2003). A region of mesial prefrontal cortex tracks monetarily rewarding outcomes: Characterization with rapid event-related fMRI. *Neuroimage*, 18(2), 263–72.

Knutson, Brian, Rick, Scott, Wimmer, G. Elliott, Prelec, Drazen, & Loewenstein, George (2007). Neural predictors of purchases. *Neuron*, 53(1), 147–56.

Knutson, B., Westdorp, A., Kaiser, E., & Hommer, D. (2000). fFMRI visualization of brain activity during a monetary incentive delay task. *Neuroimage*, 12(1), 20–27.

Koenigs, Michael, & Tranel, Daniel (2008). Prefrontal cortex damage abolishes brand-cued changes in cola preference. *Social Cognitive and Affective Neuroscience* 3(1), 1–6.

Kotler, P. (1973). Atmospherics as a marketing tool. *Journal of Retailing*, 49(4), 48–64.

Kyle, J., & Casasanto, D. (2012). The QWERTY Effect: How typing shapes the meanings of words. *Psychonomic Bulletin & Review*, 19(3), 499–504.

Lakhani, D. (2008). *Subliminal Persuasion: Influence and Marketing Secrets They Don't Want You to Know*. Hoboken, NJ: John Wiley.

Lakoff, George, & Johnson, Mark (2003). *Metaphors We Live By*. Chicago: University of Chicago Press.

Lanchester, J. (2012) *Capital*. London: Faber and Faber.

Langleben, Daniel D., Loughead, James W., Ruparel, Kosha, Hakun, Jonathan G., Busch-Winokur, Samantha, Holloway, Matthew B., & Lerman, Caryn (2009).

Reduced prefrontal and temporal processing and recall of high "sensation value" ads. *Neuroimage*, 46(1), 219–25.

Lauritzen, Martin, Mathiesen, Claus, Schaefer, Katharina, & Thomsen, Kirsten J. (2012). Neuronal inhibition and excitation, and the dichotomic control of brain hemodynamic and oxygen responses. *Neuroimage*, 62(2), 1040–50.

Lautman, M.R., & Pauwels, K. (2009). What is important? Identifying metrics that matter. *Journal of Advertising Research*, 339, 359.

Lears, T.J. Jackson (1994). *Fables of Abundance: A Cultural History of Advertising in America*. New York: Basic Books.

Lebergott, Stanley (1996). *Pursuing Happiness: American Consumers in the Twentieth Century*. Princeton, NJ: Princeton University Press.

LeDoux, Joseph E. (1999). *The Emotional Brain: The Mysterious Underpinnings of Emotional Life*. London: Phoenix.

Lee, Martyn J. (1993). *Consumer Culture Reborn: The Cultural Politics of Consumption*. New York: Routledge.

Lee, Nick, Broderick, Amanda J., & Chamberlain, Laura (2007). What is "neuromarketing"? A discussion and agenda for future research. *International Journal of Psychophysiology*, 63(2), 199–204.

Lees-Marshment, Jennifer (2009). *Political Marketing: Principles and Applications*. New York: Routledge.

Legrenzi, Paolo (2011). *Neuromania: On the Limits of Brain Science*. Oxford: Oxford University Press.

Leibenstein, H. (1950). Bandwagon, snob, and Veblen effects in the theory of consumers' demand. *Quarterly Journal of Economics*, 64(2), 183–207.

Lewis, D. (1978) *The Secret Language of Your Child: How Children Talk Before They Can Speak*. London: Souvenir Press.

Lewis, D. (2013) *Impulse: Why We Do What We Do without Knowing Why We Do It*. London: Random House.

Lewis, D., & Bridger, D. (2002) *The Soul of the New Consumer: What We Buy and Why in the New Economy*. London: Nicholas Brealey Publishing.

Lilienfeld, Scott O. (2010). *50 Great Myths of Popular Psychology: Shattering Widespread Misconceptions about Human Behavior*. Chichester: Wiley-Blackwell.

Lindström, Martin (2001). *Clicks, Bricks and Brands*. London: Kogan Page.

Logothetis, Nikos K. (2008). What we can do and what we cannot do with fMRI. *Nature*, 453(7197), 869–78.

Lupetin, A.R., Davis, D.A., Beckman, I., & Dash, N. (1995). Transcranial Doppler sonography. Part 1. Principles, technique, and normal appearances. *Radiographics*, 15(1), 179–91.

Lupton, Ellen, & Miller, Abbott (1999). *Design Writing Research*. London: Phaidon.

MacInnis, D.J., & Park, C.W. (1991). The differential role of characteristics of music on high- and low-involvement consumers' processing of ads. *Journal of Consumer Research*, 18 Sept., 161–73.

Malko, S. (2006) Time and decisions: Attention based perspective on temporal effects in judgment and choice. *Advances in Consumer Research*, 33, 688–91.

Mander, Jerry (1978). *Four Arguments for the Elimination of Television*. New York: Morrow.

Mark, Margaret, & Pearson, Carol (2001). *The Hero and the Outlaw: Building Extraordinary Brands through the Power of Archetypes*. New York: McGraw-Hill.

Martens, Ulla, Ansorge, Ulrich, & Kiefer, Markus (2011). Controlling the unconscious: Attentional task sets modulate subliminal semantic and visuomotor processes differentially. *Psychological Science*, 22(2), 282–91.

Mattila, A.S., & Wirtz, J. (2001) Congruency of scent and music as a driver of in-store evaluations and behavior. *Journal of Retailing*, 77, 273–89.

McClure, S.M., Li, J., Tomlin, D., Cypert, K.S., Montague, L.M., & Montague, P.R. (2004). Neural correlates of behavioral preference for culturally familiar drinks. *Neuron*, 44, 379–87.

McGovern, Gerry (1999). *The Caring Economy: Business Principles for the New Digital Age*. Dublin: Blackhall.

Miller, Daniel (1995). *Acknowledging Consumption: A Review of New Studies*. New York: Routledge.

Miller, Daniel (1998). *Shopping, Place, and Identity*. New York: Routledge.

Miller, Daniel (2005). *A Theory of Shopping*. Cambridge: Polity Press.

Miller, G. (2009). *Spent: Sex, Evolution and Consumer Behavior*. New York: Viking.

Mlodinow, Leonard (2012). *Subliminal: How Your Unconscious Mind Rules Your Behaviour*. London: Allen Lane.

Montague, P.R. (2007) Neuroeconomics: A view from neuroscience. *Functional Neurology*, 22(4), 219–34.

Montague, P.R. (2008) Free will. *Current Biology*, 18(14), R584–5.

Montague, P.R., Hyman, S.E., & Cohen, J.D. (2004). Computational roles for dopamine in behavioural control. *Nature*, 431(7010), 760–67.

Montague, P. Read, & King-Casas, Brooks (2007). Efficient statistics, common currencies and the problem of reward-harvesting. *Trends in Cognitive Science*, 11(12), 514–19.

Montague, Read (2006). *Why Choose This Book? How We Make Decisions*. New York: Dutton.

Morris, J.D., & Boone, M.A. (1998). The effects of music on emotional response, brand attitude, and purchase intent in an emotional advertising condition. *Advances in Consumer Research*, 25(1), 518–26.

Morris, N. (2009). Understanding digital marketing: Marketing strategies for engaging the digital generation. *Journal of Direct, Data and Digital Marketing Practice*, 10(4), 384–7.

Morrison, M. (2001) The power of music and its influence on international retail brands and shopper behaviour: A multi case study. New Zealand Marketing Academy Conference. Downloaded from http://www.evolvedsound.com.au/The_Power_of_Music_in_Retail.pdf, June 2013.

Morwitz, V.G., Steckel, J.H., & Gupta, A. (2007). When do purchase intentions predict sales? *International Journal of Forecasting*, 23(3), 347–64.

Mudrik, Liad, Breska, Assaf, Lamy, Dominique, & Deouell, Leon Y. (2011). Integration without awareness: Expanding the limits of unconscious processing. *Psychological Science*, 22(6), 764–70.

Murphy, E.R., Illes, J., & Reiner, P.B. (2008). Neuroethics of neuromarketing. *Journal of Consumer Behaviour*, 7(4–5), 293–302.

Nava, Mica (1997). *Buy This Book: Studies in Advertising and Consumption*. New York: Routledge.

Nevett, T.R. (1982). *Advertising in Britain: A History*. London: Heinemann.

Niedenthal, P.M. (2007). Embodying emotion. *Science*, 316(5827), 1002–5.

Nisbett, R.E., & Wilson, T.D. (1977). Telling more than we can know: Verbal reports on mental processes. *Psychological Review*, 84(3), 231.

O'Brien, Larry (1991). *Retailing: Shopping, Society, Space*. London: D. Fulton.

Odekerken-Schröder, Gaby, de Wulf, Kristof, & Reynolds, Kristy E. (2005) A cross-cultural investigation of relationship marketing effectiveness in retailing: A contingency approach. *Advances in International Marketing*, 15, 33–73.

O'Guinn, T.C., & Shrum, L.J. (1997). The role of television in the construction of consumer reality. *Journal of Consumer Research*, 23, 278–94.

O'Toole, John E. (1981). *The Trouble with Advertising*. New York: Chelsea House.

Packard, V. (1957). *The Hidden Persuaders*. New York: Pocket Books.

Pagnoni, Giuseppe, Zink, Caroline F., Montague, P. Read, & Berns, Gregory S. (2002). Activity in human ventral striatum locked to errors of reward prediction. *Nature Neuroscience*, 5(2), 97–8.

Palfrey, John G., & Gasser, Urs (2008). *Born Digital: Understanding the First Generation of Digital Natives*. New York: Basic Books.

Panksepp, J. (2001). The neuro-evolutionary cusp between emotions and cognitions. *Evolution and Cognition*, 7(2), 141–63.

Pardun, C.J., & Forde, K.R. (2006). Sexual content of television commercials watched by early adolescents. In Reichert, T., & Lambiase, J. (eds) *Sex in Consumer Culture: The Erotic Content of Media and Marketing Appeal*, 125–39. Mahwah, NJ: Lawrence Erlbaum Associates.

Pariser, Eli (2011). *The Filter Bubble: What the Internet Is Hiding from You*. New York: Penguin Press.

Pennings, Joost M.E., van Ittersum, Koert, & Wansink, Brian (2005). To spend or not to spend? The effect of budget constraints on estimation processes and spending behavior. *Advances in Consumer Research*, 32, 328–9.

Petsche, Hellmuth, & Etlinger, Susan C. (1998). *EEG and Thinking: Power and Coherence Analysis of Cognitive Processes*. Wien: Verlag der Österreichischen Akademie der Wissenschaften.

Petty, R.E., Cacioppo, J.T., & Schumann, D. (1983). Central and peripheral routes to advertising effectiveness: The moderating role of involvement. *Journal of Consumer Research*, 10 Sept., 135–46.

Plassmann, H., Kenning, P., Deppe, M., Kugel, H., Schwindt, W., & Ahlert, D. (2006). How brands twist heart and mind: Neural correlates of the affect heuristic during brand choice. Muenster: University of Muenster. Downloaded from http://128.118.178.162/eps/exp/papers/0509/0509004.pdf, June 2013.

Plassmann, H., O'Doherty, J., Shiv, B., & Rangel, A. (2008). Marketing actions can modulate neural representations of experienced utility. *Proceedings of the National Academy of the USA*, 105(3), 1050–54.

Plassmann, H., Ramsøy, T.Z., & Milosavljevic, M. Branding the brain: A critical review and outlook. *Journal of Consumer Psychology*, 22(1), 18–36.

Pooler, James A. (2003). *Why We Shop: Emotional Rewards and Retail Strategies*. Westport, CN: Praeger.

Postman, Neil (1986). *Amusing Ourselves to Death: Public Discourse in the Age of Show Business*. New York: Penguin Books.

Pradeep, A.K. (2010). *The Buying Brain: Secrets for Selling to the Subconscious Mind*. Hoboken, NJ: John Wiley.

Pratkanis, A.R., & Aronson, Elliot (1992). *Age of Propaganda: The Everyday Use and Abuse of Persuasion*. New York: W.H. Freeman.

Rangel, Antonio, Camerer, Colin, & Montague, P. Read. (2008). A framework for studying the neurobiology of value-based decision making. *Nature Neuroscience*, 9(7), 545–56.

Rank, Hugh (1982). *The Pitch*. Park Forest, IL: Counter-Propaganda Press.

Raudenbush, B. (2000). The effects of odors on objective and subjective measures of physical performance. *Aroma Chronology Review*, 9(1), 1–5.

Ray, M.L., & Batra, R. (1982). Emotion and persuasion in advertising: What we do and don't know about affect. Graduate School of Business, Stanford University.

Raymond, Martin (2003). *The Tomorrow People: Future Consumers and How to Read Them*. London: FT Prentice Hall.

Raz, O., & Ert, E. (2008) Size counts: The effect of queue length on choice between similar restaurants. *Advances in Consumer Research*, 35, 803–4.

Reeves, B., Lang, A., Thorson, E., & Rothschild, M. (1989). Emotional television scenes and hemispheric specialization. *Human Communication Research*, 15(4), 493–508.

Reeves, Byron, & Nass, Clifford Ivar (1998). *The Media Equation: How People Treat Computers, Television, and New Media Like Real People and Places*. Cambridge: Cambridge University Press.

Rheingold, Howard (1991). *Virtual Reality: Exploring the Brave New Technologies of Artificial Experience and Interactive Worlds—From Cyberspace to Teledildonics*. London: Martin Secker & Warburg.

Roberts, K. (2005). *Lovemarks: The Future beyond Brands*. New York: PowerHouse Books.

Rosenblatt, R. (1999). *Consuming Desires: Consumption, Culture, and the Pursuit of Happiness*. Washington, DC: Island Press.

Rothschild, M.L., Hyun, Y.J., Reeves, B., Thorson, E., & Goldstein, R. (1988). Hemispherically lateralized EEG as a response to television commercials. *Journal of Consumer Research*, 15(2), 185–98.

Rowan, A.J., & Tolunsky, Eugene (2003). *Primer of EEG*. Oxford: Butterworth-Heinemann.

Rozenblit, Leonid, & Keil, Frank (2002). The misunderstood limits of folk science: An illusion of explanatory depth. *Cognitive Science*, 26(5), 521–62.

Rugg, G., & McGeorge, P. (1997). The sorting techniques: A tutorial paper on card sorts, picture sorts and item sorts. *Expert Systems*, 14(2), 80–93.

Rushkoff, Douglas (2010). *Life Inc.: How the World Became a Corporation and How to Take It Back*. London: Vintage.

Rushkoff, Douglas, & Purvis, Leland (2011). *Program or Be Programmed: Ten Commands for a Digital Age*. Berkeley, CA: Counterpoint.

Russo, J.E., & Johnson, E.J. (1980). What do consumers know about familiar product? *Advances in Consumer Research*, 7, 417–23.

Saad, Gad (2007). *The Evolutionary Bases of Consumption*. Mahwah, NJ: Lawrence Erlbaum Associates.

Saad, G. (2011) *The Consuming Instinct: What Juicy Burgers, Ferraris, Pornography, and Gift Giving Reveal about Human Nature*. Amherst, NY: Prometheus Books.

Samuels, Mike, & Samuels, Nancy (1975). *Seeing with the Mind's Eye: The History, Techniques, and Uses of Visualization*. New York: Random House.

Savani, K., Stephens, N.M., & Markus, H.R. (2011). The unanticipated interpersonal and societal consequences of choice: Victim blaming and reduced support for the public good. *Psychological Science*, 22(6), 795–802.

Schor, J.B. (1999). *The Overspent American: Why We Want What We Don't Need*. New York: Harper.

Schor, J. (2004). *Born to Buy: The Commercialized Child and the New Consumer Culture*. New York: Scribner.

Schultheiss, Oliver C., Wirth, Michelle M., Waugh, Christian E., Stanton, Steven J., Meier, Elizabeth A., & Reuter-Lorenz, Patricia (2008). Exploring the motivational brain: Effects of implicit power motivation on brain activation in response to facial expressions of emotion. *Social Cognitive and Affective Neuroscience*, 3(4), 333–43.

Schultz, Wolfram, Dayan, Peter, & Montague, P. Read (1997). A neural substrate of prediction and reward. *Science*, 275, 1593–99.

Sedivy, Julie, & Carlson, Greg N. (2011). *Sold on Language: How Advertisers Talk to You and What This Says about You*. Chichester: Wiley-Blackwell.

Seth, Andrew, & Randall, Geoffrey (2001). *The Grocers: The Rise and Rise of the Supermarket Chains*. London: Kogan Page.

Seung, Sebastian (2012). *Connectome: How the Brain's Wiring Makes Us Who We Are*. London: Allen Lane.

Shallice, Tim, & Cooper, Richard P. (2011). *The Organisation of Mind*, Oxford: Oxford University Press.

Shapiro, Kimron (2001). *The Limits of Attention: Temporal Constraints in Human Information Processing*. Oxford: Oxford University Press.

Shapiro, Lawrence A. (2011). *Embodied Cognition*. New York: Routledge.

Shell, Ellen Ruppel (2009). *Cheap: The High Cost of Discount Culture*. New York: Penguin.

Shieh, M.D., Yan, W., & Chen, C.H. (2008). Soliciting customer requirements for product redesign based on picture sorts and ART2 neural network. *Expert Systems with Applications*, 34(1), 194–204.

Shrum, L.J., Wyer, R.S., & O'Guinn, T.C. (1998). The effects of television consumption on social perceptions: The use of priming procedures to investigate psychological processes. *Journal of Consumer Research*, 24, 447–58.

Smith, B.D., Meyers, M., Kline, R., & Bozman, A. (1987). Hemispheric asymmetry and emotion: Lateralized parietal processing of affect and cognition. *Biological Psychology*, 25(3), 247–60.

Sorensen, Herb (2009). *Inside the Mind of the Shopper: The Science of Retailing*. Upper Saddle River, NJ: Wharton School Publishing.

Spangenberg, Eric R., Crowley, Ayn E., & Henderson, Pamela W. (1996) Improving the store environment: Do olfactory cues affect evaluations and behaviors? *Journal of Marketing*, 60, 67–80.

Sparks, E.A., Stillman, T.F., & Vohs, K.D. (2008). Free will in consumer behavior: Self-control, ego depletion, and choice. *Journal of Consumer Psychology*, 18(1), 4–13.

Stauber, John C., & Rampton, Sheldon (1995). *Toxic Sludge Is Good for You: Lies, Damn Lies, and the Public Relations Industry*. Monroe, ME: Common Courage Press.

Stewart, P.A., & Schubert, J.N. (2006). Taking the low road with subliminal advertisements: A study testing the effect of precognitive prime RATS in a 2000 presidential advertisement. *Harvard International Journal of Press/Politics*, 11(4), 103–14.

Stiles, P. (2005). *Is the American Dream Killing You? How "the Market" Rules Our Lives*. New York: HarperCollins.

Strack, F., Martin, L.L., & Stepper, S. (1988). Inhibiting and facilitating conditions of the human smile: A non-obtrusive test of the facial feedback hypothesis. *Journal of Personality and Social Psychology*, 54(5), 768–77.

Sutherland, Max (1993). *Advertising and the Mind of the Consumer: What Works, What Doesn't, and Why*. St. Leonards, NSW: Allen & Unwin.

Sweeney, J.C., & Wyber, F. (2002). The role of cognitions and emotions in the music-approach-avoidance behavior relationship. *Journal of Services Marketing*, 16(1), 51–69.

Tallis, Raymond (2011). *Aping Mankind: Neuromania, Darwinitis and the Misrepresentation of Humanity*. Durham: Acumen.

Tarde, Gabriel (1903). *The Laws of Imitation*. Milton Keynes: Lightning Source.

Taylor, Kathleen E. (2006). *Brainwashing: The Science of Thought Control*. Oxford: Oxford University Press.

Thomson, Oliver (1977). *Mass Persuasion in History: An Historical Analysis of the Development of Propaganda Techniques*. Edinburgh: Paul Harris.

Thut, G., Schultz, W., Roelcke, U., Nienhusmeier, M., Missimer, J., Maguire, R.P., & Leenders, K.L. (1997). Activation of the human brain by monetary reward. *Neuroreport*, 8(5), 1225.

Topolinski, Sascha (2011). I 5683 you: Dialing phone numbers on cell phones activates key-concordant concepts. *Psychological Science*, 22(3), 355–60.

Trappenberg, Thomas P. (2002). *Fundamentals of Computational Neuroscience*. Oxford: Oxford University Press.

Travis, Daryl (2000). *Emotional Branding: How Successful Brands Gain the Irrational Edge*. Roseville, CA: Prima Venture.

Troisi, J.D., & Gabriel, S. (2011). Chicken soup really is good for the soul: "Comfort food" fulfills the need to belong. *Psychological Science*, 22(6) 747–53.

Turley, L.W., & Milliman, R.E. (2000). Atmospheric effects on shopping behavior: A review of the experimental evidence. *Journal of Business Research*, 49(2), 193–211.

Twitchell, James B. (1993). *Carnival Culture: The Trashing of Taste in America*. New York: Columbia University Press.

Underhill, Paco (1999). *Why We Buy: The Science of Shopping*. New York: Simon & Schuster.

Underhill, Paco (2004). *Call of the Mall: How We Shop*. London: Profile Books.

Van den Bergh, B., Schmitt, J., Dewitte, S., & Warlop, L. (2009). Bending arms, bending discounting functions: How motor actions affect intertemporal decision-making. Katholieke Universiteit Leuven.

Van den Bergh, B., Schmitt, J., & Warlop, L. (2011). Embodied myopia. *Journal of Marketing Research*, 48(6), 1033–44.

Van der Lans, R., Cote, J.A., Cole, C.A., Leong, S.M., Smidts, A., Henderson, P.W., & Fedorikhin, A. (2009). Cross-national logo evaluation analysis: An individual-level approach. *Marketing Science*, 28(5), 968–85.

Vandermerwe, Sandra (1999). *Customer Capitalism: The New Business Model of Increasing Returns in New Market Spaces*. London: Nicholas Brealey Publishing.

van Ittersum, Koert, & Pennings, Joost M.E. (2008) The effect of primed reference points on the shape of attribute-value functions, attribute importance, and choice. *Advances in Consumer Research*, 35, 701–2.

Vecchiato, G., Astolfi, L., Tabarrini, A., Salinari, S., Mattia, D., Cincotti, F., Soranzo, R., & Babiloni, F. (2010). EEG analysis of the brain activity during the observation of commercial, political, or public service announcements. *Computational Intelligence and Neuroscience*, 6. Downloaded from http://www.hindawi.com/journals/cin/2010/985867, June 2013.

Villarino, R.R., & Otero-Lopez, J.M. (2001). Review of Benson, A. (Ed.) *I Shop Therefore I Am: Compulsive Buying and the Search for Self, Journal of Consumer Policy*, 24(3–4), 441–7.

Walford, Rosie, Benson, Paula, & West, Paul (2004). *Shelf Life*. London: Bloomsbury.

Walsh, D., & Gentile, D.A. (2002). Slipping under the radar: Advertising and the mind. Paper presented at the WHO symposium: Marketing to Young People. Treviso, Italy.

Ward, Philippa, Davies, Barry J., & Kooijman, Dion (2003). Ambient smell and the retail environment: Relating olfaction research to consumer behaviour. *Journal of Business and Management*, 9(3), 289.

Weinberger, J., & Westen, D. (2008). RATS, we should have used Clinton: Subliminal priming in political campaigns. *Political Psychology*, 29(5), 631–51.

Weinstein, S., Weinstein, C., & Drozdenko, R. (1984). Brain wave analysis: An electroencephalographic technique used for evaluating the communications-effect of advertising. *Psychology and Marketing*, 1(1), 17–42.

Weinzembaum, J. (1984). *Computer Power and Human Reason: From Judgement to Calculation*. London: Penguin.

Westen, Drew, Blagov, Pavel S., Harenski, Keith, Kilts, Clint, & Hamann, Stephan (2006). Neural bases of motivated reasoning: An fMRI study of emotional constraints on partisan political judgment in the 2004 U.S. Presidential election. *Journal of Cognitive Neuroscience*, 18(11), 1947–58.

Westin, Alan F. (1967). *Privacy and Freedom*. New York: Atheneum.

Williamson, J. (1978). *Decoding Advertisements: Ideology and Meaning in Advertising*. London: Marion Boyars.

Williamson, Judith (1986). *Consuming Passions: The Dynamics of Popular Culture*. London: Marion Boyars.

Williamson, J. (1994) *Decoding Advertisements*. London: Marion Boyars.

Wilson, R., Gaines, J., & Hill, R.P. (2008). Neuromarketing and consumer free will. *Journal of Consumer Affairs*, 42(3), 389–410.

Winkielman, P., Knutson, B., Paulus, M., & Trujillo, J.L. (2007). Affective influence on judgments and decisions: Moving towards core mechanisms. *Review of General Psychology*, 11(2), 179.

Wolf, Michael J. (1999). *The Entertainment Economy: How Mega-Media Forces Are Transforming Our Lives*. New York: Times Books.

Wood, James Playsted (1958). *The Story of Advertising*. New York: Ronald Press.

Wright, Ronald (2005). *A Short History of Progress*. New York: Canongate.

Young, C. (2002). Brain waves, picture sorts®, and branding moments. *Journal of Advertising Research*, 42(4), 42–53.

Yuksel, A. (2007). Tourist shopping habitat: Effects on emotions, shopping value and behaviours. *Tourism Management*, 28(1), 58–69.

Zaltman, Gerald (2003). *How Customers Think: Essential Insights into the Mind of the Market*. Boston: Harvard Business School Press.

Zander, M.F. (2006). Musical influences in advertising: How music modifies first impressions of product endorsers and brands. *Psychology of Music*, 34(4), 465–80.

Zepp, Ira G. (1997). *The New Religious Image of Urban America: The Shopping Mall as Ceremonial Center*. Niwot, CO: University Press of Colorado.

Zhu, Dajiang, Li, Kaiming, Guo, Lei, et al. (2012). DICCCOL: Dense Individualized and Common Connectivity-Based Cortical Landmarks. *Cerebral Cortex*, 7 April.

Index

Acknowledgments

I am most grateful to the very large number of business and science professionals who have taken the time to assist me in writing this book.

I would especially like to thank my colleagues at Mindlab International, especially MD Duncan Smith, Director of Analysis Joseph Hilling, and Director of Neuroscience Amy Maddock, for their valuable contributions. That said, I should also make it clear that the views expressed in this book are entirely my own and do not necessarily reflect those of the board of Mindlab International Ltd or its employees, nor of the many industry executives and academics who have been kind enough to assist in my research.

My research associate, Tom Dixon, has tirelessly traveled the country to interview many of those who were kind enough to offer their views, opinions, and experiences in the fast-growing fields of neuromarketing and neuroscience. In alphabetical order these were: Terry Ayling, the artist who created the illustrations on pages 78–9, 97, and 147; Phil Barden, Managing Director of Decode Marketing Ltd and author of *Decoded: The Science Behind Why We Buy*; Yavuz Bayraktar (Mindlab, Istanbul); Michael Bevans, Head of Advertising and Publisher Solutions at Yahoo!; August Bullock, who provided the image on page 174 from his book *The Secret Sales Pitch* (for further information on embedded images and numerous examples go to http://www.subliminalsex.com); Ed Burke, Director of Marketing, ScentAir, Charlotte, NC; Victor Conde (Mindlab, Madrid); Dr. Dana R. Carney, Columbia University; Dr Amy J.C. Cuddy, Harvard; Roger Dooley, author of the informative and entertaining book *Brainfluence*, a neuromarketing blogger and critic; Bailey Dougherty, Account Director at BOOM! Marketing, Canada's respected experiential marketing agency; Ugur Erdogan (Mindlab, Istanbul); Emi Gal, CEO and Founder of Brainient; Pedro Galvan (Mindlab, Madrid); Erwin Hartsuiker, CEO Mindmedia; Jessica Howells, Kavanagh Communications; ITV Studios/Channel

4/Screenocean for permission to use the image from *Come Dine With Me* on page 240; Dan Jones, hypnotherapist; Dr. Richard Lilley, Director at Tracksys Ltd, suppliers of behavioral research solutions, including eye tracking; Jon D. Morris, CEO AdSAM Marketing, Professor, University of Florida; Tom Noble, former Managing Director of NeuroFocus Europe and now an independent adviser and consultant in applied consumer neuroscience; Dag Rasmussen and Vincent Romet, Legardère Services Retail, Paris; Professor Geraint Rees, Director of UCL Institute of Cognitive Neuroscience; Rui Rubeiro, QSP and Mindlab Portugal; Nick Thornton, retail specialist, Bluewater; Professor Jamie Ward, Editor in Chief, Cognitive Neuroscience and Professor of Cognitive Neuroscience at Sussex University; Jon Ward, Director at Acuity Eye Tracking Solutions and Acuity Intelligence; Ron Wright, CEO, Sands Research Inc., USA; Dr. Andy Yap, Columbia University.

Last but by no means least, I would like to extend my sincere thanks to my inspirational publisher Nick Brealey and his remarkable editor Sally Lansdell for the many stimulating discussions and hands-on collaboration involved in the writing and editing of this book.